Dreamweaver® 4

- In an Instant -

by Michael Toot and Mike Wooldridge

Visual™

From
maranGraphics®

&

Hungry Minds™

HUNGRY MINDS, INC.
New York, NY • Cleveland, OH • Indianapolis, IN

Dreamweaver® 4 In an Instant

Published by
Hungry Minds, Inc.
909 Third Avenue
New York, NY 10022
www.hungryminds.com

Copyright © 2001 Hungry Minds, Inc.

Certain designs and text Copyright © 1992-2001 maranGraphics, Inc., used with maranGraphics' permission.

maranGraphics, Inc.
5755 Coopers Avenue
Mississauga, Ontario, Canada
L4Z 1R9

Library of Congress Control Number: 2001091945

ISBN: 0-7645-3628-1

Printed in the United States of America

10 9 8 7 6 5 4 3 2 1

1B/QW/QY/QR/IN

Distributed in the United States by Hungry Minds, Inc.

Distributed by CDG Books Canada Inc. for Canada; by Transworld Publishers Limited in the United Kingdom; by IDG Norge Books for Norway; by IDG Sweden Books for Sweden; by IDG Books Australia Publishing Corporation Pty. Ltd. for Australia and New Zealand; by TransQuest Publishers Pte Ltd. for Singapore, Malaysia, Thailand, Indonesia, and Hong Kong; by Gotop Information Inc. for Taiwan; by ICG Muse, Inc. for Japan; by Intersoft for South Africa; by Eyrolles for France; by International Thomson Publishing for Germany, Austria, and Switzerland; by Distribuidora Cuspide for Argentina; by LR International for Brazil; by Galileo Libros for Chile; by Ediciones ZETA S.C.R. Ltda. for Peru; by WS Computer Publishing Corporation, Inc., for the Philippines; by Contemporanea de Ediciones for Venezuela; by Express Computer Distributors for the Caribbean and West Indies; by Micronesia Media Distributor, Inc., for Micronesia; by Chips Computadoras S.A. de C.V. for Mexico; by Editorial Norma de Panama S.A. for Panama; by American Bookshops for Finland.

For corporate orders, please call maranGraphics at 800-469-6616 or fax 905-890-9434.

For general information on Hungry Minds' products and services, please contact our Customer Care Department within the U.S. at 800-762-2974, outside the U.S. at 317-572-3993, or fax 317-572-4002.

For sales inquiries and reseller information, including discounts, premium and bulk quantity sales, and foreign-language translations, please contact our Customer Care Department at 800-434-3422, fax 317-572-4002, or write to Hungry Minds, Inc., Attn: Customer Care Department, 10475 Crosspoint Boulevard, Indianapolis, IN 46256.

For information on licensing foreign or domestic rights, please contact our Sub-Rights Customer Care Department at 212-884-5000.

For information on using Hungry Minds' products and services in the classroom or for ordering examination copies, please contact our Educational Sales Department at 800-434-2086 or fax 317-572-4005.

For press review copies, author interviews, or other publicity information, please contact our Public Relations department at 317-572-3168 or fax 317-572-4168.

For authorization to photocopy items for corporate, personal, or educational use, please contact Copyright Clearance Center, 222 Rosewood Drive, Danvers, MA 01923, or fax 978-750-4470.

Screen shots displayed in this book are based on pre-released software and are subject to change.

Trademark Acknowledgments

Hungry Minds, the Hungry Minds logo, Visual, the Visual logo, Master VISUALLY, Teach Yourself VISUALLY, Read Less-Learn More, and related trade dress are registered trademarks or trademarks of Hungry Minds, Inc., in the United States and/or other countries and may not be used without written permission. The maranGraphics logo is a registered trademark or trademark of maranGraphics, Inc. Dreamweaver is a registered trademark of Macromedia, Inc., in the United States and/or other countries. All other trademarks are property of their respective owners. Hungry Minds, Inc., and maranGraphics, Inc., are not associated with any product or vendor mentioned in this book.

FOR PURPOSES OF ILLUSTRATING THE CONCEPTS AND TECHNIQUES DESCRIBED IN THIS BOOK, THE AUTHOR HAS CREATED VARIOUS NAMES, COMPANY NAMES, MAILING, E-MAIL AND INTERNET ADDRESSES, PHONE AND FAX NUMBERS AND SIMILAR INFORMATION, ALL OF WHICH ARE FICTITIOUS. ANY RESEMBLANCE OF THESE FICTITIOUS NAMES, ADDRESSES, PHONE AND FAX NUMBERS AND SIMILAR INFORMATION TO ANY ACTUAL PERSON, COMPANY AND/OR ORGANIZATION IS UNINTENTIONAL AND PURELY COINCIDENTAL.

Permissions

maranGraphics
Certain text and Illustrations by maranGraphics, Inc., used with maranGraphics' permission.

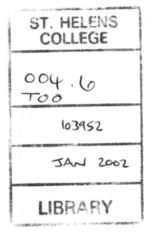
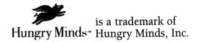

is a trademark of
Hungry Minds, Inc.

Some comments from our readers...

"I have to praise you and your company on the fine products you turn out. I have twelve of the *Teach Yourself VISUALLY* and *Simplified* books in my house. They were instrumental in helping me pass a difficult computer course. Thank you for creating books that are easy to follow."

—*Gordon Justin (Brielle, NJ)*

"I commend your efforts and your success. I teach in an outreach program for the Dr. Eugene Clark Library in Lockhart, TX. Your *Teach Yourself VISUALLY* books are incredible and I use them in my computer classes. All my students love them!"

—*Michele Schalin (Lockhart, TX)*

"Thank you so much for helping people like me learn about computers. The Maran family is just what the doctor ordered. Thank you, thank you, thank you."

—*Carol Moten (New Kensington, PA)*

"I would like to take this time to compliment maranGraphics on creating such great books. Thank you for making it clear. Keep up the good work."

—*Kirk Santoro (Burbank, CA)*

"I write to extend my thanks and appreciation for your books. They are clear, easy to follow, and straight to the point. Keep up the good work!"

—*Seward Kollie (Dakar, Senegal)*

"What fantastic teaching books you have produced! Congratulations to you and your staff. You deserve the Nobel prize in Education in the Software category. Thanks for helping me to understand computers."

—*Bruno Tonon (Melbourne, Australia)*

"Over time, I have bought a number of your 'Read Less-Learn More' books. For me, they are THE way to learn anything easily."

—*José A. Mazón (Cuba, NY)*

"I was introduced to maranGraphics about four years ago and YOU ARE THE GREATEST THING THAT EVER HAPPENED TO INTRODUCTORY COMPUTER BOOKS!"

—*Glenn Nettleton (Huntsville, AL)*

"Compliments To The Chef!! Your books are extraordinary! Or, simply put, Extra-Ordinary, meaning way above the rest! THANK YOU THANK YOU THANK YOU! for creating these."

—*Christine J. Manfrin (Castle Rock, CO)*

"I'm a grandma who was pushed by an 11-year-old grandson to join the computer age. I found myself hopelessly confused and frustrated until I discovered the Visual series. I'm no expert by any means now, but I'm a lot further along than I would have been otherwise. Thank you!"

—*Carol Louthain (Logansport, IN)*

"Thank you, thank you, thank you...for making it so easy for me to break into this high-tech world. I now own four of your books. I recommend them to anyone who is a beginner like myself. Now... if you could just do one for programming VCRs, it would make my day!"

—*Gay O'Donnell (Calgary, Alberta, Canada)*

"You're marvelous! I am greatly in your debt."

—*Patrick Baird (Lacey, WA)*

maranGraphics is a family-run business located near Toronto, Canada.

At maranGraphics, we believe in producing great computer books – one book at a time.

Each maranGraphics book uses the award-winning communication process that we have been developing over the last 25 years. Using this process, we organize screen shots and text in a way that makes it easy for you to learn new concepts and tasks.

We spend hours deciding the best way to perform each task, so you don't have to!

Our clear, easy-to-follow screen shots and instructions walk you through each task from beginning to end.

We want to thank you for purchasing what we feel are the best computer books money can buy. We hope you enjoy using this book as much as we enjoyed creating it!

Sincerely,

The Maran Family

CREDITS

Major Contributors
Michael Toot
Mike Wooldridge

Project Editor
Dana Rhodes Lesh

Acquisitions Editor
Jen Dorsey

**Product Development
Supervisor**
Lindsay Sandman

Copy Editor
Tim Borek

Technical Editor
Yolanda Burrell

Editorial Manager
Rev Mengle

Editorial Assistant
Amanda Foxworth

Book Design
maranGraphics®

Production Coordinator
Nancee Reeves

Layout
LeAndra Johnson
Kristin Pickett
Kendra Span
Brian Torwelle

Screen Artists
Ronda David-Burroughs
David E. Gregory
Mark Harris
Jill A. Proll

Proofreader
Murray Montague

Indexer
Sharon Hilgenberg

GENERAL AND ADMINISTRATIVE

Hungry Minds, Inc.: John Kilcullen, CEO; Bill Barry, President and COO; John Ball, Executive VP, Operations & Administration; John Harris, Executive VP and CFO

Hungry Minds Technology Publishing Group: Richard Swadley, Senior Vice President and Publisher; Mary Bednarek, Vice President and Publisher; Walter R. Bruce III, Vice President and Publisher; Joseph Wikert, Vice President and Publisher; Mary C. Corder, Editorial Director; Andy Cummings, Publishing Director, General User Group; Barry Pruett, Publishing Director, Visual Group

Hungry Minds Manufacturing: Ivor Parker, Vice President, Manufacturing

Hungry Minds Marketing: John Helmus, Assistant Vice President, Director of Marketing

Hungry Minds Production for Branded Press: Debbie Stailey, Production Director

Hungry Minds Sales: Michael Violano, Vice President, International Sales and Sub Rights

*The publisher would like to give special thanks to Patrick J. McGovern,
without whom this book would not have been possible.*

TABLE OF CONTENTS

TABLE OF CONTENTS

START DREAMWEAVER

You can start Dreamweaver and begin building
pages that you can publish on the Web. The
startup method depends on whether you are
using a PC or a Macintosh.

START DREAMWEAVER ON A PC

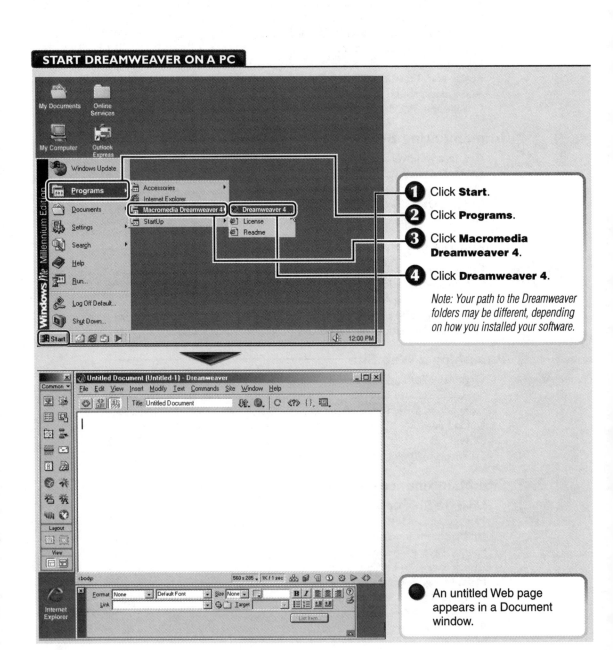

1 Click **Start**.

2 Click **Programs**.

3 Click **Macromedia
Dreamweaver 4**.

4 Click **Dreamweaver 4**.

*Note: Your path to the Dreamweaver
folders may be different, depending
on how you installed your software.*

■ An untitled Web page
appears in a Document
window.

in an *instant*

START DREAMWEAVER ON A MACINTOSH

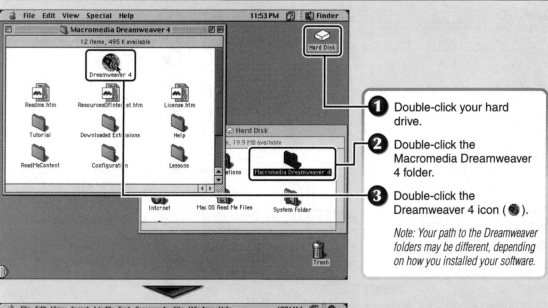

1. Double-click your hard drive.

2. Double-click the Macromedia Dreamweaver 4 folder.

3. Double-click the Dreamweaver 4 icon (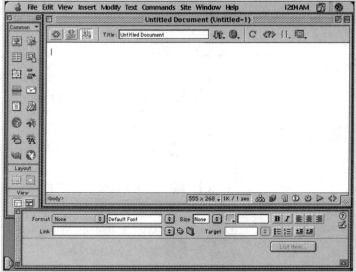).

   Note: Your path to the Dreamweaver folders may be different, depending on how you installed your software.

● An untitled Web page appears in a Document window.

CUSTOMIZE THE DOCUMENT WINDOW

The Document window is where you insert and arrange text, images, and other Web page elements. Each page that you open will have its own Document window.

CUSTOMIZE THE DOCUMENT WINDOW

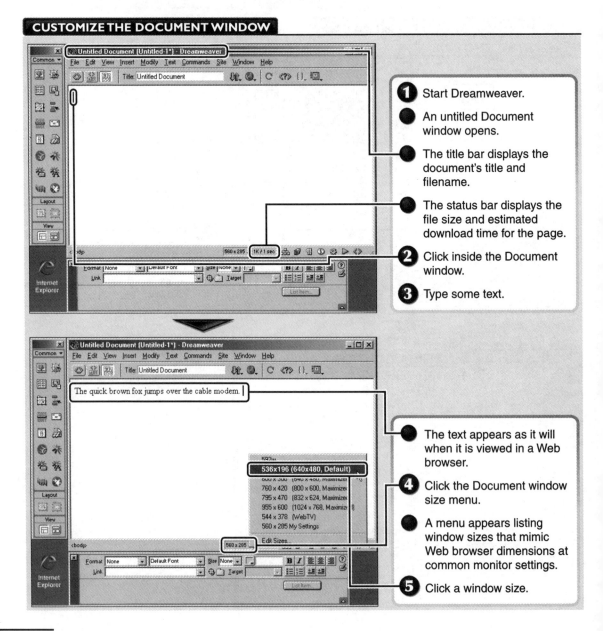

1 Start Dreamweaver.

● An untitled Document window opens.

● The title bar displays the document's title and filename.

● The status bar displays the file size and estimated download time for the page.

2 Click inside the Document window.

3 Type some text.

● The text appears as it will when it is viewed in a Web browser.

4 Click the Document window size menu.

● A menu appears listing window sizes that mimic Web browser dimensions at common monitor settings.

5 Click a window size.

in an *instant*

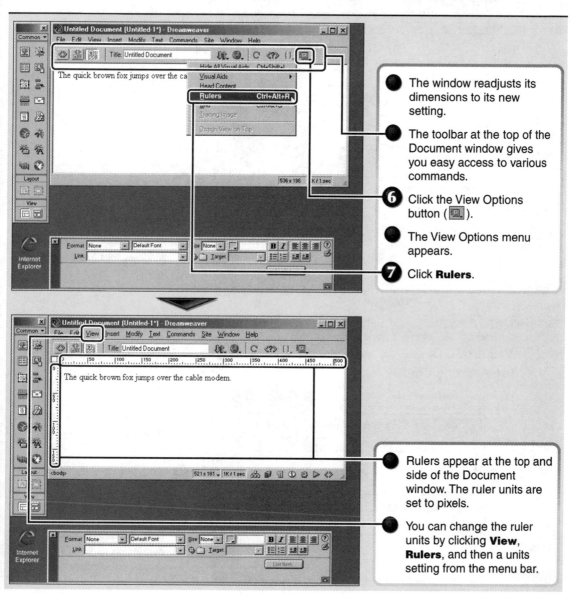

- The window readjusts its dimensions to its new setting.

- The toolbar at the top of the Document window gives you easy access to various commands.

6 Click the View Options button ( ).

- The View Options menu appears.

7 Click **Rulers**.

- Rulers appear at the top and side of the Document window. The ruler units are set to pixels.

- You can change the ruler units by clicking **View**, **Rulers**, and then a units setting from the menu bar.

SHOW OR HIDE A PANEL

You can show or hide accessory windows, also called *panels* or *inspectors,* by using commands in the Window menu.

SHOW OR HIDE A PANEL

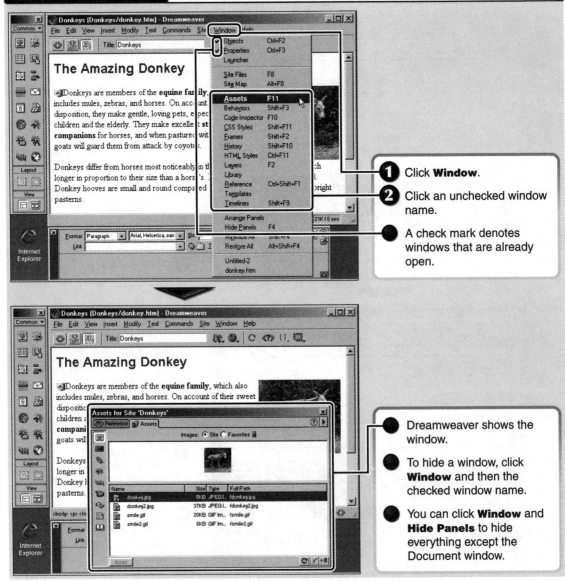

1 Click **Window**.

2 Click an unchecked window name.

■ A check mark denotes windows that are already open.

■ Dreamweaver shows the window.

■ To hide a window, click **Window** and then the checked window name.

■ You can click **Window** and **Hide Panels** to hide everything except the Document window.

REARRANGE PANELS

You can rearrange, combine, or dock panels
or inspectors to keep your on-screen
workspace from being cluttered.

REARRANGE PANELS

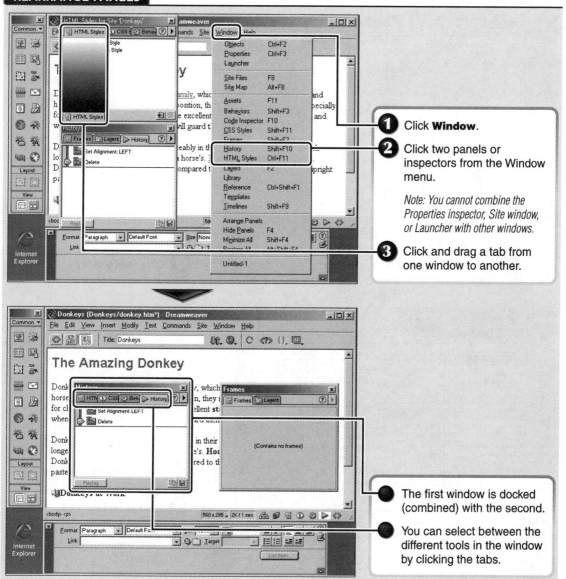

1 Click **Window**.

2 Click two panels or inspectors from the Window menu.

Note: You cannot combine the Properties inspector, Site window, or Launcher with other windows.

3 Click and drag a tab from one window to another.

● The first window is docked (combined) with the second.

● You can select between the different tools in the window by clicking the tabs.

SET PREFERENCES

You can change Dreamweaver's
default appearance and behavior
by using the Preferences dialog box.
The Preferences dialog box lets you
modify the workspace appearance
to better suit how you like to work.

SET PREFERENCES

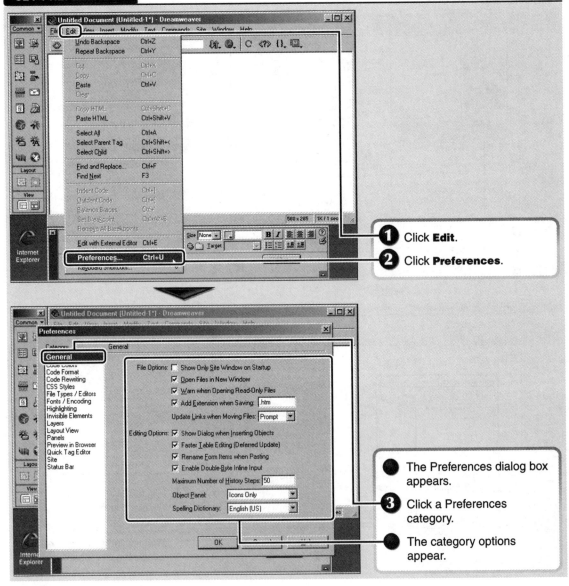

1 Click **Edit**.

2 Click **Preferences**.

■ The Preferences dialog box
appears.

3 Click a Preferences
category.

■ The category options
appear.

in an instant

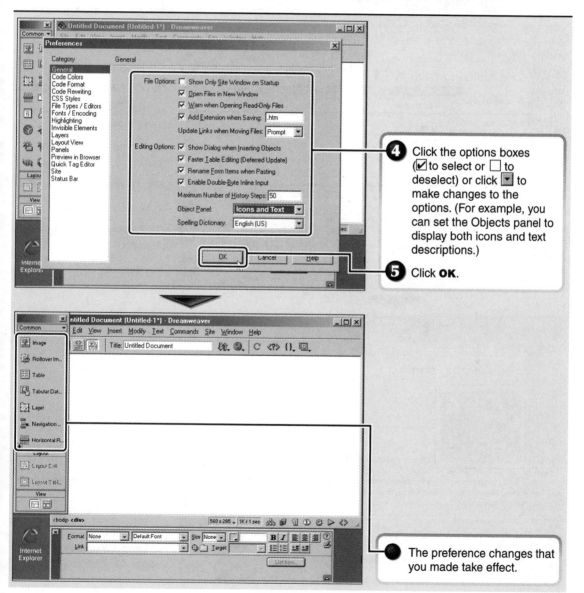

④ Click the options boxes (☑ to select or ☐ to deselect) or click ▼ to make changes to the options. (For example, you can set the Objects panel to display both icons and text descriptions.)

⑤ Click **OK**.

● The preference changes that you made take effect.

ADD OBJECTS TO A DOCUMENT

You can use the Objects panel to insert images, tables, and layers into the Document window. The panel has a drop-down menu at the top, enabling you to view different sets of object-insertion buttons.

ADD OBJECTS TO A DOCUMENT

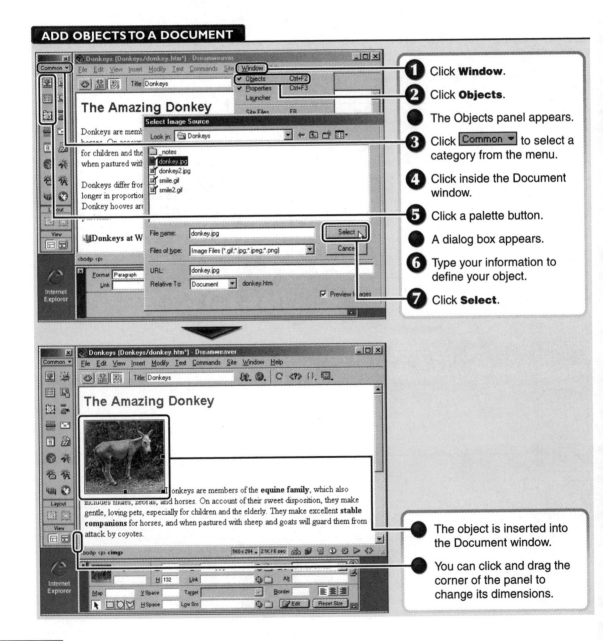

① Click **Window**.

② Click **Objects**.

● The Objects panel appears.

③ Click [Common ▼] to select a category from the menu.

④ Click inside the Document window.

⑤ Click a palette button.

● A dialog box appears.

⑥ Type your information to define your object.

⑦ Click **Select**.

● The object is inserted into the Document window.

● You can click and drag the corner of the panel to change its dimensions.

The Properties inspector lets you view and edit object properties such as text fields, drop-down menus, buttons, and other form elements.

VIEW AND EDIT OBJECT PROPERTIES

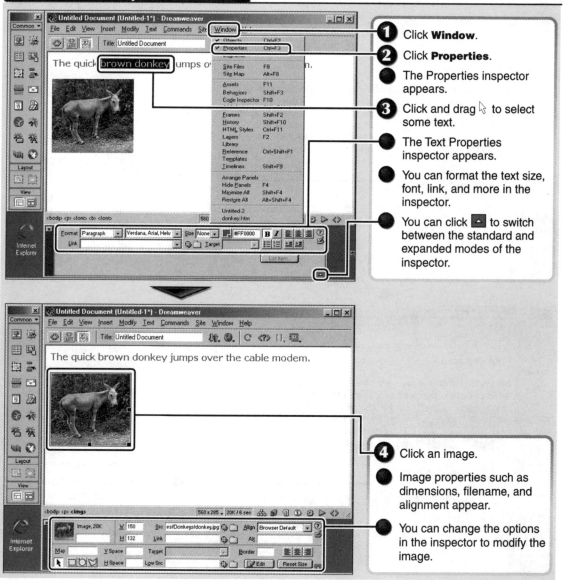

① Click **Window**.

② Click **Properties**.

● The Properties inspector appears.

③ Click and drag ↳ to select some text.

● The Text Properties inspector appears.

● You can format the text size, font, link, and more in the inspector.

● You can click ▲ to switch between the standard and expanded modes of the inspector.

④ Click an image.

● Image properties such as dimensions, filename, and alignment appear.

● You can change the options in the inspector to modify the image.

CREATE AND APPLY A CUSTOM COMMAND

You can select a sequence of commands that has been recorded in the History panel and save it as a custom command. The new command will appear under the Commands menu.

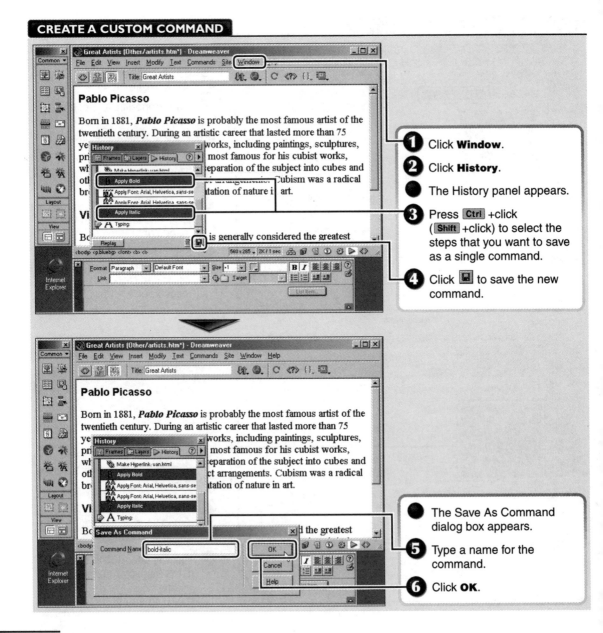

1 Click **Window**.

2 Click **History**.

● The History panel appears.

3 Press **Ctrl** +click (**Shift** +click) to select the steps that you want to save as a single command.

4 Click 🖫 to save the new command.

● The Save As Command dialog box appears.

5 Type a name for the command.

6 Click **OK**.

in an instant

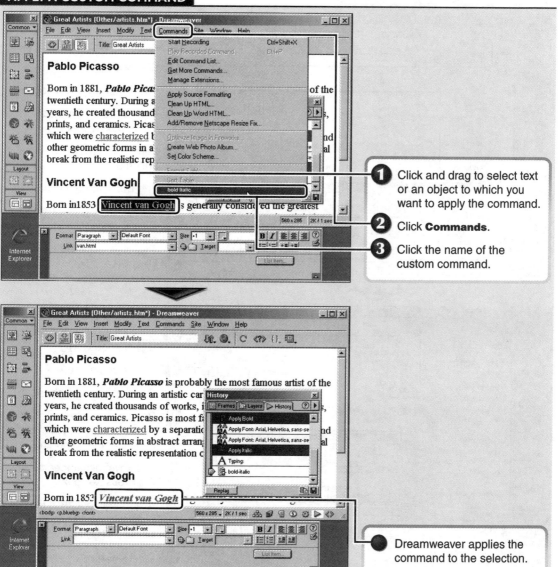

1. Click and drag to select text or an object to which you want to apply the command.

2. Click **Commands**.

3. Click the name of the custom command.

● Dreamweaver applies the command to the selection.

CREATE A KEYBOARD SHORTCUT

You can use the Keyboard Shortcuts Editor to define shortcut commands or edit existing shortcuts. You can then save time by executing the shortcut using the keystroke sequence that you defined.

CREATE A KEYBOARD SHORTCUT

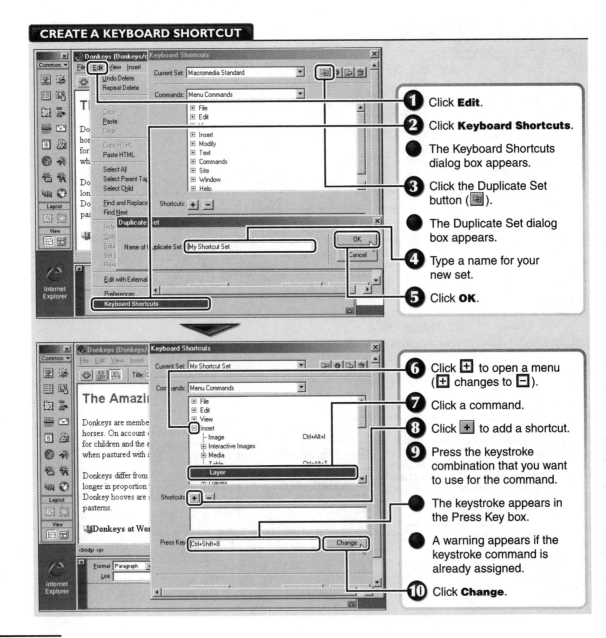

1 Click **Edit**.

2 Click **Keyboard Shortcuts**.

● The Keyboard Shortcuts dialog box appears.

3 Click the Duplicate Set button (▣).

● The Duplicate Set dialog box appears.

4 Type a name for your new set.

5 Click **OK**.

6 Click ⊞ to open a menu (⊞ changes to ⊟).

7 Click a command.

8 Click ⊞ to add a shortcut.

9 Press the keystroke combination that you want to use for the command.

● The keystroke appears in the Press Key box.

● A warning appears if the keystroke command is already assigned.

10 Click **Change**.

in an *instant*

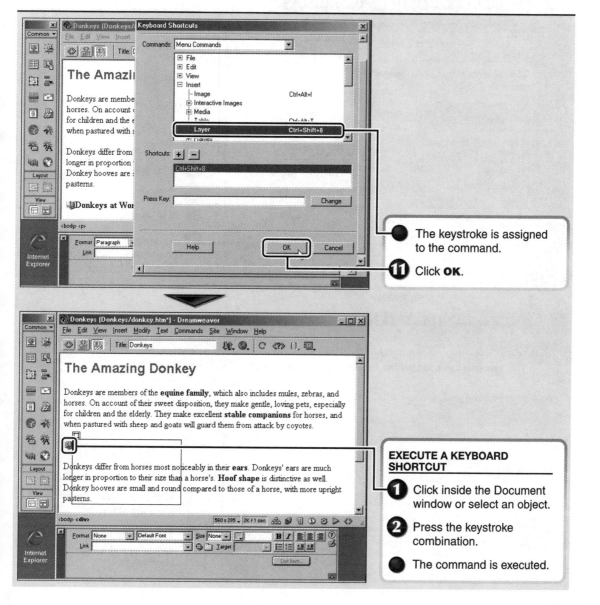

The keystroke is assigned to the command.

11 Click **OK**.

EXECUTE A KEYBOARD SHORTCUT

1 Click inside the Document window or select an object.

2 Press the keystroke combination.

The command is executed.

UNDO COMMANDS WITH THE HISTORY PANEL

The History panel keeps track of the commands that you perform and enables you to undo your changes by backtracking through those commands. This is a convenient way to correct errors.

UNDO COMMANDS WITH THE HISTORY PANEL

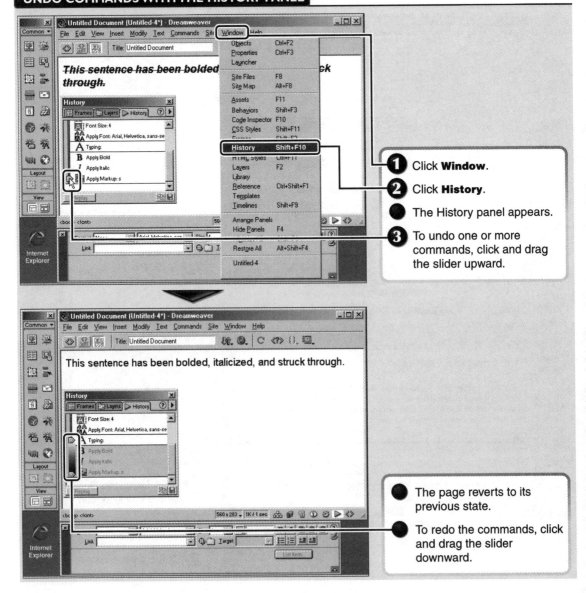

1 Click **Window**.

2 Click **History**.

● The History panel appears.

3 To undo one or more commands, click and drag the slider upward.

● The page reverts to its previous state.

● To redo the commands, click and drag the slider downward.

EXIT DREAMWEAVER

You can exit Dreamweaver after you finish using the program.

EXIT DREAMWEAVER

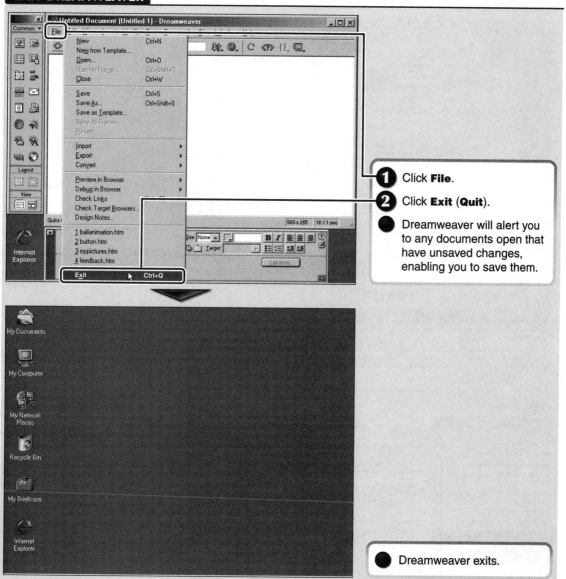

① Click **File**.

② Click **Exit (Quit)**.

● Dreamweaver will alert you to any documents open that have unsaved changes, enabling you to save them.

● Dreamweaver exits.

GET HELP

Dreamweaver comes with extensive Help documentation. There are tips, suggestions, and ways to make your Web page creation tasks easier in case you ever need help.

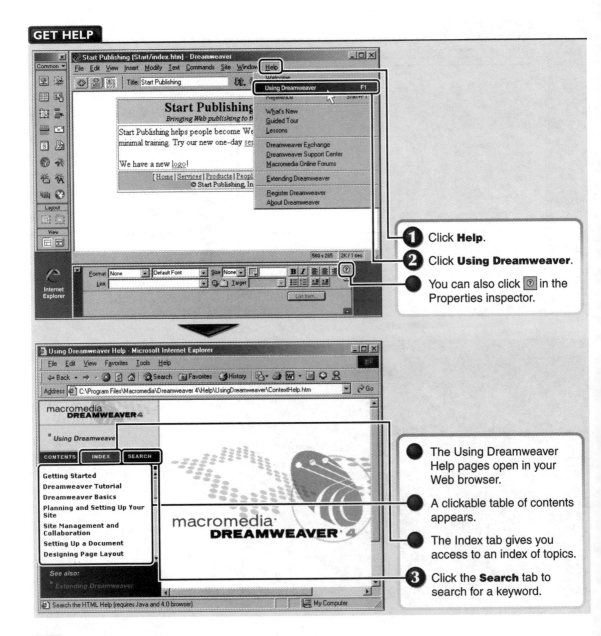

1 Click **Help**.

2 Click **Using Dreamweaver**.

You can also click ⊙ in the Properties inspector.

The Using Dreamweaver Help pages open in your Web browser.

A clickable table of contents appears.

The Index tab gives you access to an index of topics.

3 Click the **Search** tab to search for a keyword.

in an *instant*

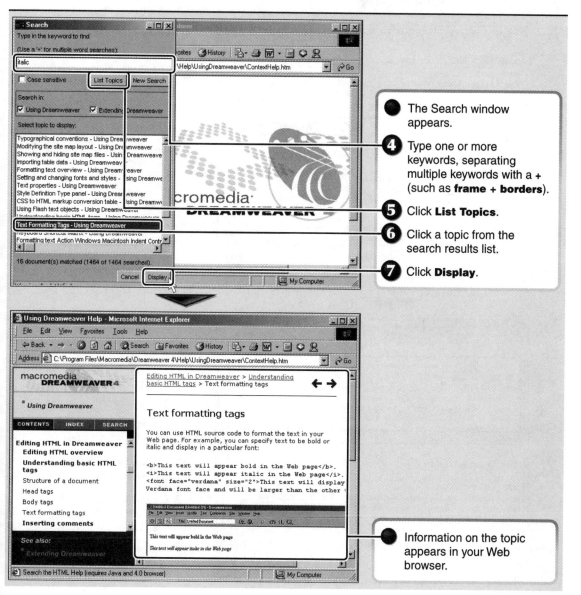

● The Search window appears.

❹ Type one or more keywords, separating multiple keywords with a + (such as **frame + borders**).

❺ Click **List Topics**.

❻ Click a topic from the search results list.

❼ Click **Display**.

● Information on the topic appears in your Web browser.

VIEW AND EDIT SOURCE CODE

You can switch to the Code view in the Document window to inspect and edit the HTML and other code of a Web page.

VIEW AND EDIT SOURCE CODE

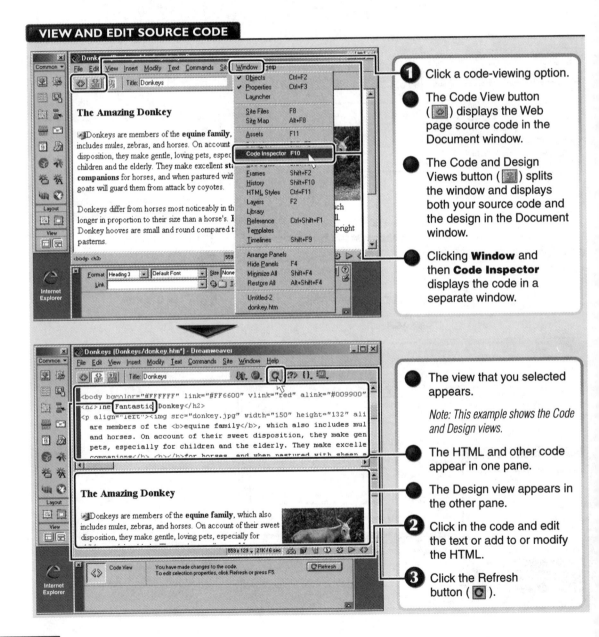

1 Click a code-viewing option.

● The Code View button (⬦) displays the Web page source code in the Document window.

● The Code and Design Views button (▦) splits the window and displays both your source code and the design in the Document window.

● Clicking **Window** and then **Code Inspector** displays the code in a separate window.

● The view that you selected appears.

Note: This example shows the Code and Design views.

● The HTML and other code appear in one pane.

● The Design view appears in the other pane.

2 Click in the code and edit the text or add to or modify the HTML.

3 Click the Refresh button (🔄).

20

in an *instant*

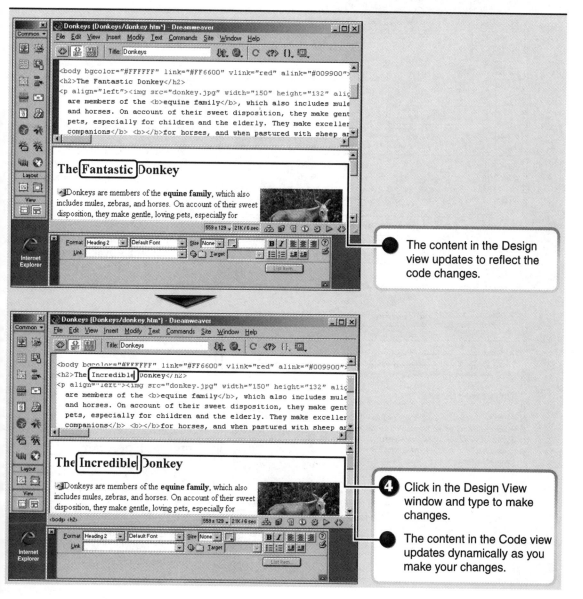

The content in the Design view updates to reflect the code changes.

④ Click in the Design View window and type to make changes.

The content in the Code view updates dynamically as you make your changes.

VIEW AND EDIT HEAD CONTENT

You can view or edit a Web page's head content, where special descriptive information about the page is stored.

VIEW AND EDIT HEAD CONTENT

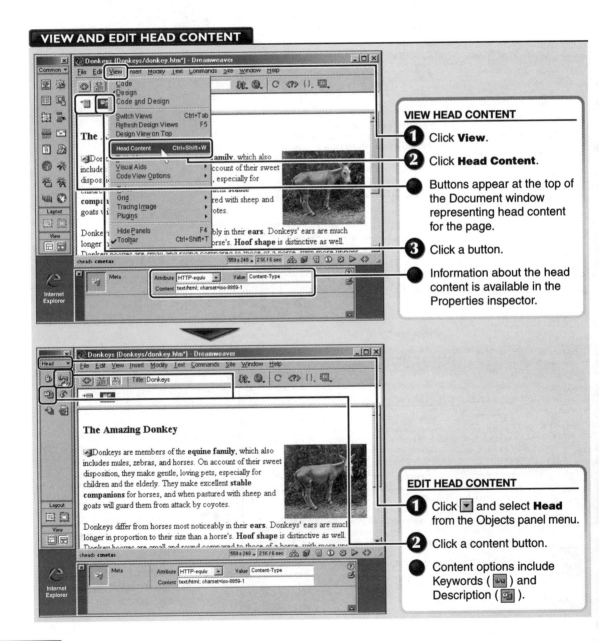

VIEW HEAD CONTENT

1 Click **View**.

2 Click **Head Content**.

Buttons appear at the top of the Document window representing head content for the page.

3 Click a button.

Information about the head content is available in the Properties inspector.

EDIT HEAD CONTENT

1 Click and select **Head** from the Objects panel menu.

2 Click a content button.

Content options include Keywords ( ) and Description ( ).

in an instant

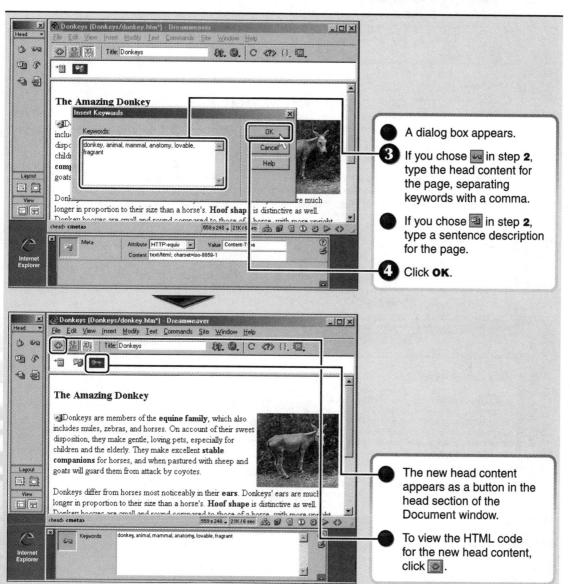

A dialog box appears.

3 If you chose 🖼 in step **2**, type the head content for the page, separating keywords with a comma.

If you chose 🖼 in step **2**, type a sentence description for the page.

4 Click **OK**.

The new head content appears as a button in the head section of the Document window.

To view the HTML code for the new head content, click 🖾.

23

USING THE QUICK TAG EDITOR

The Quick Tag Editor gives you easy access to HTML without having to switch to the Code view. You use the editor to add or modify HTML tags when you are working inside the Document window.

USING THE QUICK TAG EDITOR

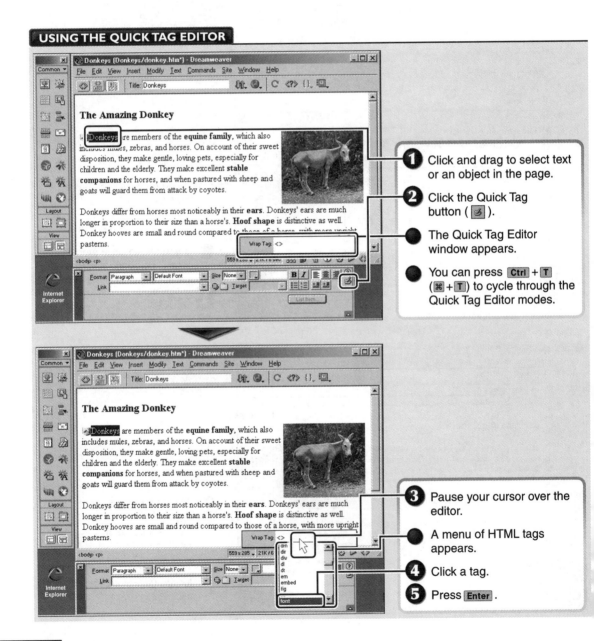

1 Click and drag to select text or an object in the page.

2 Click the Quick Tag button ( ).

● The Quick Tag Editor window appears.

● You can press Ctrl + T (⌘ + T) to cycle through the Quick Tag Editor modes.

3 Pause your cursor over the editor.

● A menu of HTML tags appears.

4 Click a tag.

5 Press Enter.

in an *instant*

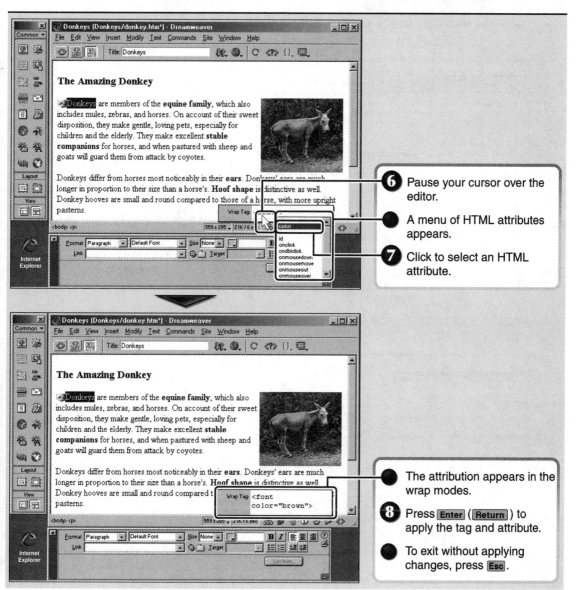

6 Pause your cursor over the editor.

A menu of HTML attributes appears.

7 Click to select an HTML attribute.

The attribution appears in the wrap modes.

8 Press Enter (Return) to apply the tag and attribute.

To exit without applying changes, press Esc.

USING THE REFERENCE PANEL

You can get quick access to reference information
about HTML tags and their attributes by using
the Reference panel.

USING THE REFERENCE PANEL

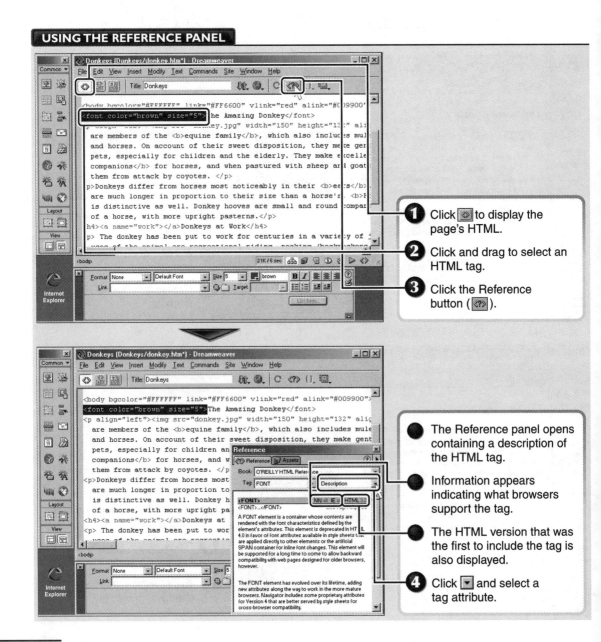

1 Click to display the page's HTML.

2 Click and drag to select an HTML tag.

3 Click the Reference button (<?>).

■ The Reference panel opens containing a description of the HTML tag.

■ Information appears indicating what browsers support the tag.

■ The HTML version that was the first to include the tag is also displayed.

4 Click ▼ and select a tag attribute.

in an instant

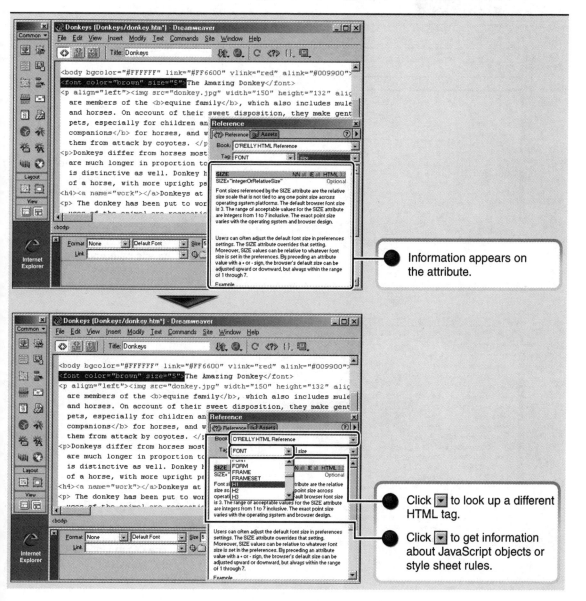

Information appears on the attribute.

Click ▾ to look up a different HTML tag.

Click ▾ to get information about JavaScript objects or style sheet rules.

CLEAN UP YOUR HTML

You can optimize HTML in your Web page by deleting extraneous or nonfunctional tags. This can decrease a page's file size and make the source code easier to read in the Code view.

CLEAN UP YOUR HTML

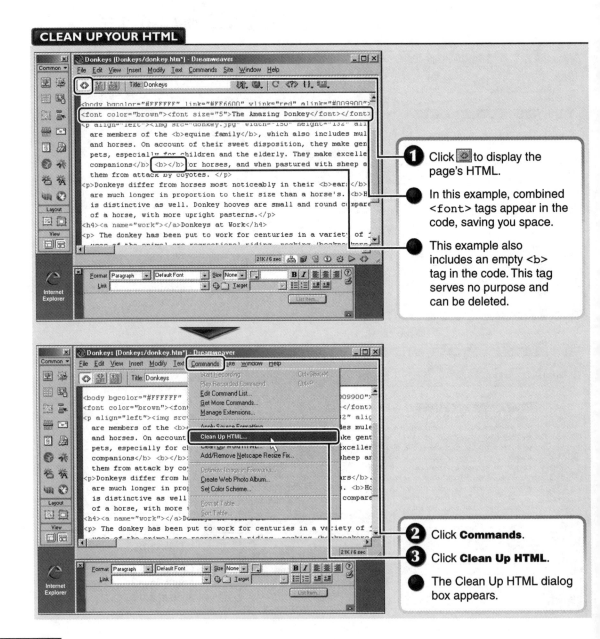

1 Click ◇ to display the page's HTML.

● In this example, combined <font> tags appear in the code, saving you space.

● This example also includes an empty <b> tag in the code. This tag serves no purpose and can be deleted.

2 Click **Commands**.

3 Click **Clean Up HTML**.

● The Clean Up HTML dialog box appears.

in an *instant*

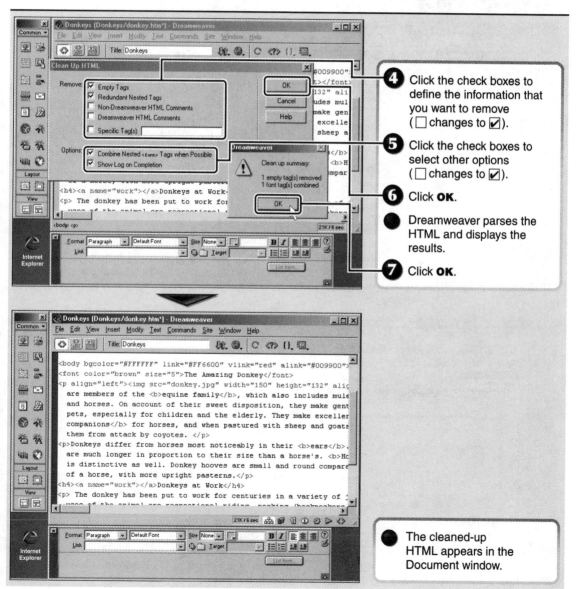

4 Click the check boxes to define the information that you want to remove (☐ changes to ☑).

5 Click the check boxes to select other options (☐ changes to ☑).

6 Click **OK**.

● Dreamweaver parses the HTML and displays the results.

7 Click **OK**.

● The cleaned-up HTML appears in the Document window.

SET UP A LOCAL SITE

Before creating your Web pages, you need to
define a local site for storing the information
in your site. Defining a local site enables you
to store and manage your Web page files.

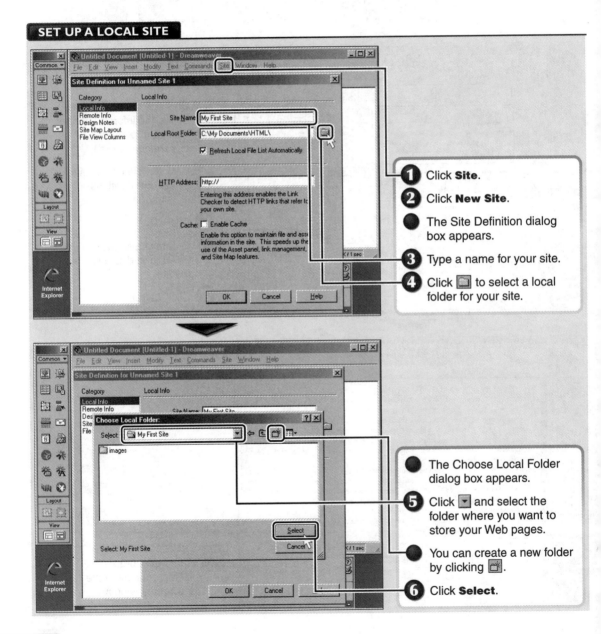

1 Click **Site**.

2 Click **New Site**.

● The Site Definition dialog
box appears.

3 Type a name for your site.

4 Click ▣ to select a local
folder for your site.

● The Choose Local Folder
dialog box appears.

5 Click ▾ and select the
folder where you want to
store your Web pages.

● You can create a new folder
by clicking ▣.

6 Click **Select**.

in an *instant*

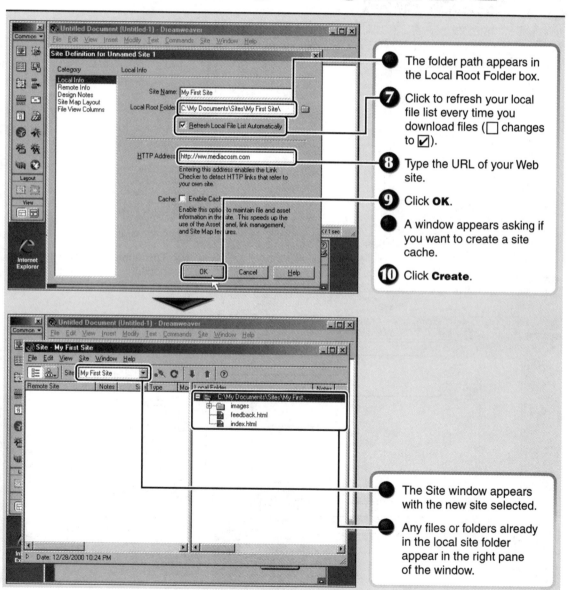

The folder path appears in the Local Root Folder box.

7 Click to refresh your local file list every time you download files (☐ changes to ☑).

8 Type the URL of your Web site.

9 Click **OK**.

A window appears asking if you want to create a site cache.

10 Click **Create**.

The Site window appears with the new site selected.

Any files or folders already in the local site folder appear in the right pane of the window.

OPEN AN EXISTING WEB PAGE

You can open an existing Web page to view
and modify its contents.

OPEN AN EXISTING WEB PAGE

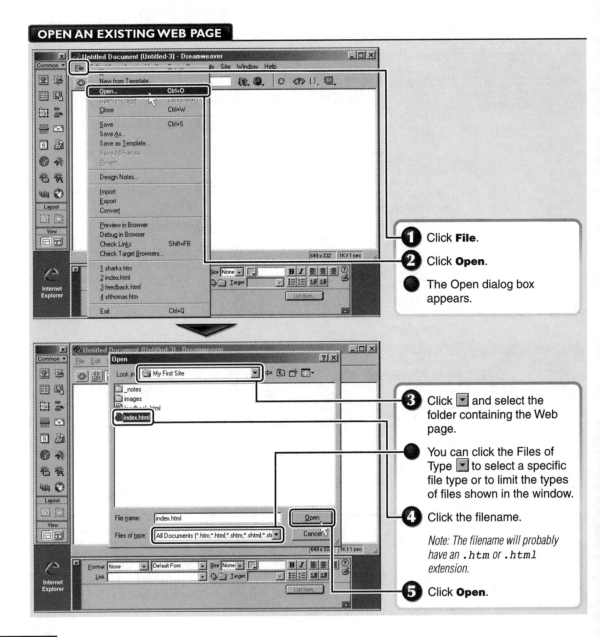

1 Click **File**.

2 Click **Open**.

● The Open dialog box
appears.

3 Click ▼ and select the
folder containing the Web
page.

● You can click the Files of
Type ▼ to select a specific
file type or to limit the types
of files shown in the window.

4 Click the filename.

*Note: The filename will probably
have an .htm or .html
extension.*

5 Click **Open**.

in an *instant*

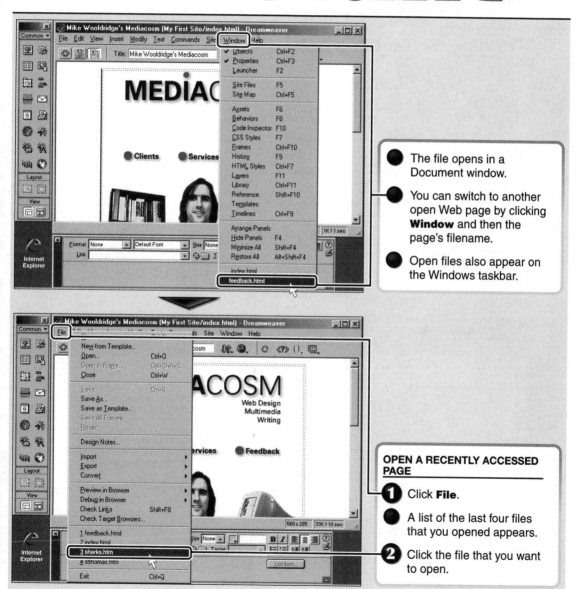

The file opens in a
Document window.

You can switch to another
open Web page by clicking
Window and then the
page's filename.

Open files also appear on
the Windows taskbar.

**OPEN A RECENTLY ACCESSED
PAGE**

1 Click **File**.

A list of the last four files
that you opened appears.

2 Click the file that you want
to open.

CREATE A NEW WEB PAGE

You can open a new Web page and then add text, images, and other elements to create a new Web page design.

CREATE A NEW WEB PAGE

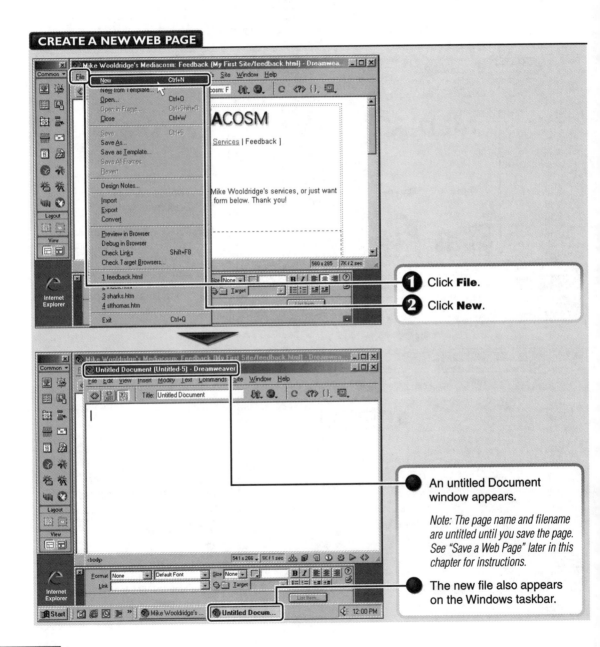

1 Click **File**.

2 Click **New**.

An untitled Document window appears.

Note: The page name and filename are untitled until you save the page. See "Save a Web Page" later in this chapter for instructions.

The new file also appears on the Windows taskbar.

ADD A WEB PAGE TITLE

A Web page title appears in the title bar when the page is opened in a Web browser. Adding a Web page title makes the page easily identifiable to viewers and search engines.

ADD A WEB PAGE TITLE

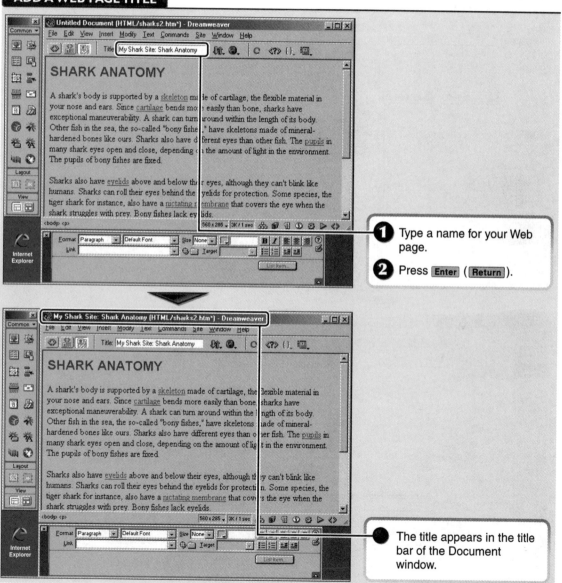

1 Type a name for your Web page.

2 Press `Enter` (`Return`).

The title appears in the title bar of the Document window.

SAVE A WEB PAGE

You should save your Web page
before closing it or transferring it
to a remote site. If you accidentally
save a wrong version, you can revert
back to the previously saved file
version.

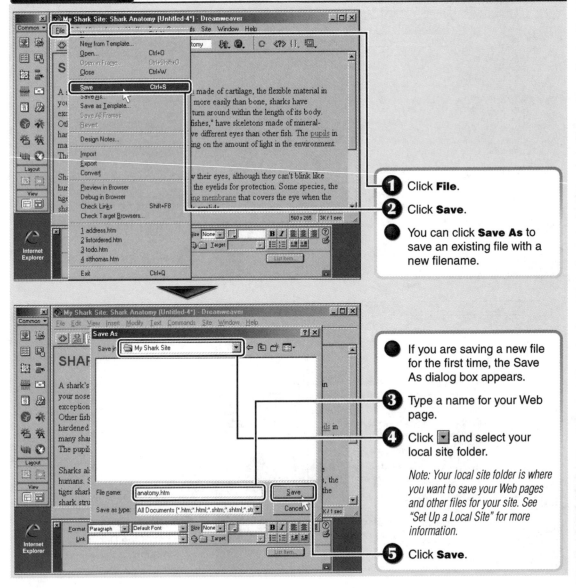

1 Click **File**.

2 Click **Save**.

● You can click **Save As** to
save an existing file with a
new filename.

● If you are saving a new file
for the first time, the Save
As dialog box appears.

3 Type a name for your Web
page.

4 Click ▼ and select your
local site folder.

*Note: Your local site folder is where
you want to save your Web pages
and other files for your site. See
"Set Up a Local Site" for more
information.*

5 Click **Save**.

in an *instant*

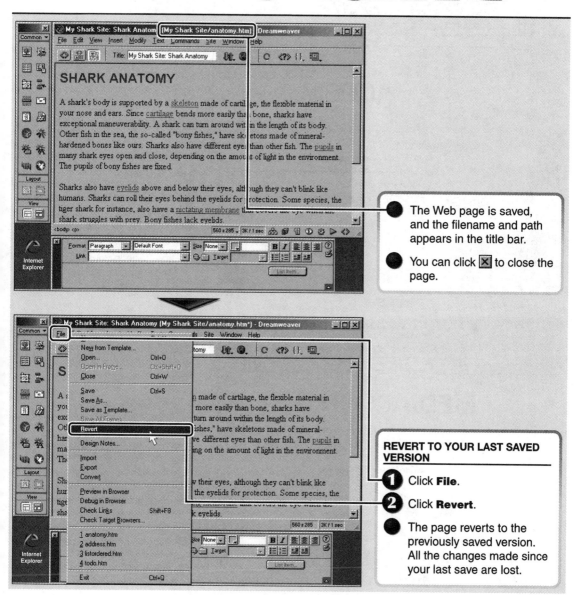

The Web page is saved, and the filename and path appears in the title bar.

You can click ☒ to close the page.

REVERT TO YOUR LAST SAVED VERSION

1 Click **File**.

2 Click **Revert**.

The page reverts to the previously saved version. All the changes made since your last save are lost.

PREVIEW A WEB PAGE IN A BROWSER

You can see how your page will appear online by previewing it in a Web browser. The Preview in Browser command works with the Web browsers installed on your computer.

PREVIEW A WEB PAGE IN A BROWSER

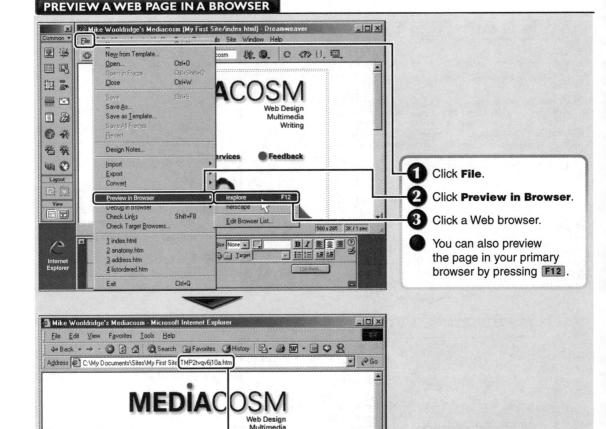

1 Click **File**.

2 Click **Preview in Browser**.

3 Click a Web browser.

● You can also preview the page in your primary browser by pressing **F12**.

● Your Web browser starts and opens the current page.

● The file has a temporary filename for viewing in the browser.

in an  *instant*

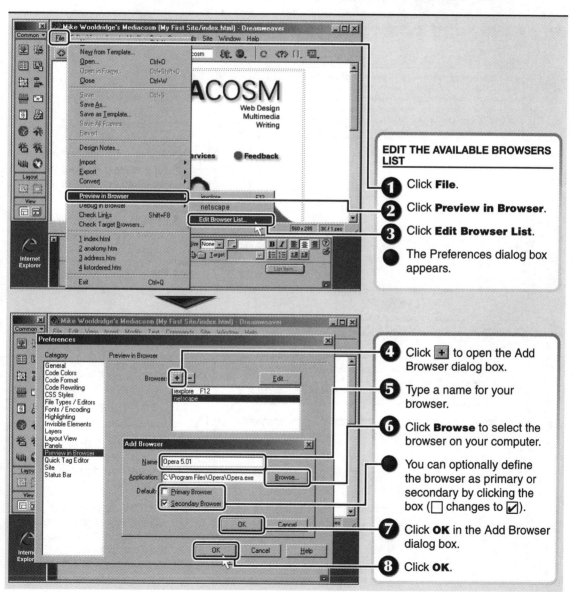

EDIT THE AVAILABLE BROWSERS LIST

1 Click **File**.

2 Click **Preview in Browser**.

3 Click **Edit Browser List**.

● The Preferences dialog box appears.

4 Click ⊞ to open the Add Browser dialog box.

5 Type a name for your browser.

6 Click **Browse** to select the browser on your computer.

● You can optionally define the browser as primary or secondary by clicking the box (☐ changes to ☑).

7 Click **OK** in the Add Browser dialog box.

8 Click **OK**.

CREATE AND ALIGN PARAGRAPHS

You can organize text on your Web page by creating and aligning paragraphs. This makes it easier to display and read information.

CREATE A PARAGRAPH

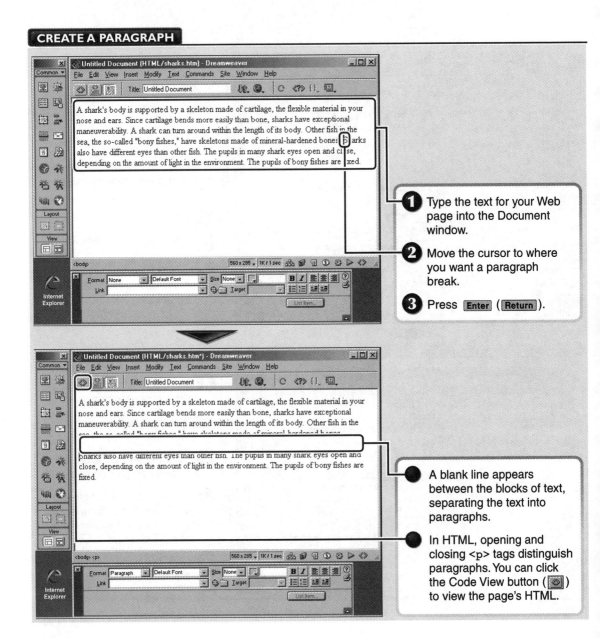

1. Type the text for your Web page into the Document window.

2. Move the cursor to where you want a paragraph break.

3. Press Enter (Return).

● A blank line appears between the blocks of text, separating the text into paragraphs.

● In HTML, opening and closing <p> tags distinguish paragraphs. You can click the Code View button ([⬚]) to view the page's HTML.

in an *instant*

ALIGN A PARAGRAPH

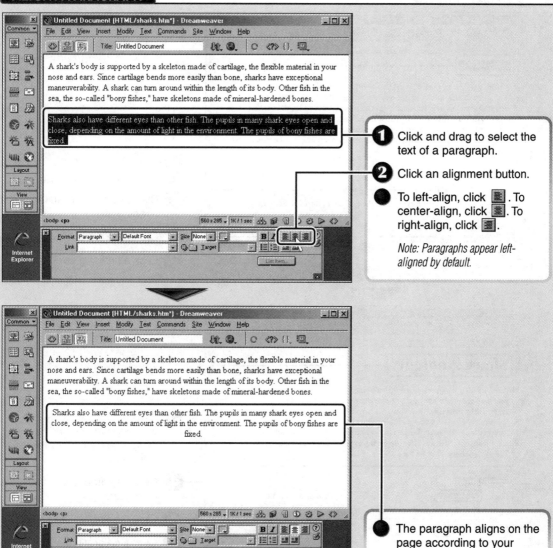

1 Click and drag to select the text of a paragraph.

2 Click an alignment button.

To left-align, click 🔳. To center-align, click 🔳. To right-align, click 🔳.

Note: Paragraphs appear left-aligned by default.

● The paragraph aligns on the page according to your selection.

CREATE A HEADING

You can add headings to structure the text on your Web page hierarchically with titles and subtitles. You can also align headings to add emphasis to your text.

CREATE A HEADING

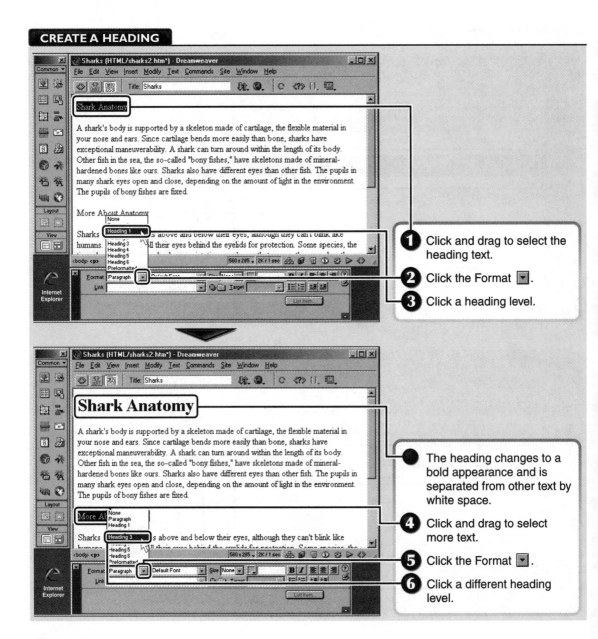

① Click and drag to select the heading text.

② Click the Format ▾.

③ Click a heading level.

■ The heading changes to a bold appearance and is separated from other text by white space.

④ Click and drag to select more text.

⑤ Click the Format ▾.

⑥ Click a different heading level.

in an *instant*

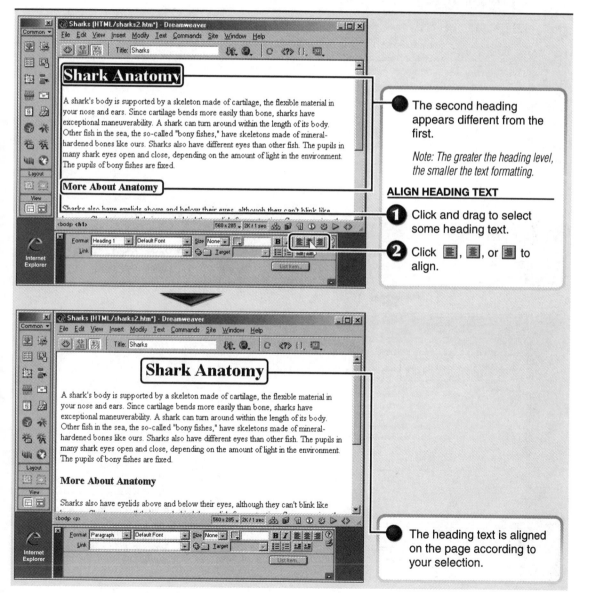

The second heading appears different from the first.

Note: The greater the heading level, the smaller the text formatting.

ALIGN HEADING TEXT

1 Click and drag to select some heading text.

2 Click ▤, ▤, or ▤ to align.

The heading text is aligned on the page according to your selection.

CREATE LINE BREAKS

You can add line breaks to your page if you
want to break up text into separate lines but
keep adjacent lines of related text close
together. Line breaks are an alternative to
paragraph breaks, which add more space
between lines of text.

CREATE LINE BREAKS

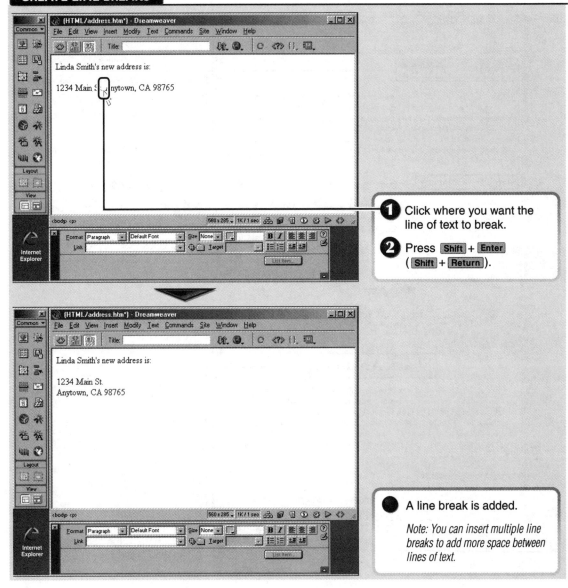

1 Click where you want the
line of text to break.

2 Press **Shift** + **Enter**
(**Shift** + **Return**).

● A line break is added.

*Note: You can insert multiple line
breaks to add more space between
lines of text.*

INDENT PARAGRAPHS

You can make selected paragraphs stand out
from the rest of the text on your Web page
by indenting them. Indents are often used for
displaying quotations.

INDENT PARAGRAPHS

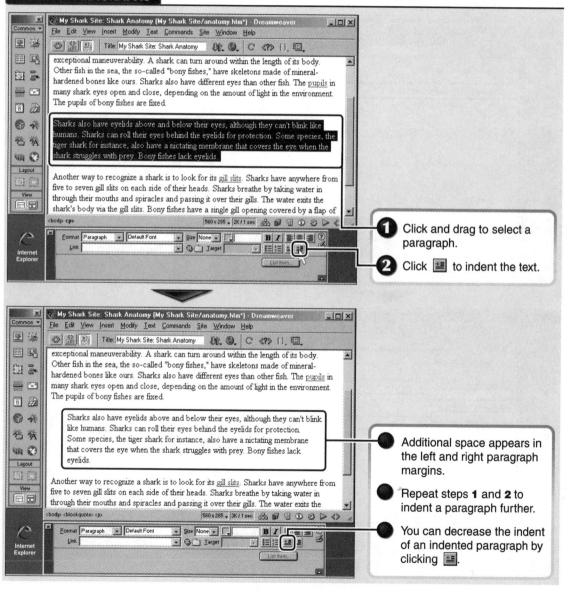

1 Click and drag to select a
paragraph.

2 Click 🗏 to indent the text.

● Additional space appears in
the left and right paragraph
margins.

● Repeat steps **1** and **2** to
indent a paragraph further.

● You can decrease the indent
of an indented paragraph by
clicking 🗏.

CREATE UNORDERED LISTS

You can organize text items into unordered lists.
Unordered lists have items that are indented and
bulleted.

CREATE UNORDERED LISTS

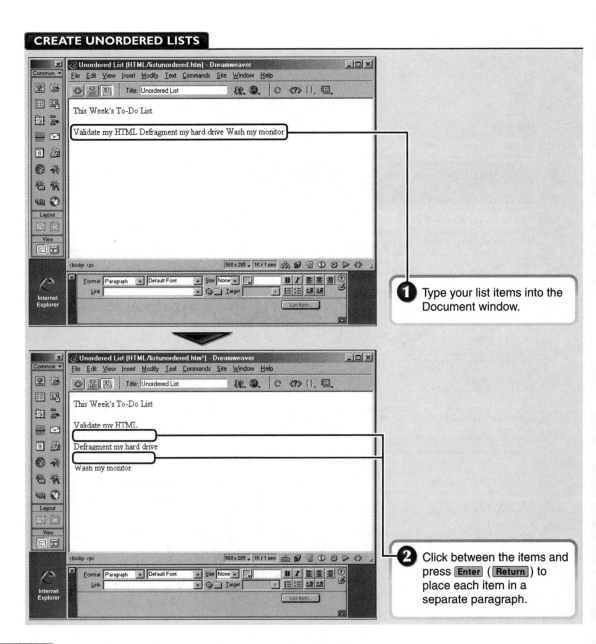

1 Type your list items into the Document window.

2 Click between the items and press **Enter** (**Return**) to place each item in a separate paragraph.

in an *instant*

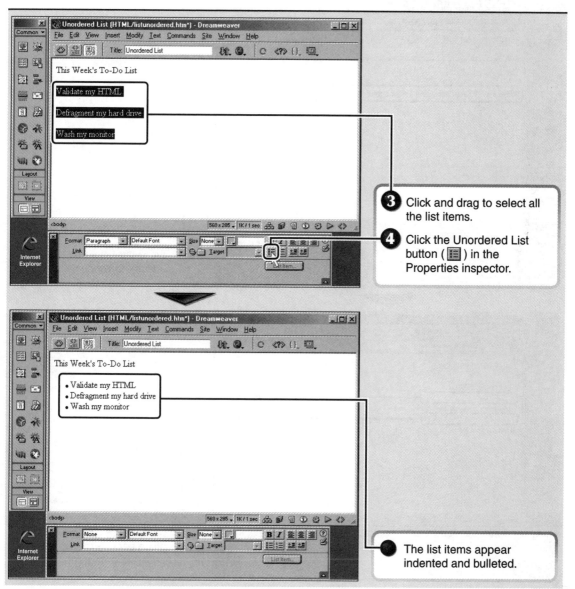

3 Click and drag to select all the list items.

4 Click the Unordered List button ( ) in the Properties inspector.

● The list items appear indented and bulleted.

CREATE ORDERED LISTS

You can organize text items into ordered lists, which have items that are indented and numbered. One example of a good use of ordered lists is to display step-by-step instructions on your Web page.

CREATE ORDERED LISTS

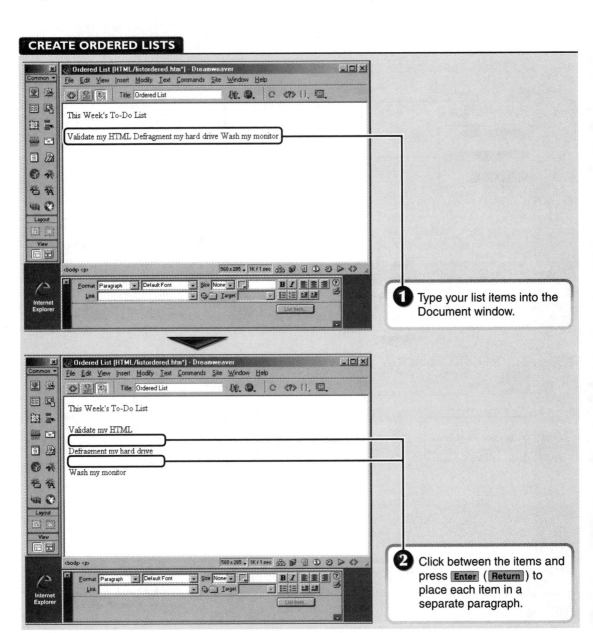

1 Type your list items into the Document window.

2 Click between the items and press **Enter** (**Return**) to place each item in a separate paragraph.

in an *instant*

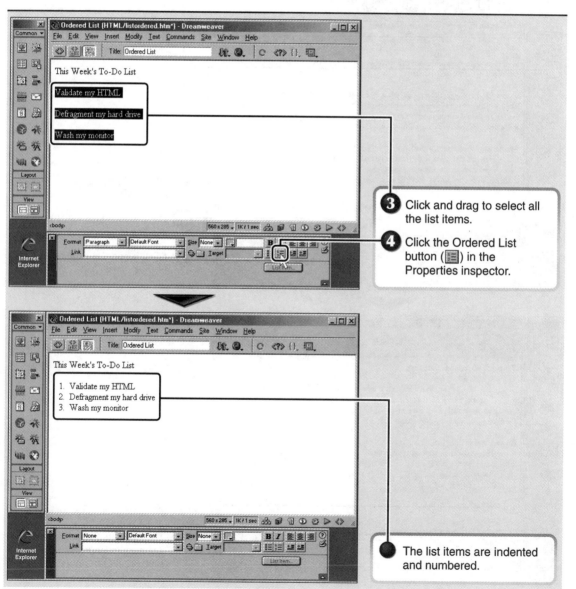

3 Click and drag to select all the list items.

4 Click the Ordered List button (⊞) in the Properties inspector.

● The list items are indented and numbered.

INSERT SPECIAL CHARACTERS

You can insert special characters that do not appear on your keyboard into your Web page.

INSERT SPECIAL CHARACTERS

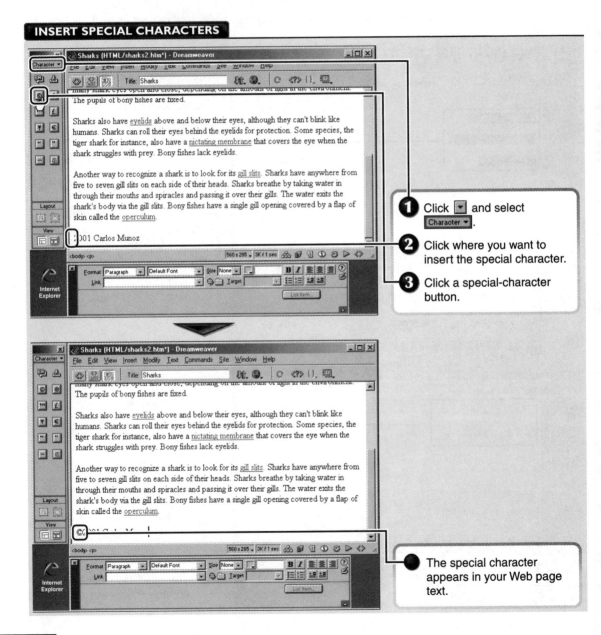

1 Click ▼ and select `Character ▼`.

2 Click where you want to insert the special character.

3 Click a special-character button.

● The special character appears in your Web page text.

in an *instant*

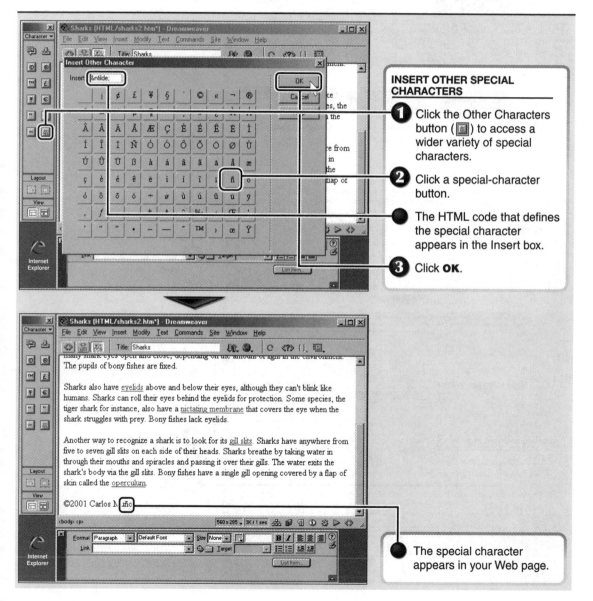

INSERT OTHER SPECIAL CHARACTERS

1 Click the Other Characters button (▣) to access a wider variety of special characters.

2 Click a special-character button.

● The HTML code that defines the special character appears in the Insert box.

3 Click **OK**.

● The special character appears in your Web page.

CHANGE THE FONT

To add variety or to emphasize certain elements to your Web page, you can change the font style of your text.

CHANGE THE FONT

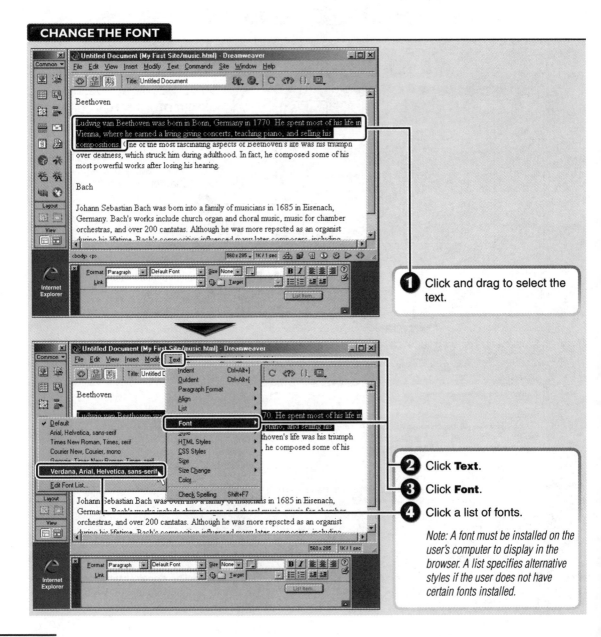

1 Click and drag to select the text.

2 Click **Text**.

3 Click **Font**.

4 Click a list of fonts.

Note: A font must be installed on the user's computer to display in the browser. A list specifies alternative styles if the user does not have certain fonts installed.

in an instant

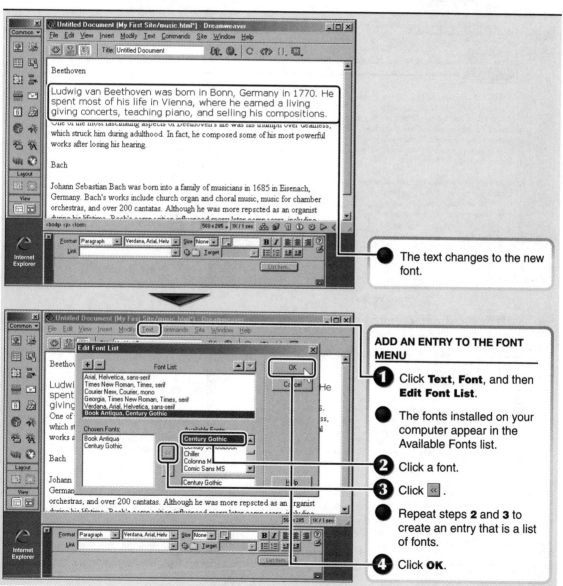

The text changes to the new font.

ADD AN ENTRY TO THE FONT MENU

1 Click **Text**, **Font**, and then **Edit Font List**.

● The fonts installed on your computer appear in the Available Fonts list.

2 Click a font.

3 Click ⟨⟨ .

● Repeat steps **2** and **3** to create an entry that is a list of fonts.

4 Click **OK**.

CHANGE FONT SIZE

You can emphasize or de-emphasize sections of text by changing the font size. Absolute font sizes on a Web page range from 1 to 7.

CHANGE FONT SIZE

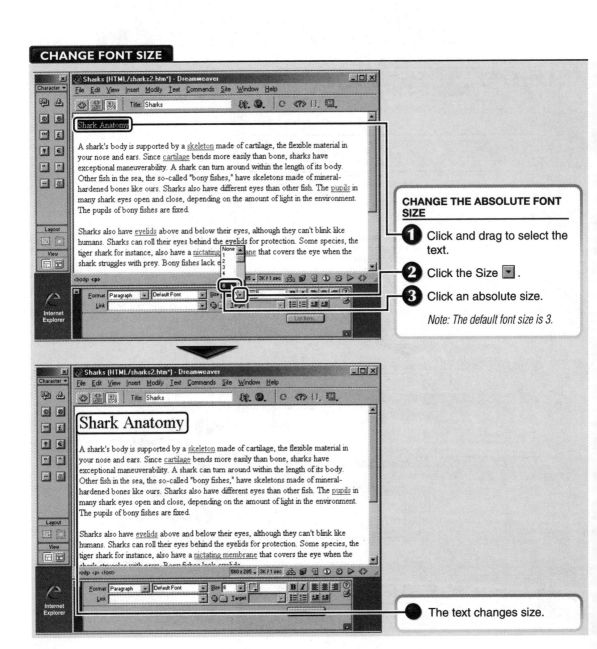

CHANGE THE ABSOLUTE FONT SIZE

1 Click and drag to select the text.

2 Click the Size ▾.

3 Click an absolute size.

Note: The default font size is 3.

● The text changes size.

in an *instant*

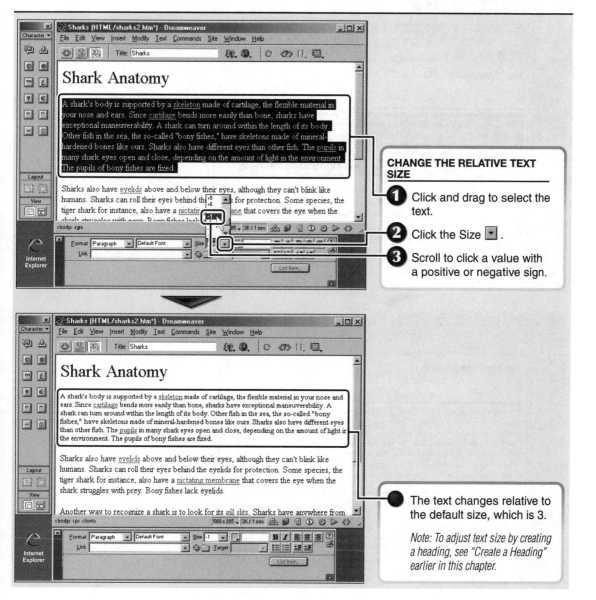

CHANGE THE RELATIVE TEXT SIZE

1 Click and drag to select the text.

2 Click the Size ▾.

3 Scroll to click a value with a positive or negative sign.

● The text changes relative to the default size, which is 3.

Note: To adjust text size by creating a heading, see "Create a Heading" earlier in this chapter.

55

FORMAT TEXT AS BOLD OR ITALIC

You can emphasize text on your Web
page with bold or italic styles.

FORMAT TEXT AS BOLD

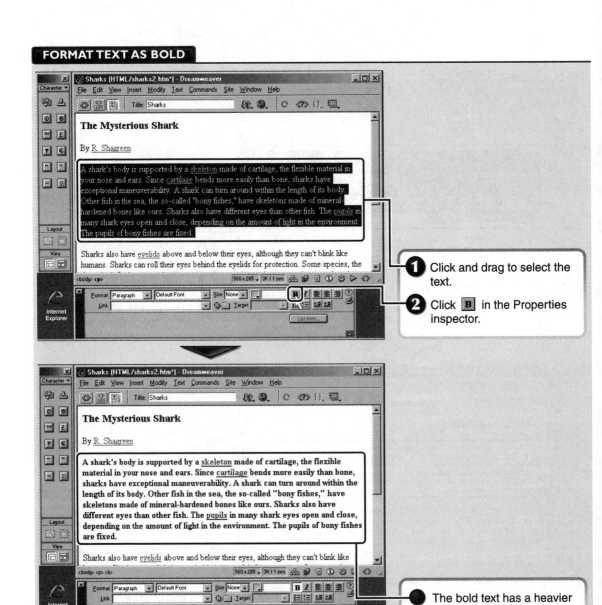

1 Click and drag to select the text.

2 Click **B** in the Properties inspector.

● The bold text has a heavier weight.

in an *instant*

FORMAT TEXT AS ITALIC

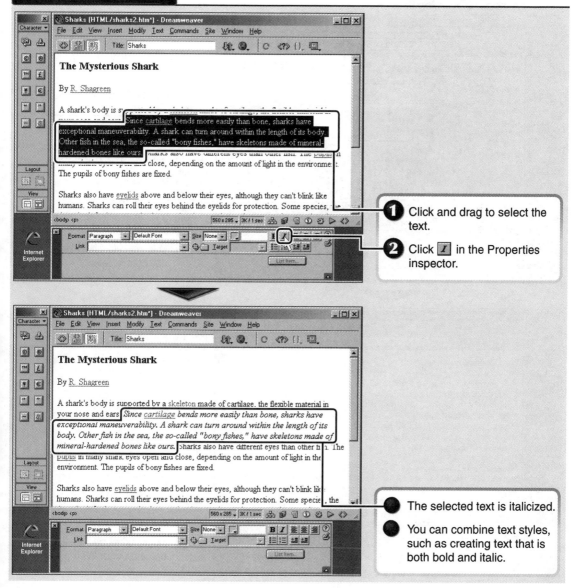

1 Click and drag to select the text.

2 Click *I* in the Properties inspector.

● The selected text is italicized.

● You can combine text styles, such as creating text that is both bold and italic.

CHANGE FONT COLOR

You can change the color of the text on all or part of your Web page so that it complements the background and other page elements.

CHANGE FONT COLOR

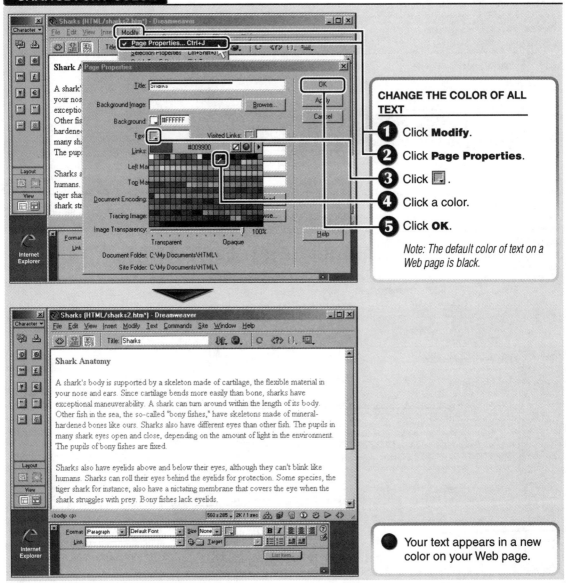

CHANGE THE COLOR OF ALL TEXT

1. Click **Modify**.

2. Click **Page Properties**.

3. Click 🔲 .

4. Click a color.

5. Click **OK**.

Note: The default color of text on a Web page is black.

● Your text appears in a new color on your Web page.

in an *instant*

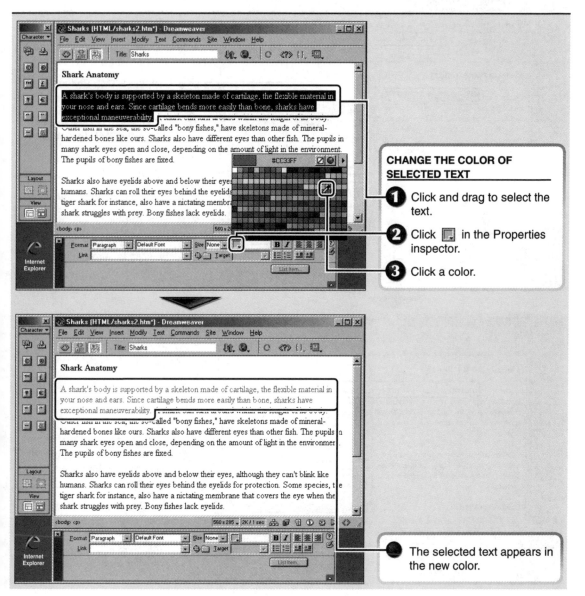

**CHANGE THE COLOR OF
SELECTED TEXT**

1 Click and drag to select the text.

2 Click in the Properties inspector.

3 Click a color.

The selected text appears in the new color.

APPLY HTML STYLES

You can format text by using the HTML Styles panel, which enables you to easily apply complicated styles.

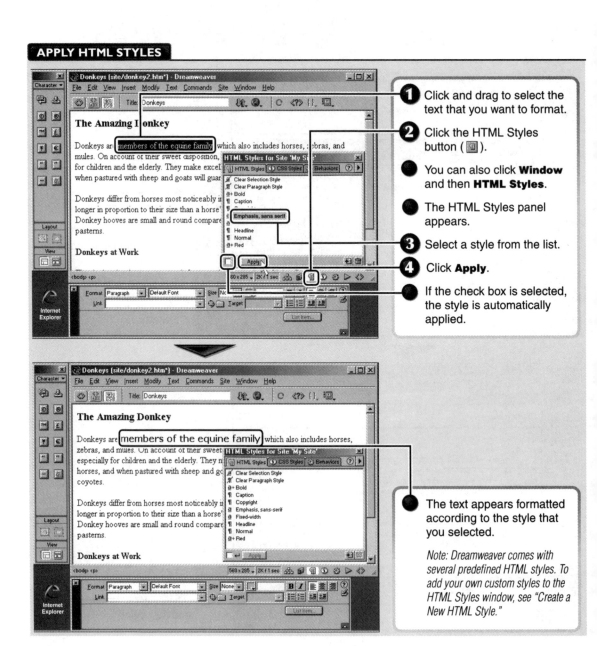

1 Click and drag to select the text that you want to format.

2 Click the HTML Styles button (▦).

● You can also click **Window** and then **HTML Styles**.

● The HTML Styles panel appears.

3 Select a style from the list.

4 Click **Apply**.

● If the check box is selected, the style is automatically applied.

● The text appears formatted according to the style that you selected.

Note: Dreamweaver comes with several predefined HTML styles. To add your own custom styles to the HTML Styles window, see "Create a New HTML Style."

Dreamweaver allows you to save time by saving
complicated text styles in the HTML Styles
window. You can then easily use them later.

CREATE A NEW HTML STYLE

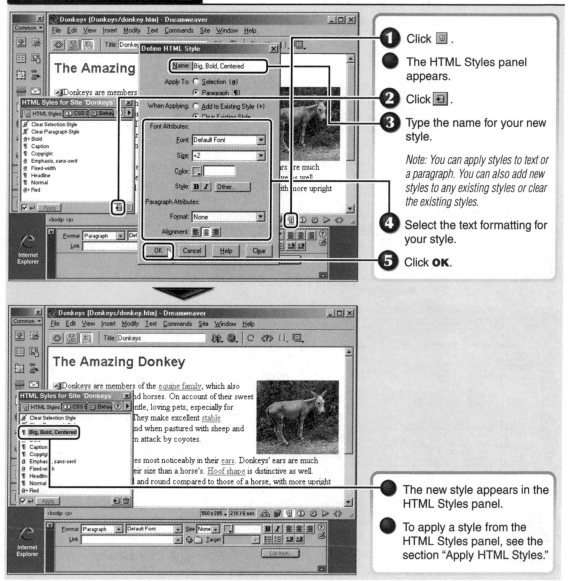

1 Click 🔲 .

The HTML Styles panel
appears.

2 Click 🔲 .

3 Type the name for your new
style.

*Note: You can apply styles to text or
a paragraph. You can also add new
styles to any existing styles or clear
the existing styles.*

4 Select the text formatting for
your style.

5 Click **OK**.

● The new style appears in the
HTML Styles panel.

● To apply a style from the
HTML Styles panel, see the
section "Apply HTML Styles."

INSERT AN IMAGE INTO A WEB PAGE

Different types of images, including clip art, digital camera images, and scanned photos, can be inserted into your Web page. You can also place a border around your image after you have placed it on the page.

INSERT AN IMAGE INTO A WEB PAGE

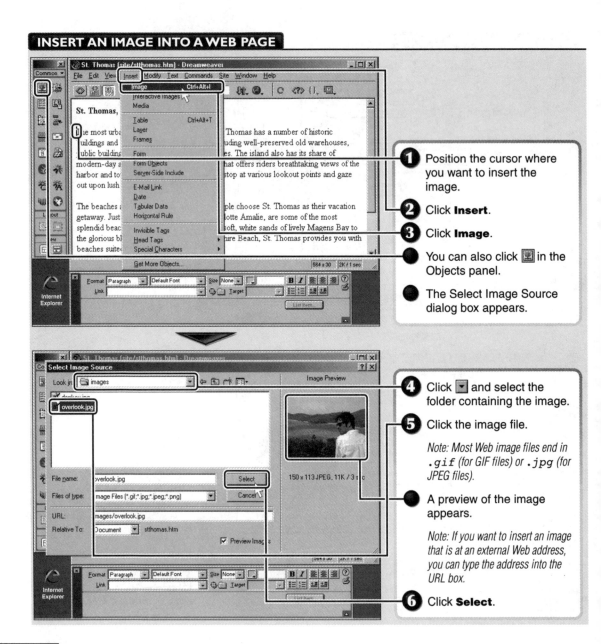

1 Position the cursor where you want to insert the image.

2 Click **Insert**.

3 Click **Image**.

You can also click ▦ in the Objects panel.

The Select Image Source dialog box appears.

4 Click ▾ and select the folder containing the image.

5 Click the image file.

Note: Most Web image files end in .gif (for GIF files) or .jpg (for JPEG files).

A preview of the image appears.

Note: If you want to insert an image that is at an external Web address, you can type the address into the URL box.

6 Click **Select**.

in an *instant*

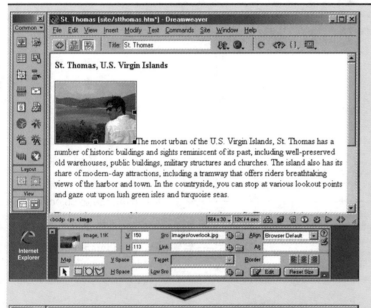

- The image appears where you positioned your cursor in the Web page.

- To delete an image, click the image and press Delete.

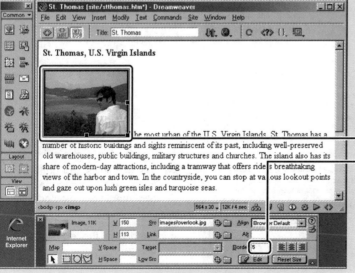

ADD A BORDER TO AN IMAGE

1. Click the image to select it.

2. Type the width (in pixels) into the Border box.

3. Press Enter (Return).

- A border that is the same color as the text appears around the image.

WRAP TEXT AROUND AN IMAGE

Wrapping text around images enables you to fit more information onto the screen and gives your Web pages a professional look.

WRAP TEXT AROUND AN IMAGE

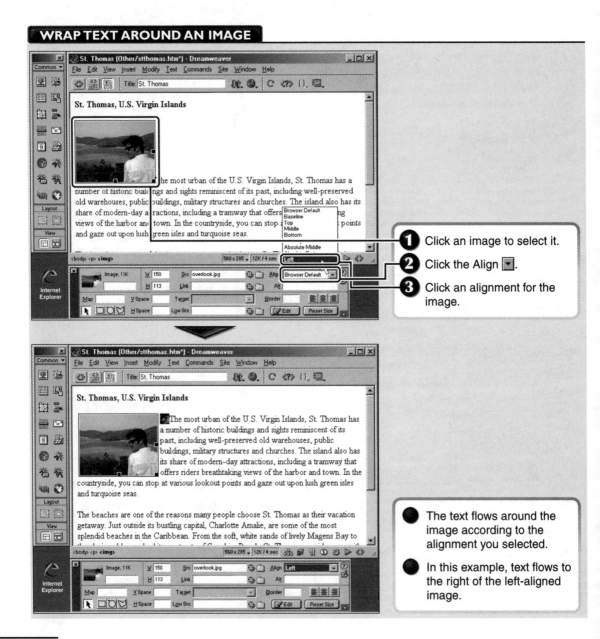

1 Click an image to select it.

2 Click the Align ▾.

3 Click an alignment for the image.

● The text flows around the image according to the alignment you selected.

● In this example, text flows to the right of the left-aligned image.

in an *instant*

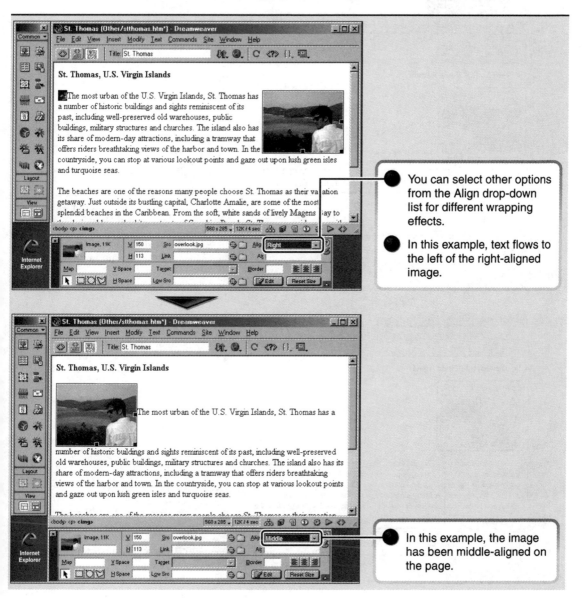

You can select other options from the Align drop-down list for different wrapping effects.

In this example, text flows to the left of the right-aligned image.

In this example, the image has been middle-aligned on the page.

CENTER AN IMAGE

Centering an image can give a photo or banner prominence on your page.

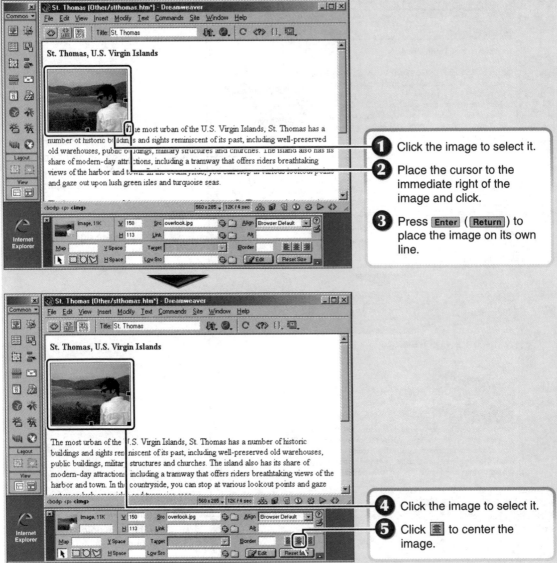

1 Click the image to select it.

2 Place the cursor to the immediate right of the image and click.

3 Press Enter (Return) to place the image on its own line.

4 Click the image to select it.

5 Click 🖼 to center the image.

in an instant

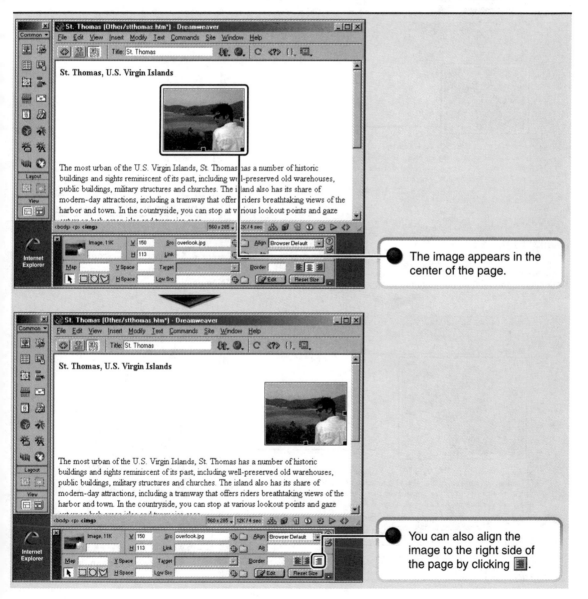

The image appears in the center of the page.

You can also align the image to the right side of the page by clicking 🔲.

RESIZE AN IMAGE

You can resize an image for your
Web page by changing the image's
pixel dimensions, clicking and dragging
the corner of the image, or changing
the image's proportional size.

RESIZE AN IMAGE

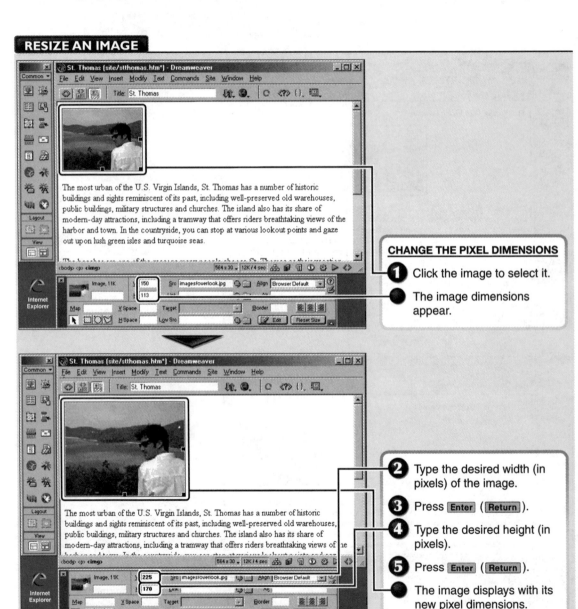

CHANGE THE PIXEL DIMENSIONS

1 Click the image to select it.

■ The image dimensions
appear.

2 Type the desired width (in
pixels) of the image.

3 Press Enter (Return).

4 Type the desired height (in
pixels).

5 Press Enter (Return).

■ The image displays with its
new pixel dimensions.

in an *instant*

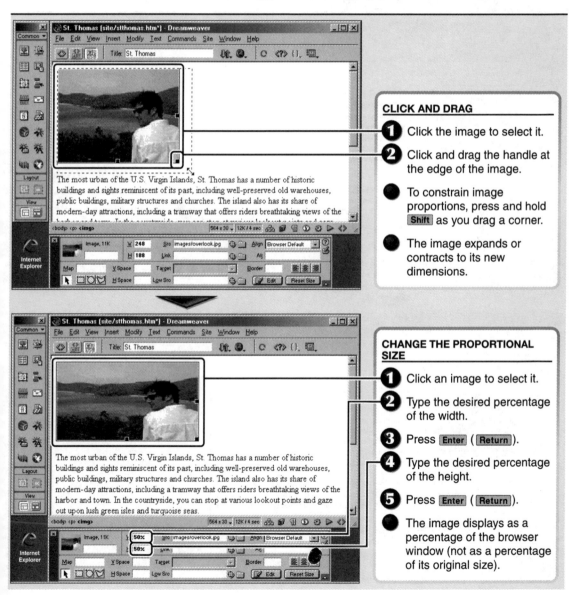

ADD SPACE AROUND AN IMAGE

Adding space around an image distinguishes it from the text and other images on your Web page.

ADD SPACE AROUND AN IMAGE

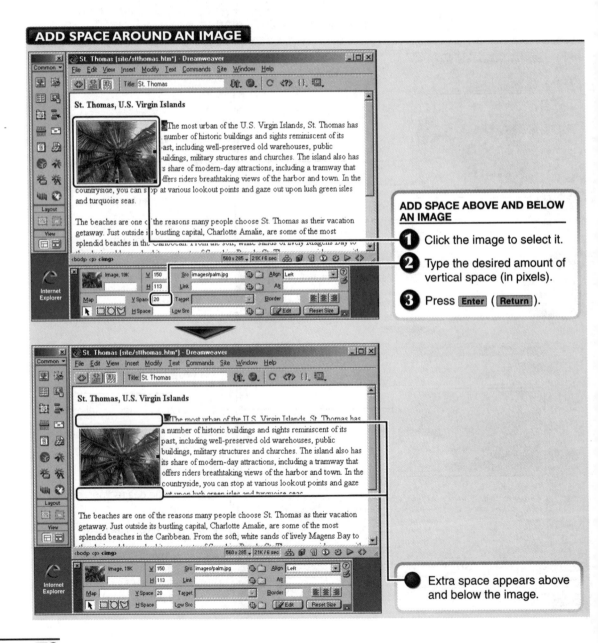

ADD SPACE ABOVE AND BELOW AN IMAGE

1 Click the image to select it.

2 Type the desired amount of vertical space (in pixels).

3 Press Enter (Return).

■ Extra space appears above and below the image.

in an instant

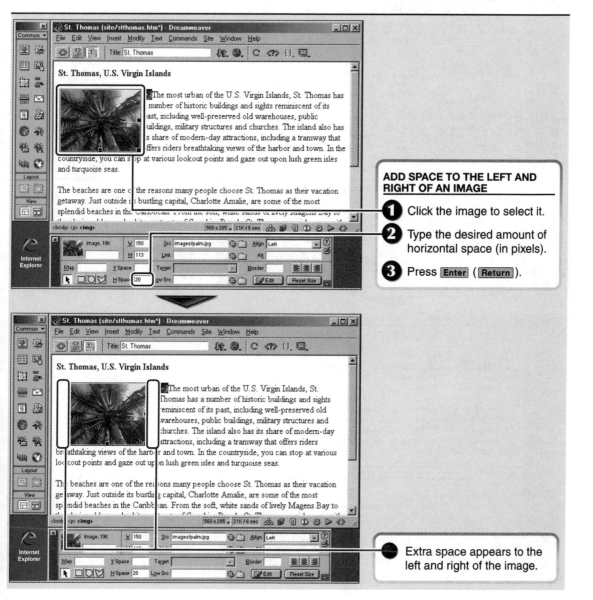

**ADD SPACE TO THE LEFT AND
RIGHT OF AN IMAGE**

1 Click the image to select it.

2 Type the desired amount of
horizontal space (in pixels).

3 Press Enter (Return).

● Extra space appears to the
left and right of the image.

ADD A HORIZONTAL RULE

You can add a horizontal rule to your Web page to separate sections of content. You can customize the appearance of the rule according to your preferences.

ADD A HORIZONTAL RULE

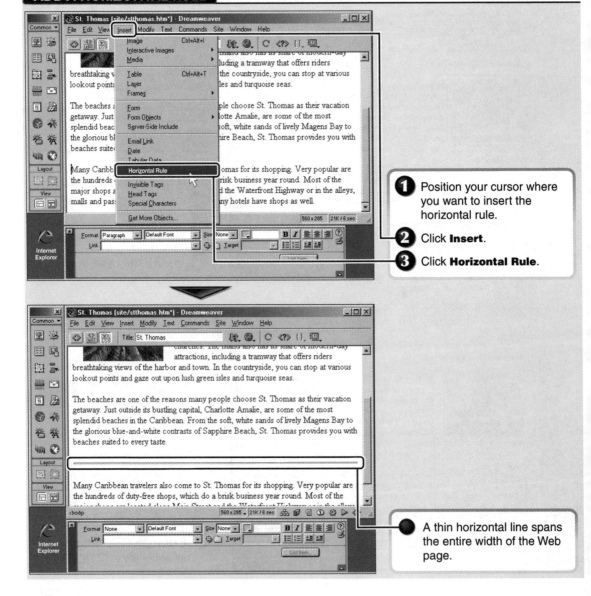

1 Position your cursor where you want to insert the horizontal rule.

2 Click **Insert**.

3 Click **Horizontal Rule**.

A thin horizontal line spans the entire width of the Web page.

in an *instant*

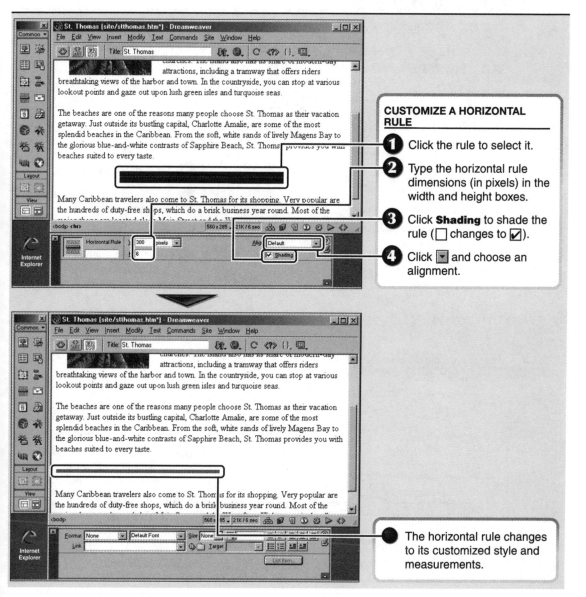

CUSTOMIZE A HORIZONTAL RULE

1. Click the rule to select it.

2. Type the horizontal rule dimensions (in pixels) in the width and height boxes.

3. Click **Shading** to shade the rule (☐ changes to ☑).

4. Click ▾ and choose an alignment.

● The horizontal rule changes to its customized style and measurements.

BACKGROUND IMAGE

...rate a background image to add texture to
...background images appear beneath any text
...r page.

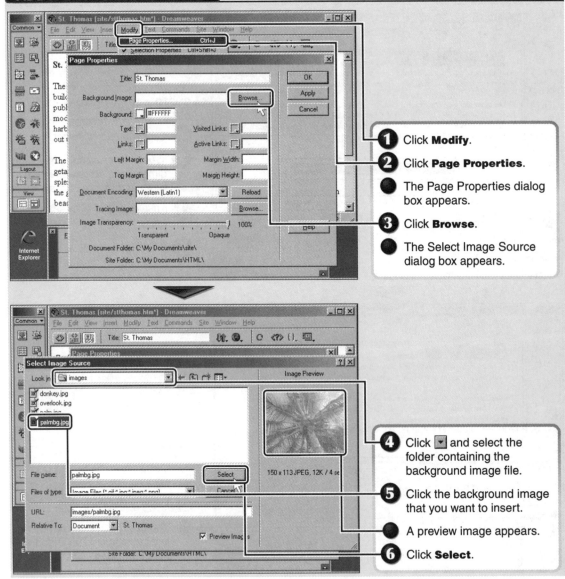

1 Click **Modify**.

2 Click **Page Properties**.

● The Page Properties dialog box appears.

3 Click **Browse**.

● The Select Image Source dialog box appears.

4 Click ▼ and select the folder containing the background image file.

5 Click the background image that you want to insert.

● A preview image appears.

6 Click **Select**.

in an instant

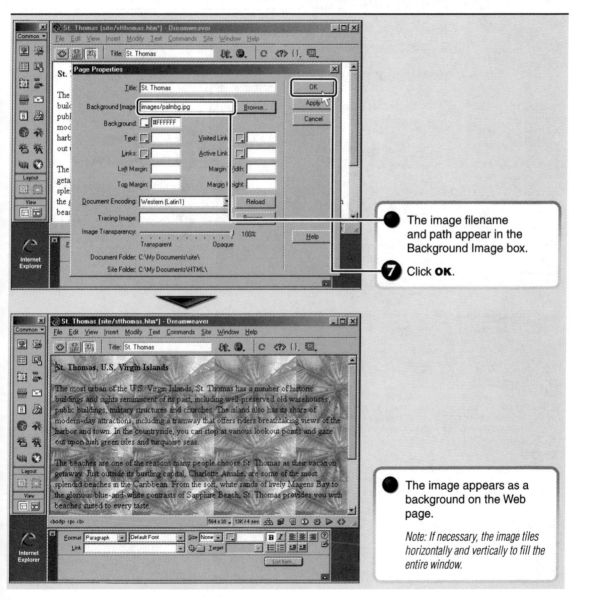

The image filename and path appear in the Background Image box.

7 Click **OK**.

The image appears as a background on the Web page.

Note: If necessary, the image tiles horizontally and vertically to fill the entire window.

CHANGE THE BACKGROUND COLOR

For variety, you can change the background color of your Web page. The default background color of Dreamweaver Web pages is white.

CHANGE THE BACKGROUND COLOR

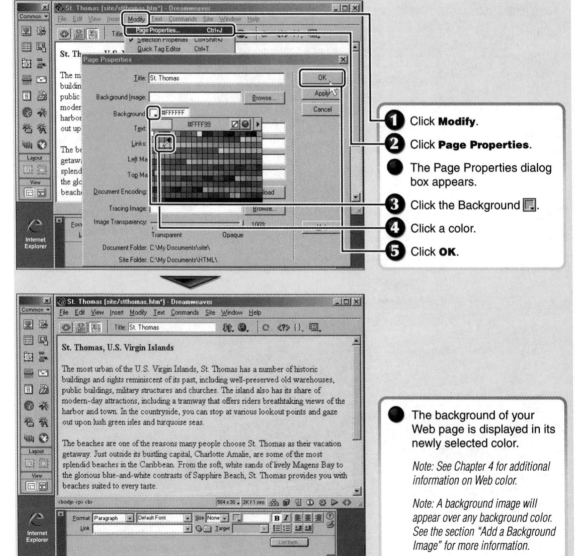

1 Click **Modify**.

2 Click **Page Properties**.

● The Page Properties dialog box appears.

3 Click the Background.

4 Click a color.

5 Click **OK**.

● The background of your Web page is displayed in its newly selected color.

Note: See Chapter 4 for additional information on Web color.

Note: A background image will appear over any background color. See the section "Add a Background Image" for more information.

You can add alternate text for users to read when
your image does not appear in their browsers.
Some Web browsers cannot display images, and
some users surf the Web with images turned off.

ADD ALTERNATE TEXT

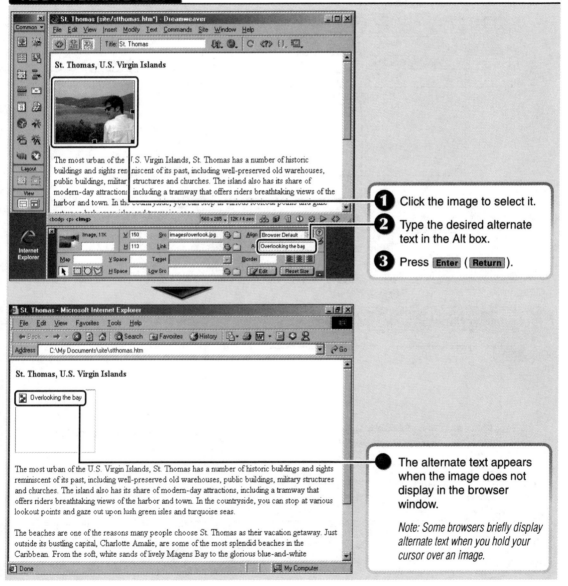

1 Click the image to select it.

2 Type the desired alternate text in the Alt box.

3 Press **Enter** (**Return**).

● The alternate text appears when the image does not display in the browser window.

Note: Some browsers briefly display alternate text when you hold your cursor over an image.

INSERT MULTIMEDIA

You can insert video clips and other multimedia to add life to your Web page.

INSERT MULTIMEDIA

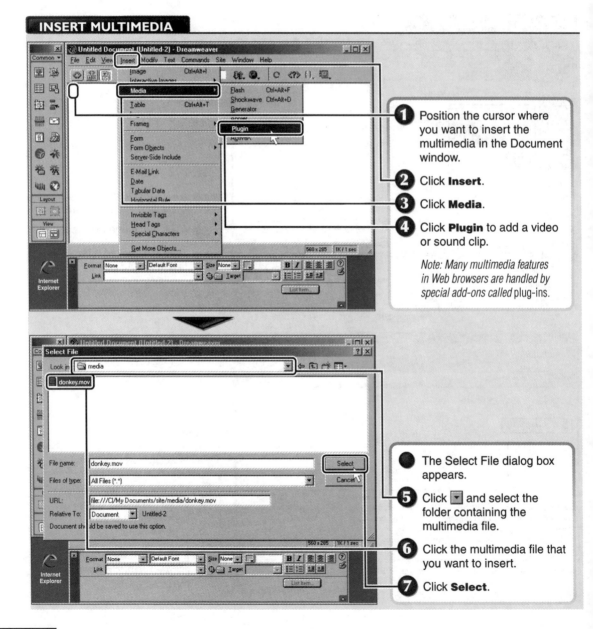

1 Position the cursor where you want to insert the multimedia in the Document window.

2 Click **Insert**.

3 Click **Media**.

4 Click **Plugin** to add a video or sound clip.

Note: Many multimedia features in Web browsers are handled by special add-ons called plug-ins.

■ The Select File dialog box appears.

5 Click ▼ and select the folder containing the multimedia file.

6 Click the multimedia file that you want to insert.

7 Click **Select**.

in an instant

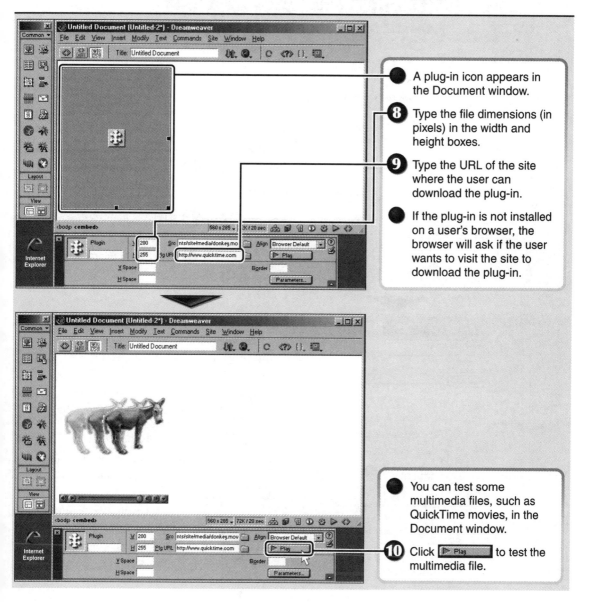

A plug-in icon appears in the Document window.

8 Type the file dimensions (in pixels) in the width and height boxes.

9 Type the URL of the site where the user can download the plug-in.

If the plug-in is not installed on a user's browser, the browser will ask if the user wants to visit the site to download the plug-in.

You can test some multimedia files, such as QuickTime movies, in the Document window.

10 Click ▶ Play to test the multimedia file.

yperlink that enables readers to move from
Web site to another.

CREATE HYPERLINKS TO OTHER PAGES IN YOUR WEB SITE

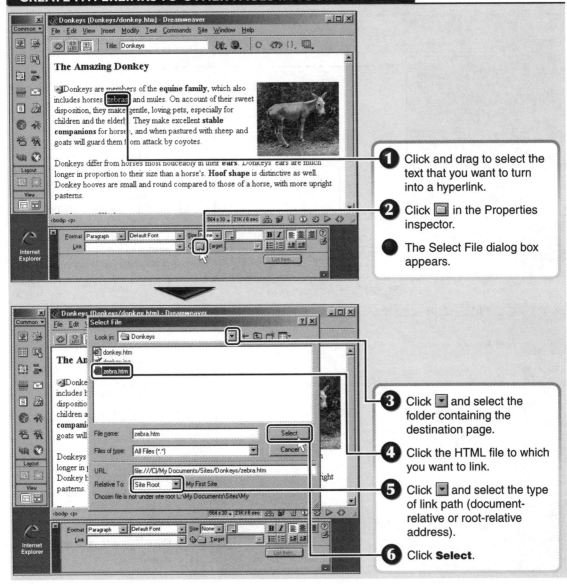

1 Click and drag to select the text that you want to turn into a hyperlink.

2 Click 📁 in the Properties inspector.

● The Select File dialog box appears.

3 Click 🔽 and select the folder containing the destination page.

4 Click the HTML file to which you want to link.

5 Click 🔽 and select the type of link path (document-relative or root-relative address).

6 Click **Select**.

in an *instant*

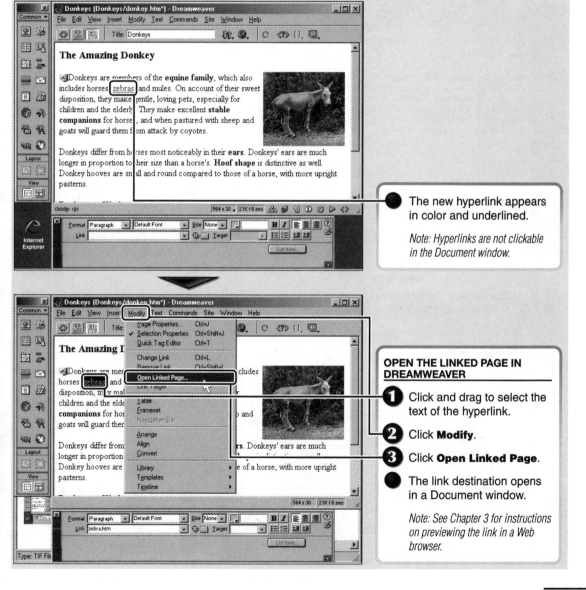

The new hyperlink appears in color and underlined.

Note: Hyperlinks are not clickable in the Document window.

OPEN THE LINKED PAGE IN DREAMWEAVER

1 Click and drag to select the text of the hyperlink.

2 Click **Modify**.

3 Click **Open Linked Page**.

The link destination opens in a Document window.

Note: See Chapter 3 for instructions on previewing the link in a Web browser.

You can give viewers access to additional information about topics by linking to pages in other Web sites.

CREATE HYPERLINKS TO ANOTHER WEB SITE

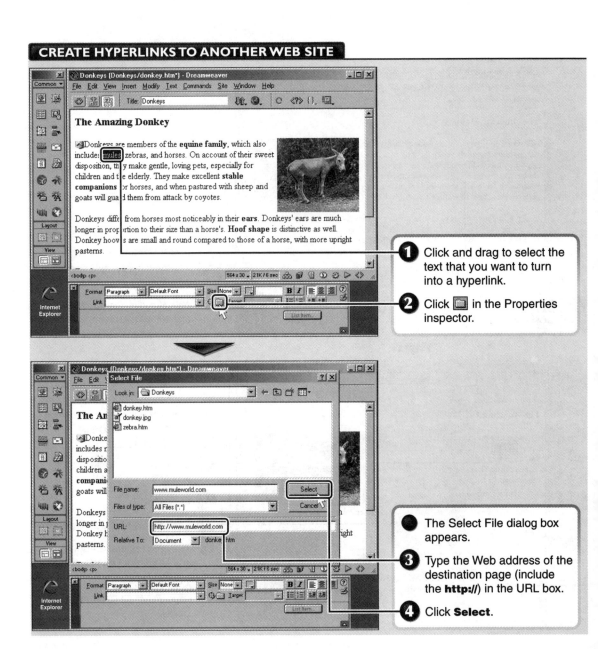

1 Click and drag to select the text that you want to turn into a hyperlink.

2 Click 🔲 in the Properties inspector.

● The Select File dialog box appears.

3 Type the Web address of the destination page (include the **http://**) in the URL box.

4 Click **Select**.

in an *instant*

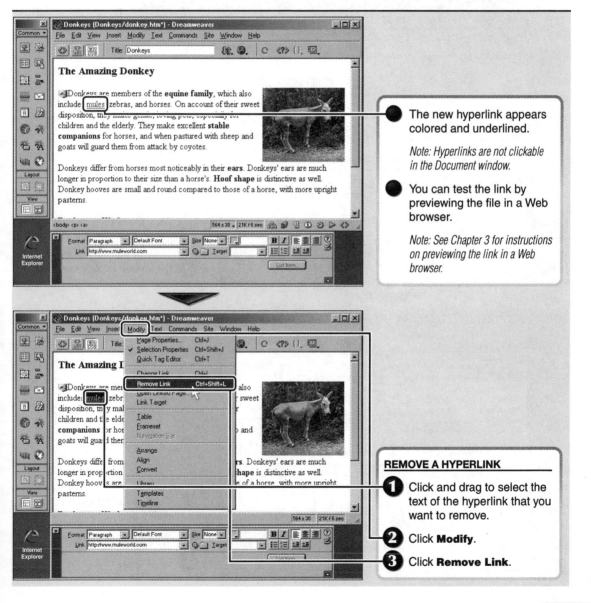

The new hyperlink appears colored and underlined.

Note: Hyperlinks are not clickable in the Document window.

You can test the link by previewing the file in a Web browser.

Note: See Chapter 3 for instructions on previewing the link in a Web browser.

REMOVE A HYPERLINK

1 Click and drag to select the text of the hyperlink that you want to remove.

2 Click **Modify**.

3 Click **Remove Link**.

CREATE HYPERLINKS TO CONTENT ON THE SAME WEB PAGE

You can create a hyperlink to other content on the same Web page.
Same-page hyperlinks are useful when a page is very long.

CREATE HYPERLINKS TO CONTENT ON THE SAME WEB PAGE

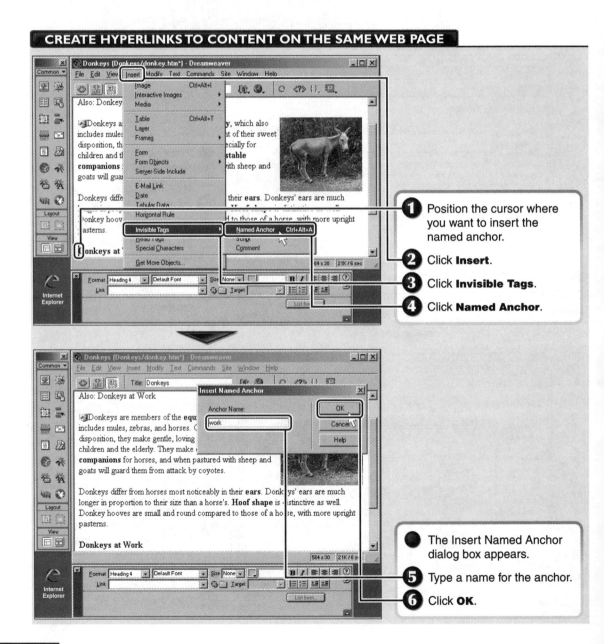

1 Position the cursor where you want to insert the named anchor.

2 Click **Insert**.

3 Click **Invisible Tags**.

4 Click **Named Anchor**.

■ The Insert Named Anchor dialog box appears.

5 Type a name for the anchor.

6 Click **OK**.

in an *instant*

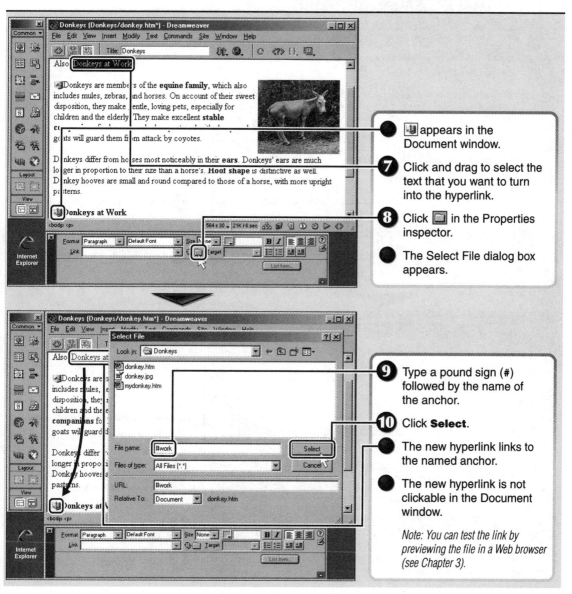

appears in the Document window.

7 Click and drag to select the text that you want to turn into the hyperlink.

8 Click in the Properties inspector.

The Select File dialog box appears.

9 Type a pound sign (#) followed by the name of the anchor.

10 Click **Select**.

The new hyperlink links to the named anchor.

The new hyperlink is not clickable in the Document window.

Note: You can test the link by previewing the file in a Web browser (see Chapter 3).

CREATE HYPERLINKS TO OTHER FILES

Hyperlinks do not have to lead just to other Web pages. You can link to other file types, such as image files, word processing documents, or multimedia files.

CREATE HYPERLINKS TO OTHER FILES

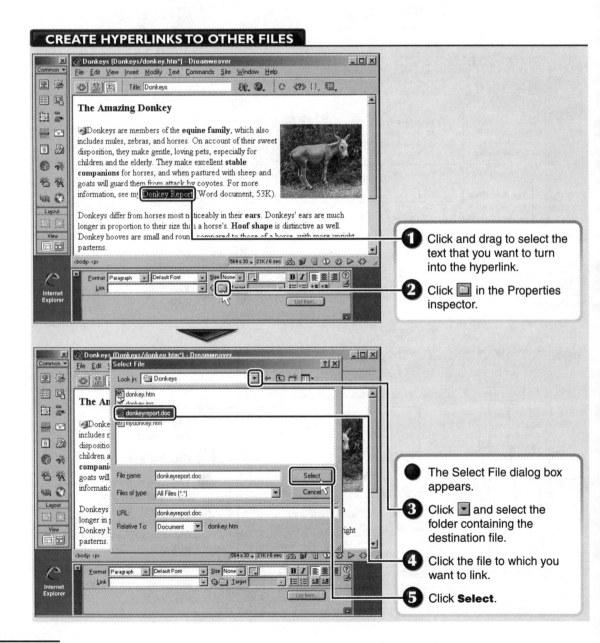

1 Click and drag to select the text that you want to turn into the hyperlink.

2 Click 🔲 in the Properties inspector.

● The Select File dialog box appears.

3 Click ▾ and select the folder containing the destination file.

4 Click the file to which you want to link.

5 Click **Select**.

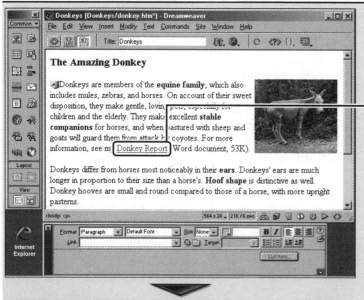

The new hyperlink appears in color and underlined.

Note: Hyperlinks are not clickable in the Document window.

You can test the link by previewing the file in a Web browser.

Note: See Chapter 3 for instructions on previewing the link in a Web browser.

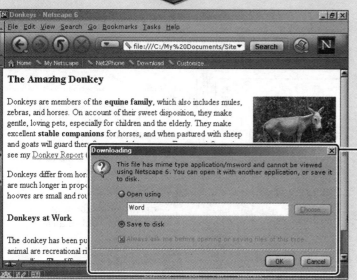

This particular browser is not configured to view the file type that was linked. When you click a Web page link in a browser, an alert box appears asking whether the user wants to open the document with another application or save it.

users to click an image to go

LINKS

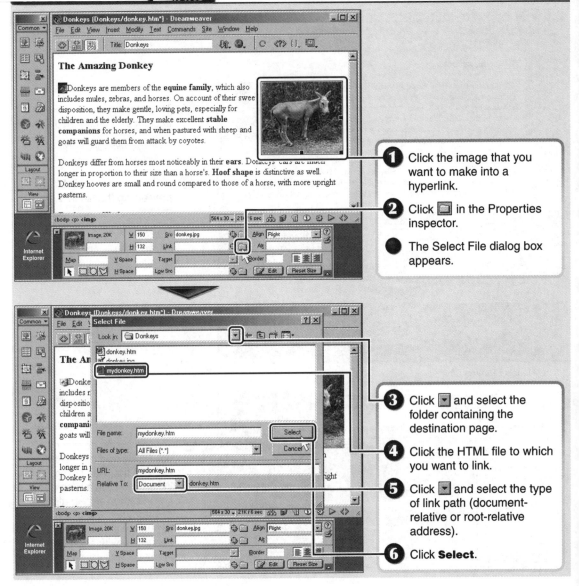

1 Click the image that you want to make into a hyperlink.

2 Click 🗀 in the Properties inspector.

● The Select File dialog box appears.

3 Click ▾ and select the folder containing the destination page.

4 Click the HTML file to which you want to link.

5 Click ▾ and select the type of link path (document-relative or root-relative address).

6 Click **Select**.

in an *instant*

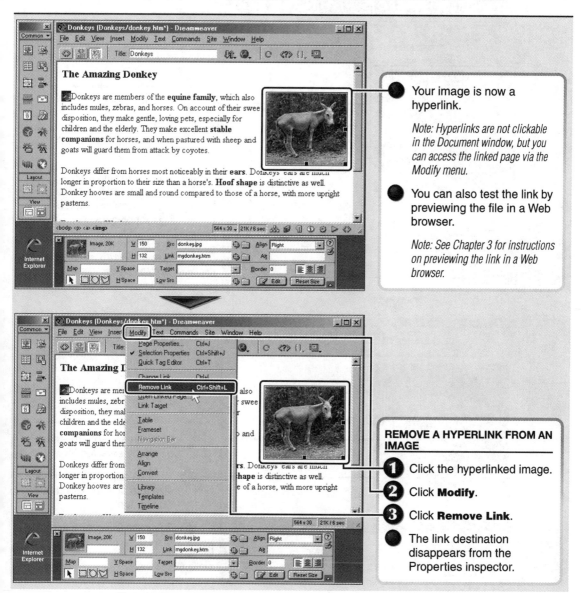

Your image is now a hyperlink.

Note: Hyperlinks are not clickable in the Document window, but you can access the linked page via the Modify menu.

You can also test the link by previewing the file in a Web browser.

Note: See Chapter 3 for instructions on previewing the link in a Web browser.

REMOVE A HYPERLINK FROM AN IMAGE

1 Click the hyperlinked image.

2 Click **Modify**.

3 Click **Remove Link**.

The link destination disappears from the Properties inspector.

CREATE HYPERLINK HOTSPOTS WITHIN AN IMAGE

To make an image serve several purposes, you can assign different hyperlinks (also called *hotspots*) to different parts of the image using the Dreamweaver image-mapping tools.

CREATE HYPERLINK HOTSPOTS WITHIN AN IMAGE

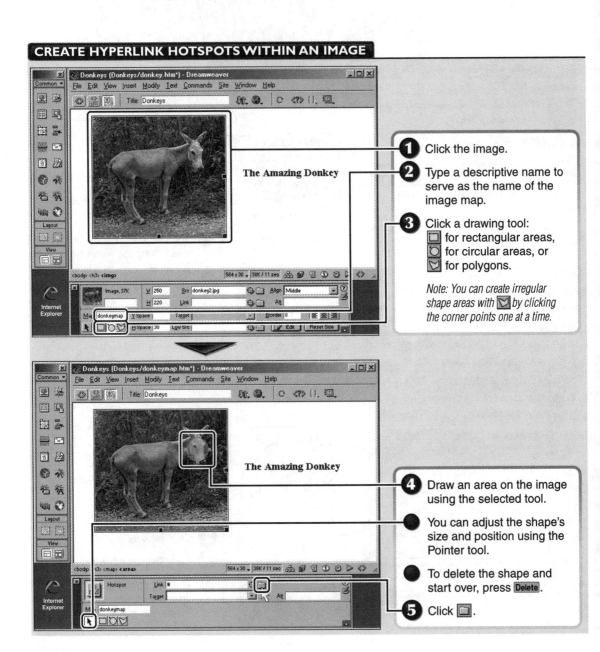

1 Click the image.

2 Type a descriptive name to serve as the name of the image map.

3 Click a drawing tool:
☐ for rectangular areas,
◯ for circular areas, or
▽ for polygons.

Note: You can create irregular shape areas with ▽ by clicking the corner points one at a time.

4 Draw an area on the image using the selected tool.

■ You can adjust the shape's size and position using the Pointer tool.

■ To delete the shape and start over, press Delete.

5 Click ☐.

in an *instant*

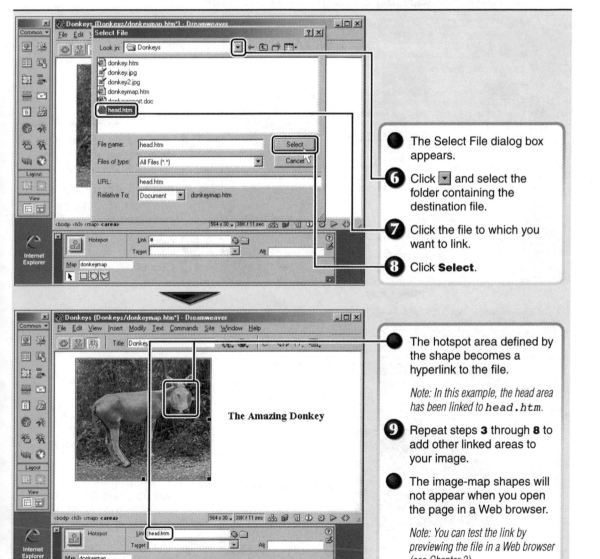

The Select File dialog box appears.

6 Click ▾ and select the folder containing the destination file.

7 Click the file to which you want to link.

8 Click **Select**.

The hotspot area defined by the shape becomes a hyperlink to the file.

Note: In this example, the head area has been linked to `head.htm`.

9 Repeat steps **3** through **8** to add other linked areas to your image.

The image-map shapes will not appear when you open the page in a Web browser.

Note: You can test the link by previewing the file in a Web browser (see Chapter 3).

CREATE A HYPERLINK THAT OPENS A NEW WINDOW

You can create a hyperlink that opens a new browser window when it is clicked. The destination page opens in the new window.

CREATE A HYPERLINK THAT OPENS A NEW WINDOW

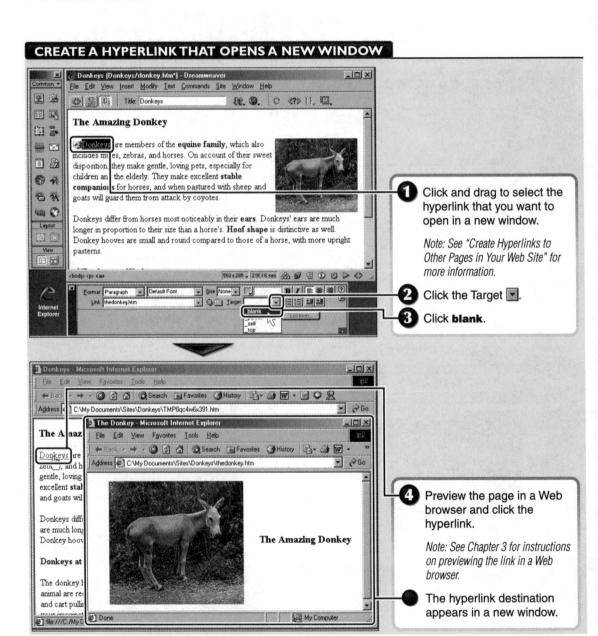

1 Click and drag to select the hyperlink that you want to open in a new window.

Note: See "Create Hyperlinks to Other Pages in Your Web Site" for more information.

2 Click the Target ▼.

3 Click **blank**.

4 Preview the page in a Web browser and click the hyperlink.

Note: See Chapter 3 for instructions on previewing the link in a Web browser.

■ The hyperlink destination appears in a new window.

CREATE A HYPERLINK USING THE SITE WINDOW

You can create hyperlinks on your page quickly and easily by using the Site window.

CREATE A HYPERLINK USING THE SITE WINDOW

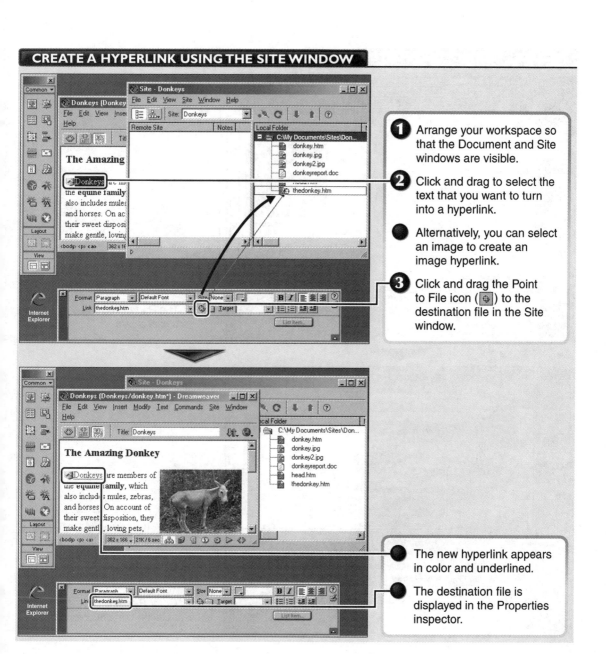

1 Arrange your workspace so that the Document and Site windows are visible.

2 Click and drag to select the text that you want to turn into a hyperlink.

- Alternatively, you can select an image to create an image hyperlink.

3 Click and drag the Point to File icon (⊕) to the destination file in the Site window.

- The new hyperlink appears in color and underlined.

- The destination file is displayed in the Properties inspector.

CHANGE THE COLOR OF HYPERLINKS

You can change the color of unvisited links, visited links, and active (clicked) links on your Web page to make them match the visual style of your page's text and images.

CHANGE THE COLOR OF HYPERLINKS

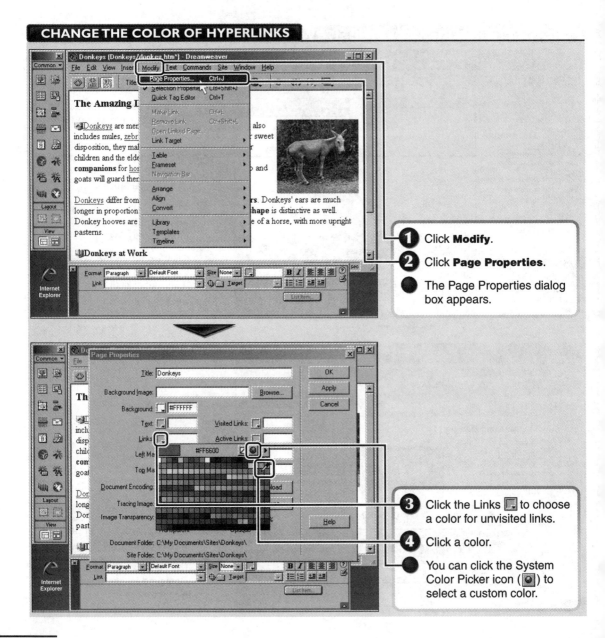

1 Click **Modify**.

2 Click **Page Properties**.

● The Page Properties dialog box appears.

3 Click the Links ▣ to choose a color for unvisited links.

4 Click a color.

● You can click the System Color Picker icon (◉) to select a custom color.

in an *instant*

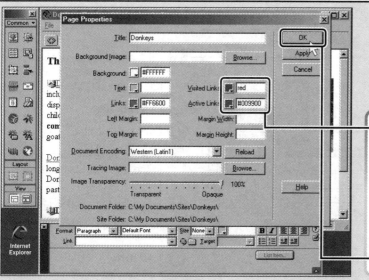

5 Click 🔲 to select the colors for visited links and active links.

● You can specify common colors on your Web page with their names. This example defines the color of visited links as **red**.

6 Click **OK**.

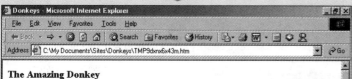

The Amazing Donkey

<u>Donkeys</u> are members of the **equine family**, which also includes mules, <u>zebras</u>, and horses. On account of their sweet disposition, they make gentle, loving pets, especially for children and the elderly. They make excellent **stable companions** for <u>horses</u>, and when pastured with sheep and goats will guard them from attack by coyotes.

<u>Donkeys</u> differ from horses most noticeably in their **ears**. Donkeys' ears are much longer in proportion to their size than a horse's. **Hoof shape** is distinctive as well. Donkey hooves are small and round compared to those of a horse, with more upright pasterns.

Donkeys at Work

The donkey has been put to work for centuries in a variety of jobs. Some common uses of the animal are recreational riding, packing (backpackers can use donkeys to carry their equipment), and cart pulling. The different kinds of work your donkey can do to help you are limited only by your imagination.

7 Preview the page in a Web browser.

Note: See Chapter 3 for instructions on previewing a page in a Web browser.

● The hyperlinks are displayed in the defined colors.

CREATE AN E-MAIL HYPERLINK

You can create a hyperlink that launches a user's e-mail message window.

CREATE AN E-MAIL HYPERLINK

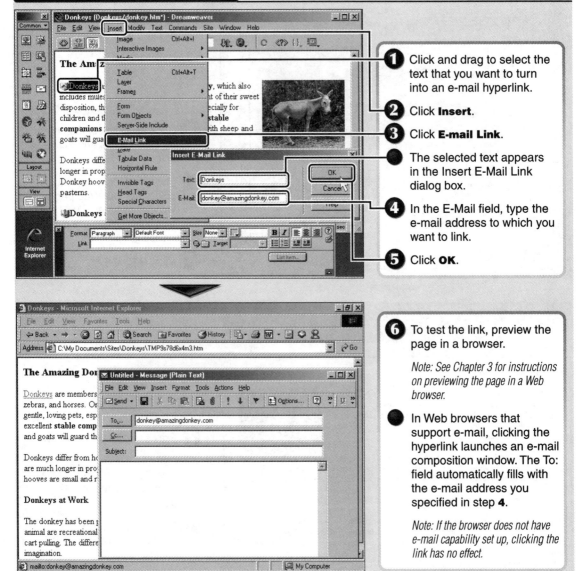

1 Click and drag to select the text that you want to turn into an e-mail hyperlink.

2 Click **Insert**.

3 Click **E-mail Link**.

■ The selected text appears in the Insert E-Mail Link dialog box.

4 In the E-Mail field, type the e-mail address to which you want to link.

5 Click **OK**.

6 To test the link, preview the page in a browser.

Note: See Chapter 3 for instructions on previewing the page in a Web browser.

■ In Web browsers that support e-mail, clicking the hyperlink launches an e-mail composition window. The To: field automatically fills with the e-mail address you specified in step **4**.

Note: If the browser does not have e-mail capability set up, clicking the link has no effect.

You can automatically verify a Web page's
links and get a report that lists any that are
broken. Note, however, that Dreamweaver
is unable to verify links to Web pages on
external sites.

CHECK HYPERLINKS

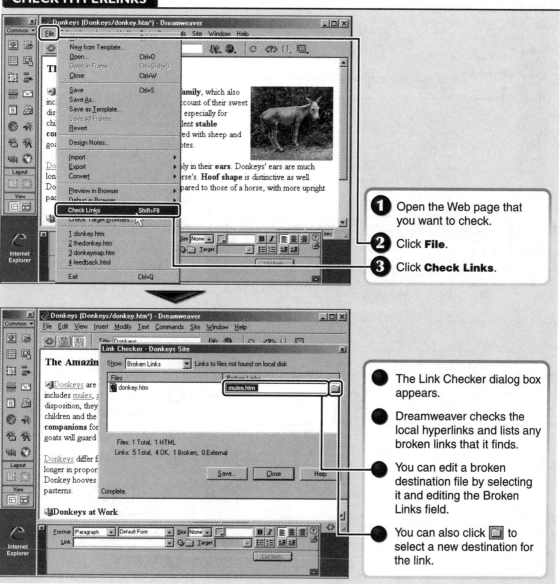

1 Open the Web page that
you want to check.

2 Click **File**.

3 Click **Check Links**.

● The Link Checker dialog box
appears.

● Dreamweaver checks the
local hyperlinks and lists any
broken links that it finds.

● You can edit a broken
destination file by selecting
it and editing the Broken
Links field.

● You can also click 📁 to
select a new destination for
the link.

You can organize content into columns and rows by inserting tables into your Web page. A default table has table borders, but you can turn these off, making them invisible.

INSERT A TABLE INTO YOUR WEB PAGE

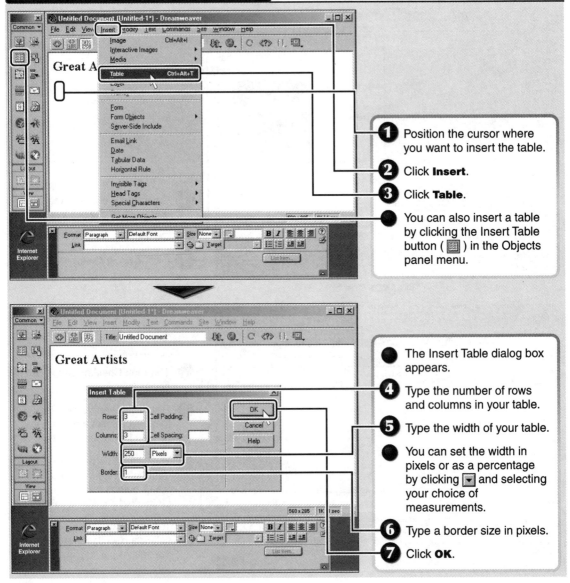

1 Position the cursor where you want to insert the table.

2 Click **Insert**.

3 Click **Table**.

● You can also insert a table by clicking the Insert Table button (▦) in the Objects panel menu.

● The Insert Table dialog box appears.

4 Type the number of rows and columns in your table.

5 Type the width of your table.

● You can set the width in pixels or as a percentage by clicking ▼ and selecting your choice of measurements.

6 Type a border size in pixels.

7 Click **OK**.

in an instant

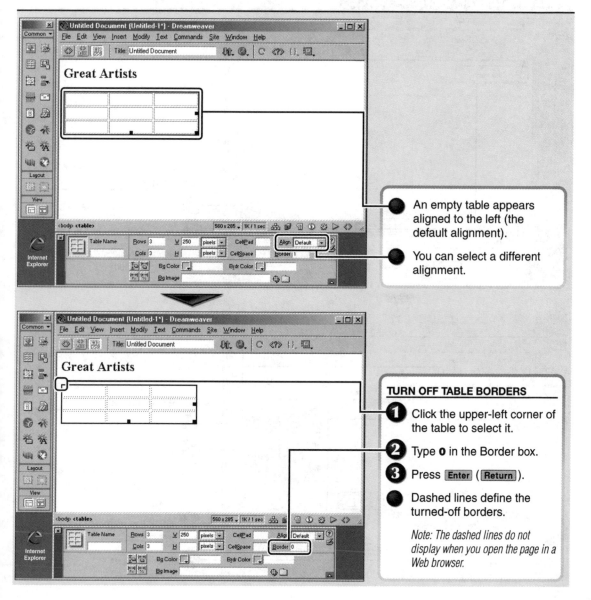

An empty table appears aligned to the left (the default alignment).

You can select a different alignment.

TURN OFF TABLE BORDERS

1 Click the upper-left corner of the table to select it.

2 Type **0** in the Border box.

3 Press **Enter** (**Return**).

Dashed lines define the turned-off borders.

Note: The dashed lines do not display when you open the page in a Web browser.

INSERT CONTENT INTO A TABLE

You can place text and images in your table. You can also nest tables within each other for more complex information.

INSERT CONTENT INTO A TABLE

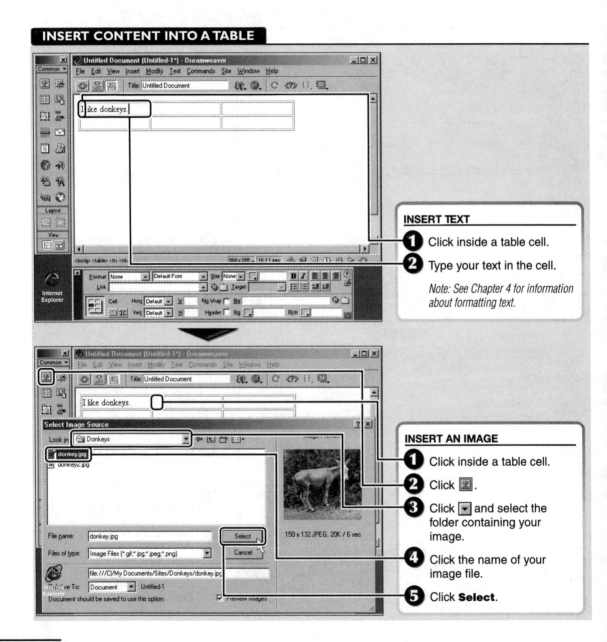

INSERT TEXT

1 Click inside a table cell.

2 Type your text in the cell.

Note: See Chapter 4 for information about formatting text.

INSERT AN IMAGE

1 Click inside a table cell.

2 Click 🖼.

3 Click ▼ and select the folder containing your image.

4 Click the name of your image file.

5 Click **Select**.

in an *instant*

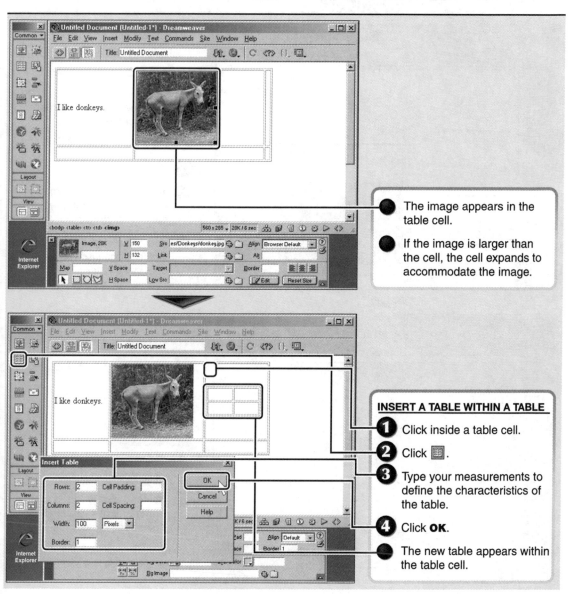

● The image appears in the table cell.

● If the image is larger than the cell, the cell expands to accommodate the image.

INSERT A TABLE WITHIN A TABLE

1 Click inside a table cell.

2 Click ▦.

3 Type your measurements to define the characteristics of the table.

4 Click **OK**.

● The new table appears within the table cell.

CHANGE THE TABLE BACKGROUND

You can change the table background to complement your Web page's style. You can change the background color or fill the background with an image.

CHANGE THE TABLE BACKGROUND

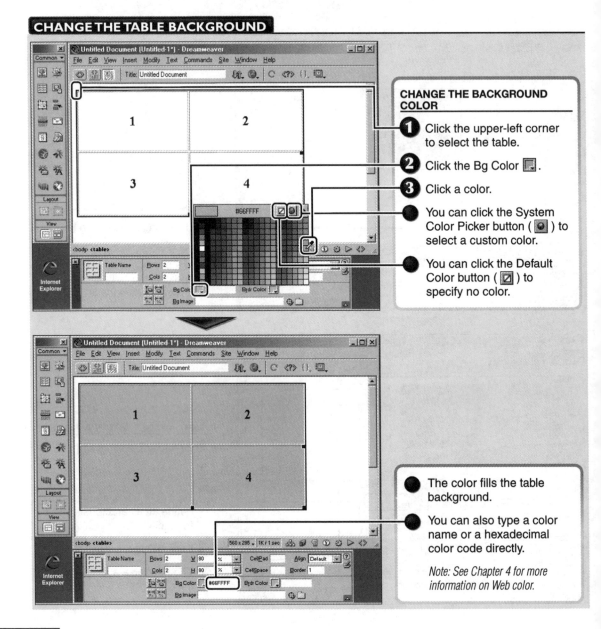

CHANGE THE BACKGROUND COLOR

① Click the upper-left corner to select the table.

② Click the Bg Color ▦.

③ Click a color.

● You can click the System Color Picker button (🔘) to select a custom color.

● You can click the Default Color button (🗹) to specify no color.

● The color fills the table background.

● You can also type a color name or a hexadecimal color code directly.

Note: See Chapter 4 for more information on Web color.

in an instant

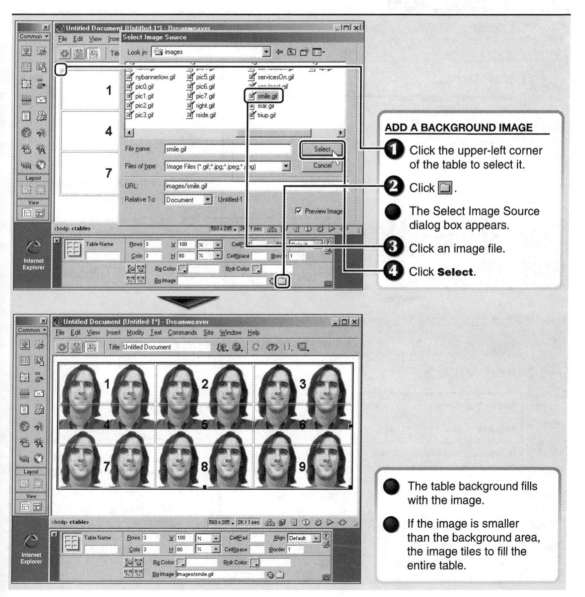

ADD A BACKGROUND IMAGE

1 Click the upper-left corner of the table to select it.

2 Click 🖿.

● The Select Image Source dialog box appears.

3 Click an image file.

4 Click **Select**.

● The table background fills with the image.

● If the image is smaller than the background area, the image tiles to fill the entire table.

CHANGE CELL PADDING

You can change the cell padding to add space between a table's content and its borders.

CHANGE CELL PADDING

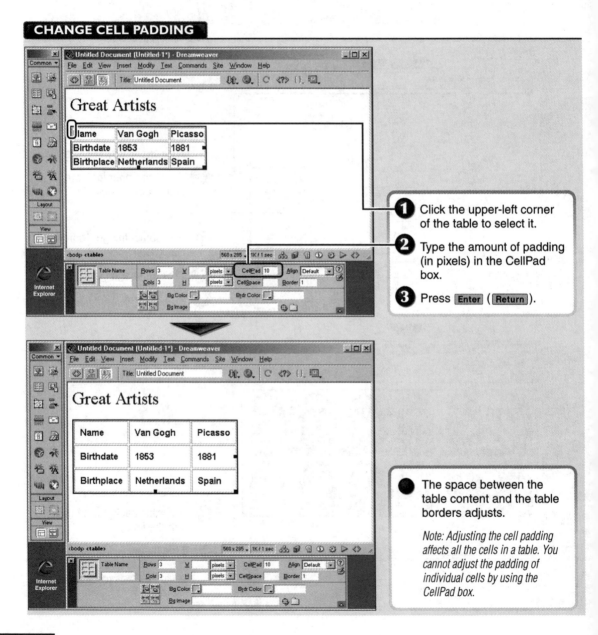

1 Click the upper-left corner of the table to select it.

2 Type the amount of padding (in pixels) in the CellPad box.

3 Press Enter (Return).

● The space between the table content and the table borders adjusts.

Note: Adjusting the cell padding affects all the cells in a table. You cannot adjust the padding of individual cells by using the CellPad box.

You can change the cell spacing to adjust the width
of your table borders.

CHANGE CELL SPACING

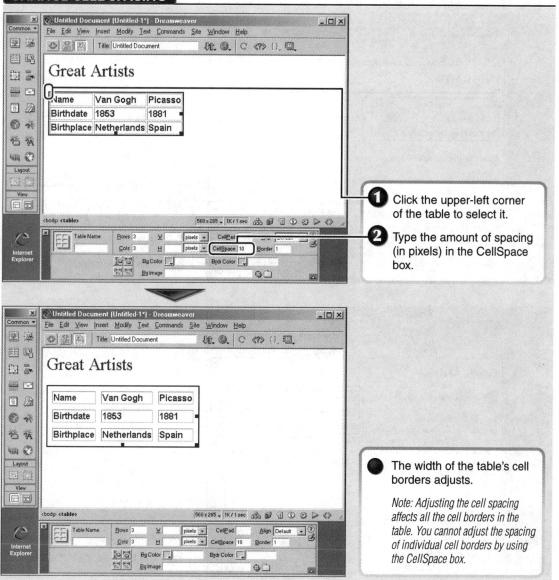

1 Click the upper-left corner of the table to select it.

2 Type the amount of spacing (in pixels) in the CellSpace box.

● The width of the table's cell borders adjusts.

Note: Adjusting the cell spacing affects all the cell borders in the table. You cannot adjust the spacing of individual cell borders by using the CellSpace box.

You can change the alignment of a table to center it or to wrap text and other content around it.

CHANGE THE TABLE ALIGNMENT

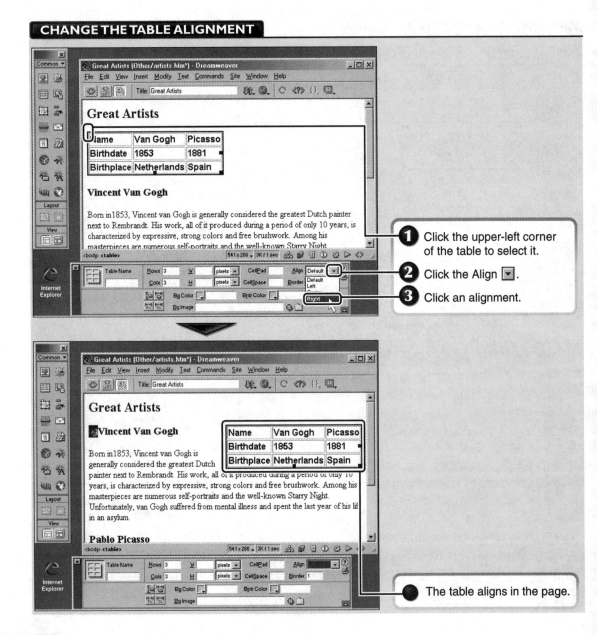

1 Click the upper-left corner of the table to select it.

2 Click the Align ▼.

3 Click an alignment.

● The table aligns in the page.

CHANGE THE ALIGNMENT OF CELL CONTENT

You can align the content in your table cells horizontally and vertically.

CHANGE THE ALIGNMENT OF CELL CONTENT

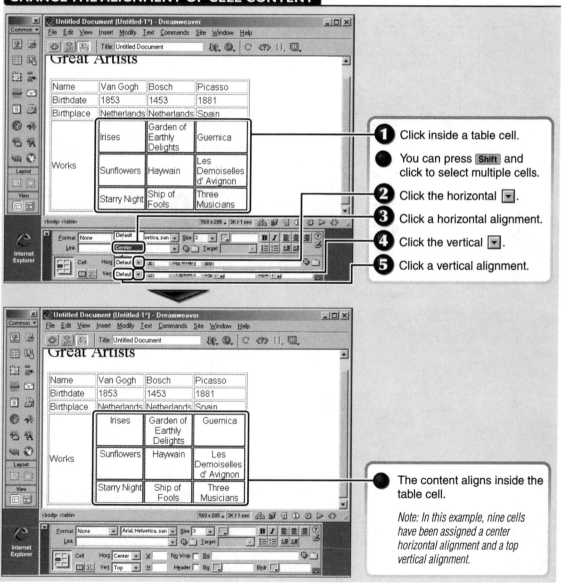

① Click inside a table cell.

● You can press Shift and click to select multiple cells.

② Click the horizontal ▼.

③ Click a horizontal alignment.

④ Click the vertical ▼.

⑤ Click a vertical alignment.

● The content aligns inside the table cell.

Note: In this example, nine cells have been assigned a center horizontal alignment and a top vertical alignment.

107

INSERT OR DELETE A ROW OR COLUMN

You can insert new rows or columns into your table to add table content or delete rows or columns to remove unused cells.

INSERT A ROW OR COLUMN

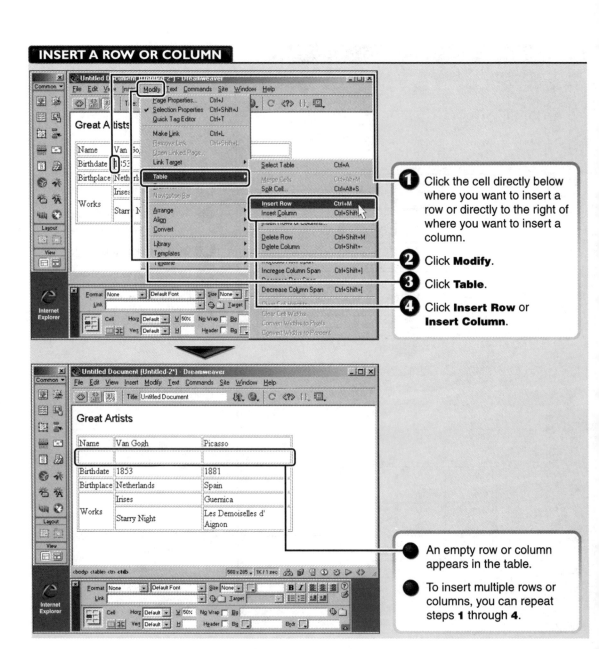

1 Click the cell directly below where you want to insert a row or directly to the right of where you want to insert a column.

2 Click **Modify**.

3 Click **Table**.

4 Click **Insert Row** or **Insert Column**.

● An empty row or column appears in the table.

● To insert multiple rows or columns, you can repeat steps **1** through **4**.

in an *instant*

DELETE A ROW OR COLUMN

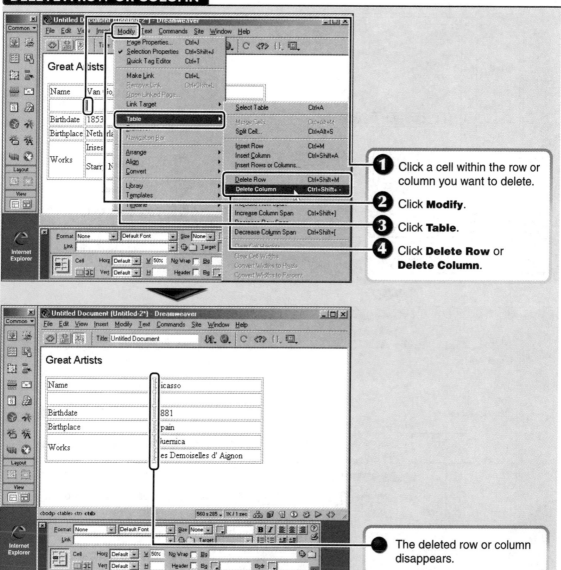

1 Click a cell within the row or column you want to delete.

2 Click **Modify**.

3 Click **Table**.

4 Click **Delete Row** or **Delete Column**.

The deleted row or column disappears.

SPLIT OR MERGE TABLE CELLS

You can create a more elaborate arrangement of cells in a table by splitting or merging its cells.

SPLIT A TABLE CELL

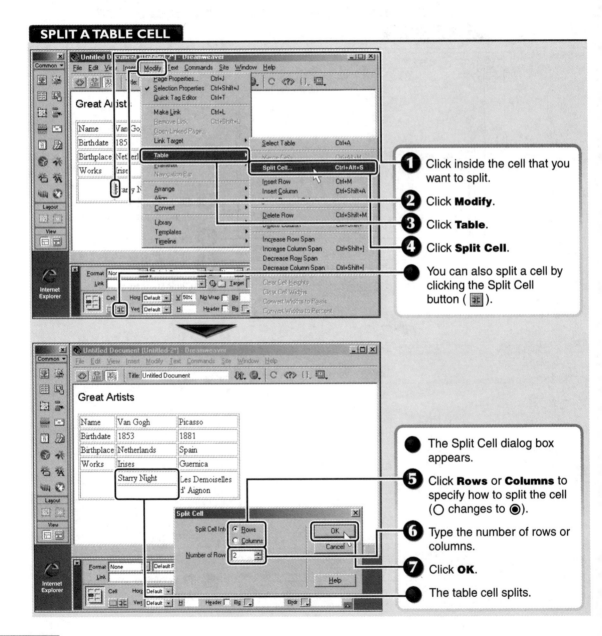

1 Click inside the cell that you want to split.

2 Click **Modify**.

3 Click **Table**.

4 Click **Split Cell**.

● You can also split a cell by clicking the Split Cell button ( ).

● The Split Cell dialog box appears.

5 Click **Rows** or **Columns** to specify how to split the cell (○ changes to ⦿).

6 Type the number of rows or columns.

7 Click **OK**.

● The table cell splits.

in an *instant*

MERGE TABLE CELLS

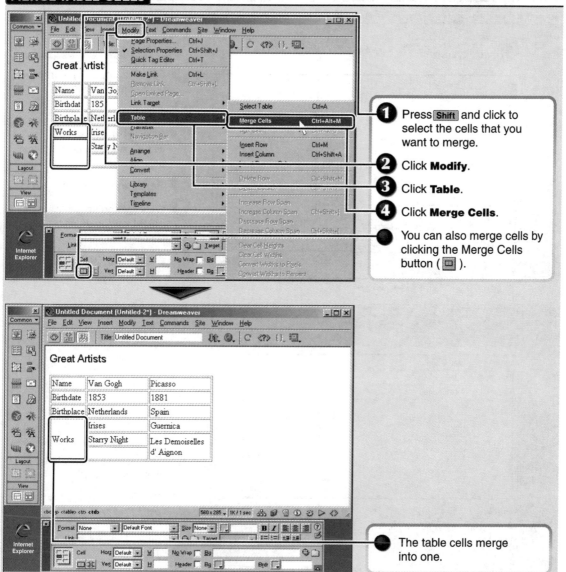

1 Press **Shift** and click to select the cells that you want to merge.

2 Click **Modify**.

3 Click **Table**.

4 Click **Merge Cells**.

● You can also merge cells by clicking the Merge Cells button (▣).

● The table cells merge into one.

CHANGE TABLE DIMENSIONS

You can change the dimensions of your table to better fit it into your Web page.

CHANGE TABLE DIMENSIONS

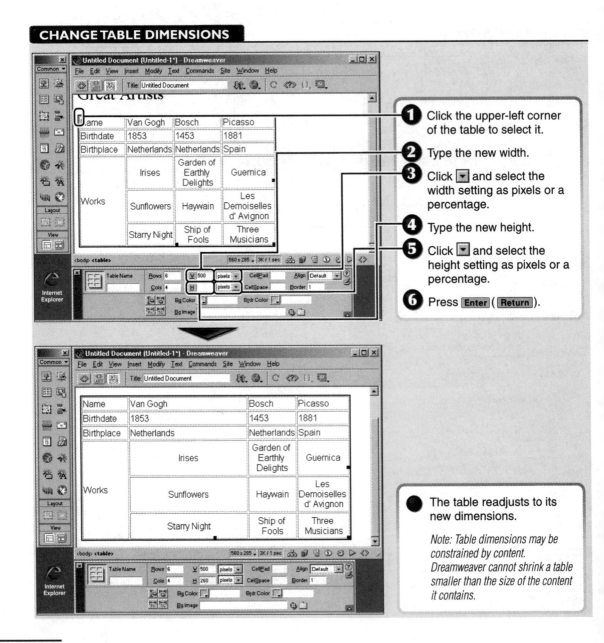

1 Click the upper-left corner of the table to select it.

2 Type the new width.

3 Click ▼ and select the width setting as pixels or a percentage.

4 Type the new height.

5 Click ▼ and select the height setting as pixels or a percentage.

6 Press Enter (Return).

● The table readjusts to its new dimensions.

Note: Table dimensions may be constrained by content. Dreamweaver cannot shrink a table smaller than the size of the content it contains.

CHANGE CELL DIMENSIONS

You can change the dimensions of individual table cells to better organize the content in your table.

CHANGE CELL DIMENSIONS

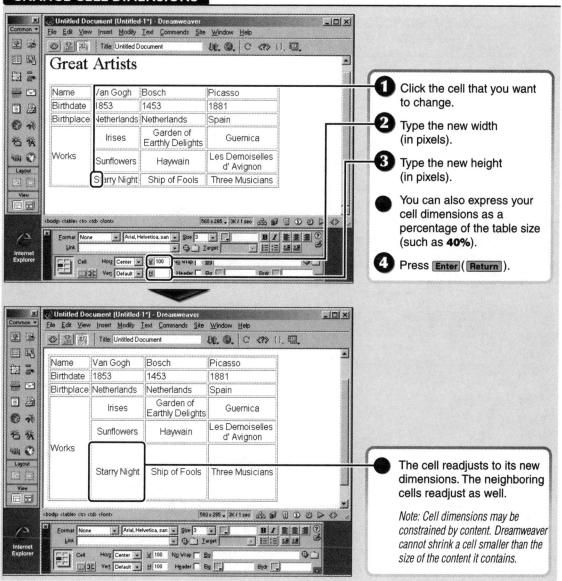

1 Click the cell that you want to change.

2 Type the new width (in pixels).

3 Type the new height (in pixels).

● You can also express your cell dimensions as a percentage of the table size (such as **40%**).

4 Press `Enter` (`Return`).

● The cell readjusts to its new dimensions. The neighboring cells readjust as well.

Note: Cell dimensions may be constrained by content. Dreamweaver cannot shrink a cell smaller than the size of the content it contains.

113

CREATE A LAYOUT TABLE

You can easily create tables that determine Web page content layout. Layout tables typically take up the entire dimensions of the page and have their borders turned off.

CREATE A LAYOUT TABLE

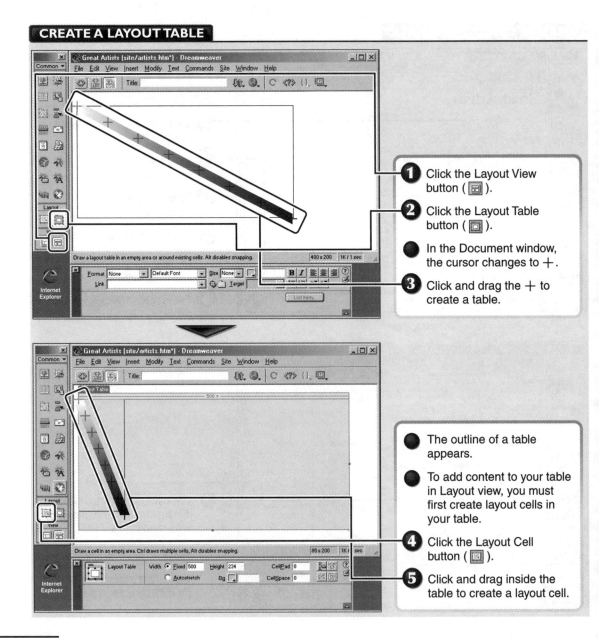

1 Click the Layout View button (▦).

2 Click the Layout Table button (▦).

● In the Document window, the cursor changes to +.

3 Click and drag the + to create a table.

● The outline of a table appears.

● To add content to your table in Layout view, you must first create layout cells in your table.

4 Click the Layout Cell button (▨).

5 Click and drag inside the table to create a layout cell.

in an *instant*

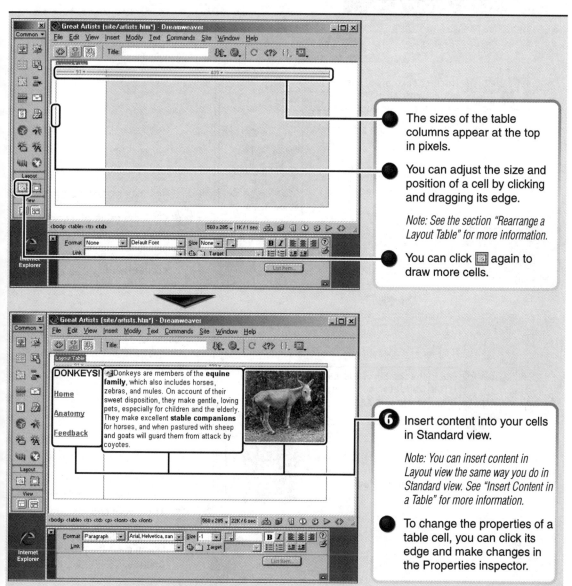

The sizes of the table columns appear at the top in pixels.

You can adjust the size and position of a cell by clicking and dragging its edge.

Note: See the section "Rearrange a Layout Table" for more information.

You can click ▦ again to draw more cells.

DONKEYS!

Home

Anatomy

Feedback

Donkeys are members of the **equine family**, which also includes horses, zebras, and mules. On account of their sweet disposition, they make gentle, loving pets, especially for children and the elderly. They make excellent **stable companions** for horses, and when pastured with sheep and goats will guard them from attack by coyotes.

6 Insert content into your cells in Standard view.

Note: You can insert content in Layout view the same way you do in Standard view. See "Insert Content in a Table" for more information.

To change the properties of a table cell, you can click its edge and make changes in the Properties inspector.

REARRANGE A LAYOUT TABLE

You can easily change the size and arrangement of a table's cells in Layout view.

REARRANGE A LAYOUT TABLE

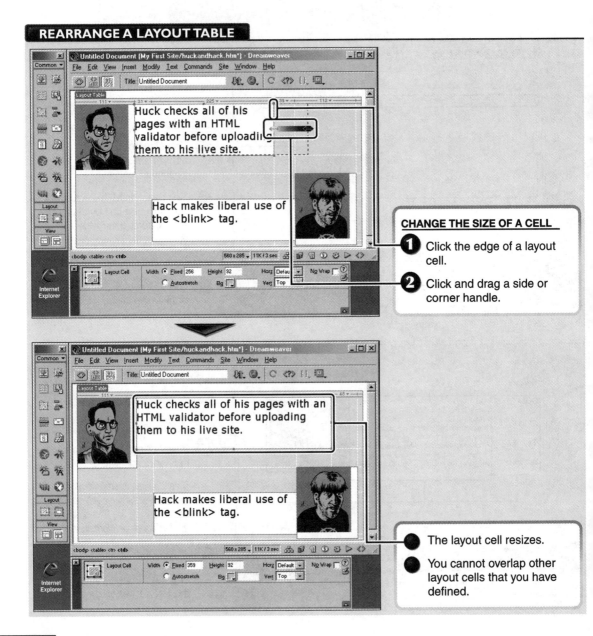

CHANGE THE SIZE OF A CELL

1️⃣ Click the edge of a layout cell.

2️⃣ Click and drag a side or corner handle.

⬤ The layout cell resizes.

⬤ You cannot overlap other layout cells that you have defined.

in an *instant*

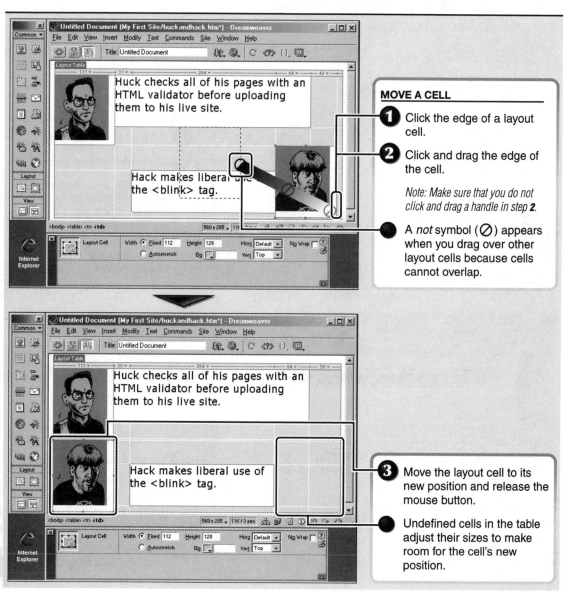

MOVE A CELL

1 Click the edge of a layout cell.

2 Click and drag the edge of the cell.

Note: Make sure that you do not click and drag a handle in step 2.

A *not* symbol (⊘) appears when you drag over other layout cells because cells cannot overlap.

3 Move the layout cell to its new position and release the mouse button.

Undefined cells in the table adjust their sizes to make room for the cell's new position.

117

ADJUST THE WIDTH OF A LAYOUT TABLE

By resizing the browser window, you can specify how
a layout table's width behaves when the browser
window is resized.

ADJUST THE WIDTH OF A LAYOUT TABLE

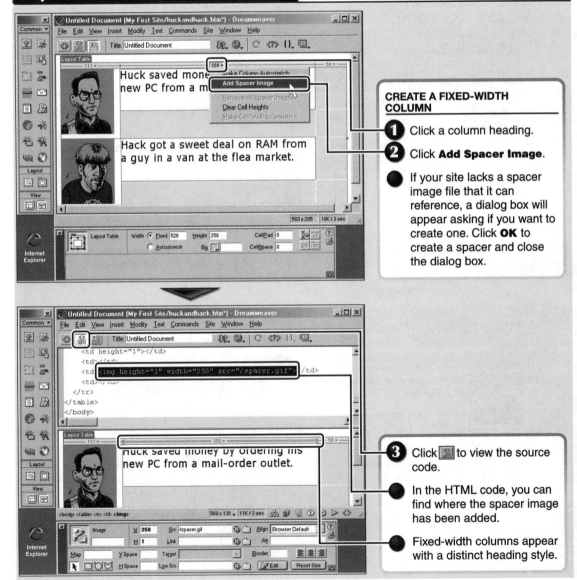

CREATE A FIXED-WIDTH COLUMN

1 Click a column heading.

2 Click **Add Spacer Image**.

● If your site lacks a spacer image file that it can reference, a dialog box will appear asking if you want to create one. Click **OK** to create a spacer and close the dialog box.

3 Click 🖩 to view the source code.

● In the HTML code, you can find where the spacer image has been added.

● Fixed-width columns appear with a distinct heading style.

118

in an *instant*

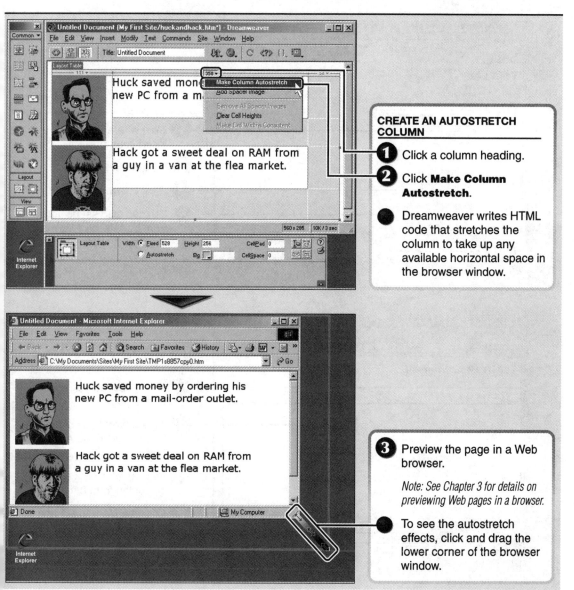

CREATE AN AUTOSTRETCH COLUMN

1 Click a column heading.

2 Click **Make Column Autostretch**.

● Dreamweaver writes HTML code that stretches the column to take up any available horizontal space in the browser window.

3 Preview the page in a Web browser.

Note: See Chapter 3 for details on previewing Web pages in a browser.

● To see the autostretch effects, click and drag the lower corner of the browser window.

SET UP A FORM

You set up a form on your Web page by first creating a container that holds the text fields, menus, and other form elements. This container gets assigned the Web address of the form handler — the program that processes the submitted form.

SET UP A FORM

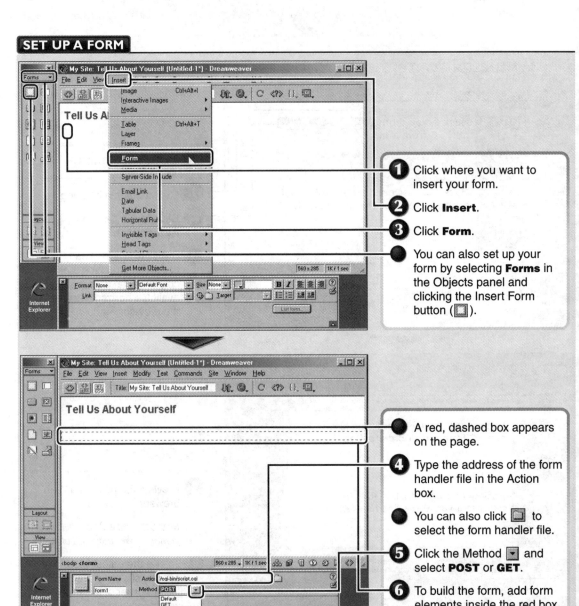

① Click where you want to insert your form.

② Click **Insert**.

③ Click **Form**.

● You can also set up your form by selecting **Forms** in the Objects panel and clicking the Insert Form button (▣).

● A red, dashed box appears on the page.

④ Type the address of the form handler file in the Action box.

● You can also click ▣ to select the form handler file.

⑤ Click the Method ▼ and select **POST** or **GET**.

⑥ To build the form, add form elements inside the red box.

ADD A TEXT FIELD TO A FORM

You can add a text field to enable viewers to submit text through your form. Text fields are probably the most common form elements, enabling users to enter names, addresses, brief answers to questions, and other short pieces of text.

ADD A TEXT FIELD TO A FORM

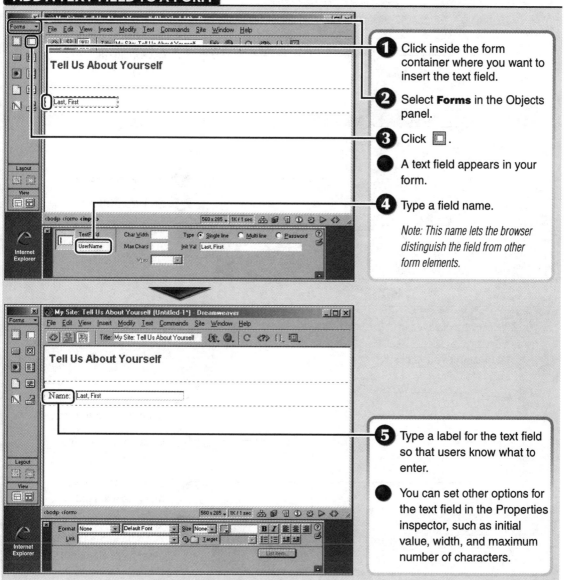

1 Click inside the form container where you want to insert the text field.

2 Select **Forms** in the Objects panel.

3 Click ▣.

● A text field appears in your form.

4 Type a field name.

Note: This name lets the browser distinguish the field from other form elements.

5 Type a label for the text field so that users know what to enter.

● You can set other options for the text field in the Properties inspector, such as initial value, width, and maximum number of characters.

ADD A MULTILINE TEXT FIELD TO A FORM

Multiline text fields enable viewers to submit large amounts of text into a form. Multiline text fields can be useful if you want to allow viewers to send you lengthy comments about your site or cut and paste large amounts of text — such as a résumé — into the form.

ADD A MULTILINE TEXT FIELD TO A FORM

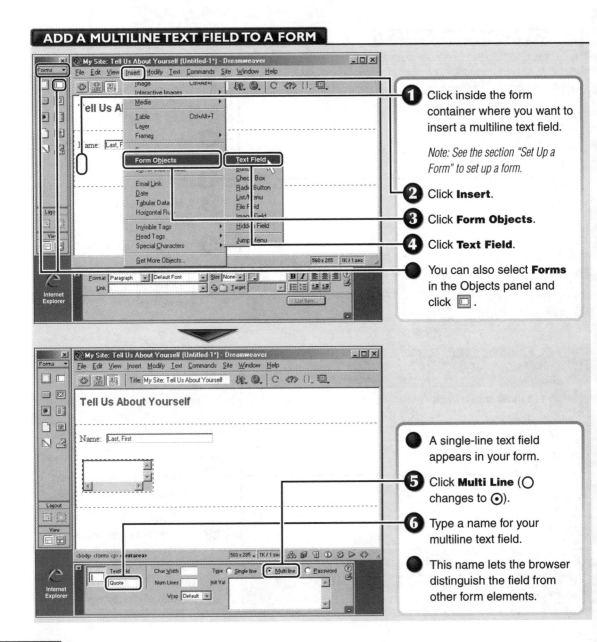

1 Click inside the form container where you want to insert a multiline text field.

Note: See the section "Set Up a Form" to set up a form.

2 Click **Insert**.

3 Click **Form Objects**.

4 Click **Text Field**.

● You can also select **Forms** in the Objects panel and click ▣.

● A single-line text field appears in your form.

5 Click **Multi Line** (○ changes to ⊙).

6 Type a name for your multiline text field.

● This name lets the browser distinguish the field from other form elements.

in an *instant*

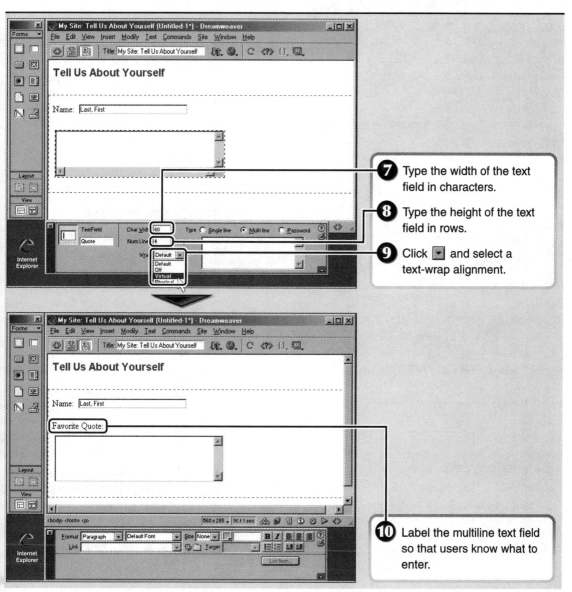

7 Type the width of the text field in characters.

8 Type the height of the text field in rows.

9 Click ▾ and select a text-wrap alignment.

10 Label the multiline text field so that users know what to enter.

123

A password field is similar to a text field, except the text in the field is hidden as the user enters it. The characters display as asterisks or bullets, depending on the type of operating system being used to view the page.

ADD A PASSWORD FIELD TO A FORM

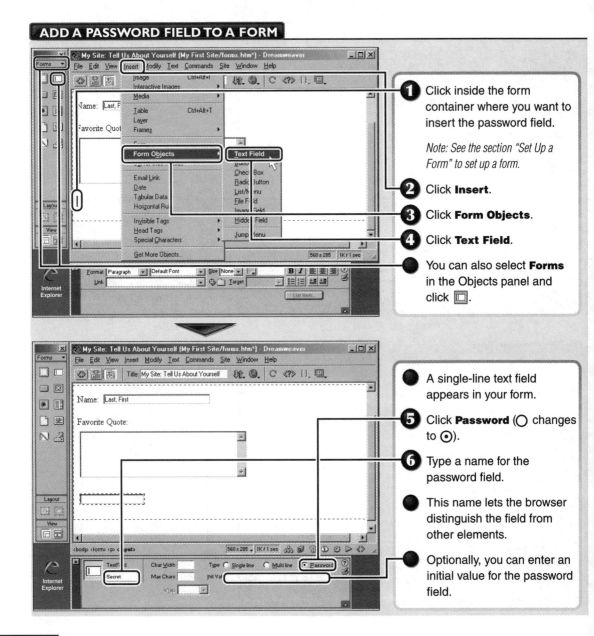

1 Click inside the form container where you want to insert the password field.

Note: See the section "Set Up a Form" to set up a form.

2 Click **Insert**.

3 Click **Form Objects**.

4 Click **Text Field**.

■ You can also select **Forms** in the Objects panel and click □.

■ A single-line text field appears in your form.

5 Click **Password** (○ changes to ⊙).

6 Type a name for the password field.

■ This name lets the browser distinguish the field from other elements.

■ Optionally, you can enter an initial value for the password field.

in an *instant*

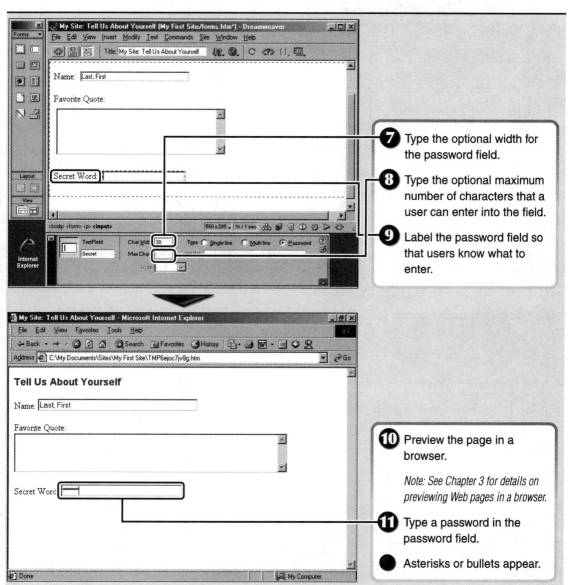

7 Type the optional width for the password field.

8 Type the optional maximum number of characters that a user can enter into the field.

9 Label the password field so that users know what to enter.

10 Preview the page in a browser.

Note: See Chapter 3 for details on previewing Web pages in a browser.

11 Type a password in the password field.

● Asterisks or bullets appear.

Check boxes enable you to present multiple options
in a form and allow the user to select one, several, or
none of the options.

ADD CHECK BOXES TO A FORM

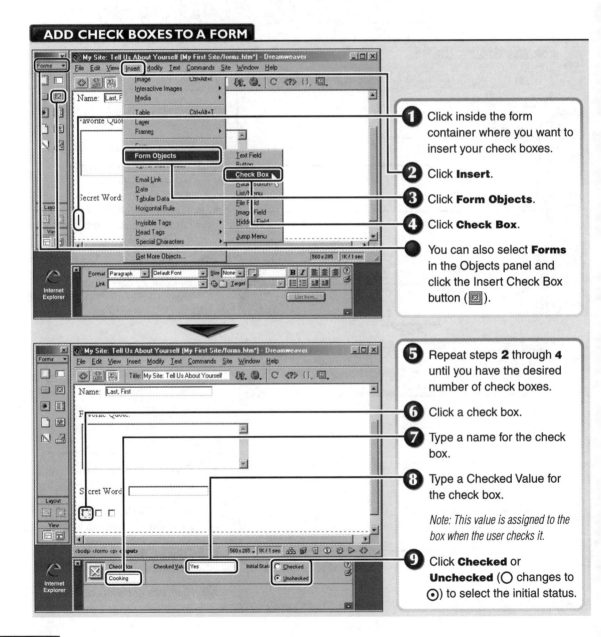

1 Click inside the form
container where you want to
insert your check boxes.

2 Click **Insert**.

3 Click **Form Objects**.

4 Click **Check Box**.

● You can also select **Forms**
in the Objects panel and
click the Insert Check Box
button (⊠).

5 Repeat steps **2** through **4**
until you have the desired
number of check boxes.

6 Click a check box.

7 Type a name for the check
box.

8 Type a Checked Value for
the check box.

*Note: This value is assigned to the
box when the user checks it.*

9 Click **Checked** or
Unchecked (○ changes to
⊙) to select the initial status.

in an instant

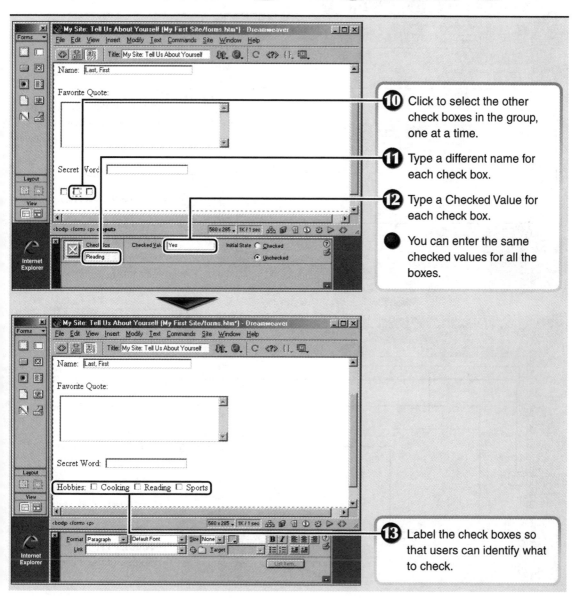

10 Click to select the other check boxes in the group, one at a time.

11 Type a different name for each check box.

12 Type a Checked Value for each check box.

● You can enter the same checked values for all the boxes.

13 Label the check boxes so that users can identify what to check.

ADD RADIO BUTTONS TO A FORM

You can let users select one option from a set of several options by adding a set of radio buttons to your form. With radio buttons, a user cannot select more that one option from a set.

ADD RADIO BUTTONS TO A FORM

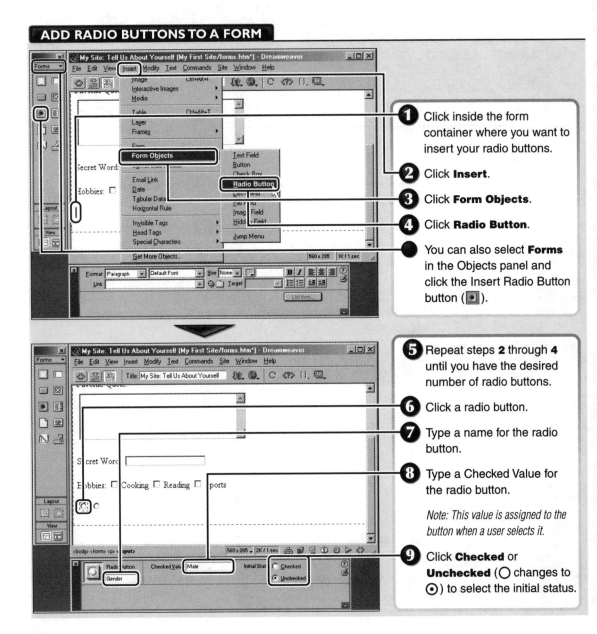

① Click inside the form container where you want to insert your radio buttons.

② Click **Insert**.

③ Click **Form Objects**.

④ Click **Radio Button**.

● You can also select **Forms** in the Objects panel and click the Insert Radio Button button (▣).

⑤ Repeat steps **2** through **4** until you have the desired number of radio buttons.

⑥ Click a radio button.

⑦ Type a name for the radio button.

⑧ Type a Checked Value for the radio button.

Note: This value is assigned to the button when a user selects it.

⑨ Click **Checked** or **Unchecked** (◯ changes to ⊙) to select the initial status.

in an *instant*

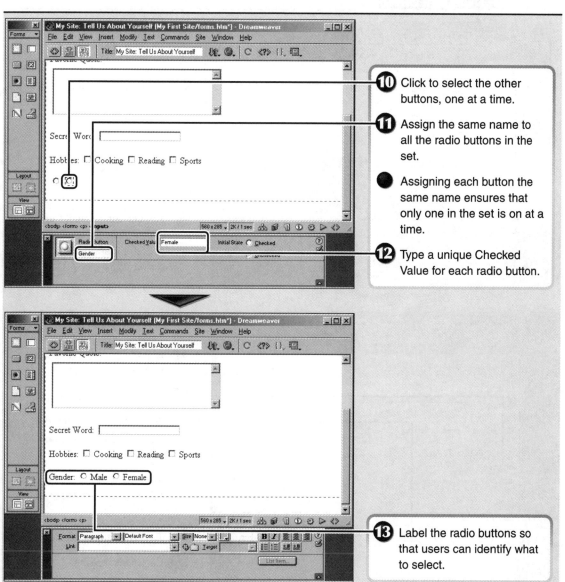

10 Click to select the other buttons, one at a time.

11 Assign the same name to all the radio buttons in the set.

● Assigning each button the same name ensures that only one in the set is on at a time.

12 Type a unique Checked Value for each radio button.

13 Label the radio buttons so that users can identify what to select.

A menu enables users to choose one option from a list of options. Because a menu hides the information until a user clicks it, a menu allows you to put a long list of options in a small amount of space.

ADD A MENU TO A FORM

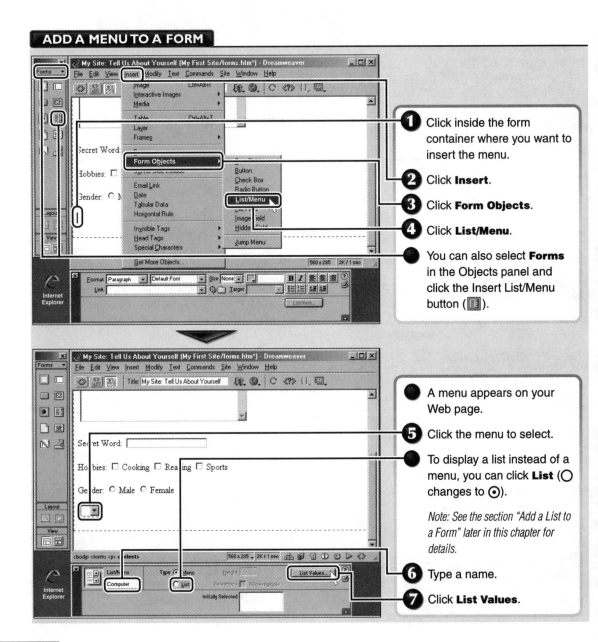

① Click inside the form container where you want to insert the menu.

② Click **Insert**.

③ Click **Form Objects**.

④ Click **List/Menu**.

● You can also select **Forms** in the Objects panel and click the Insert List/Menu button (▥).

● A menu appears on your Web page.

⑤ Click the menu to select.

● To display a list instead of a menu, you can click **List** (○ changes to ⊙).

Note: See the section "Add a List to a Form" later in this chapter for details.

⑥ Type a name.

⑦ Click **List Values**.

in an *instant*

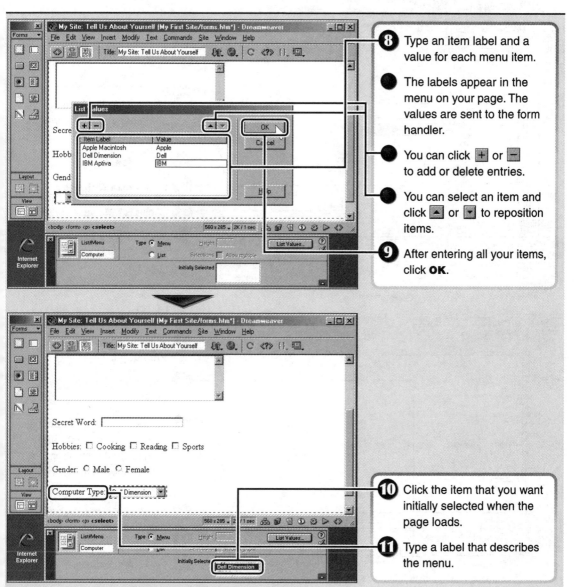

8 Type an item label and a value for each menu item.

● The labels appear in the menu on your page. The values are sent to the form handler.

● You can click ⊞ or ⊟ to add or delete entries.

● You can select an item and click ▲ or ▼ to reposition items.

9 After entering all your items, click **OK**.

10 Click the item that you want initially selected when the page loads.

11 Type a label that describes the menu.

ADD A LIST TO A FORM

A list allows a user to choose one option from a list of options. You can also create a list that allows a user to choose multiple options.

ADD A LIST TO A FORM

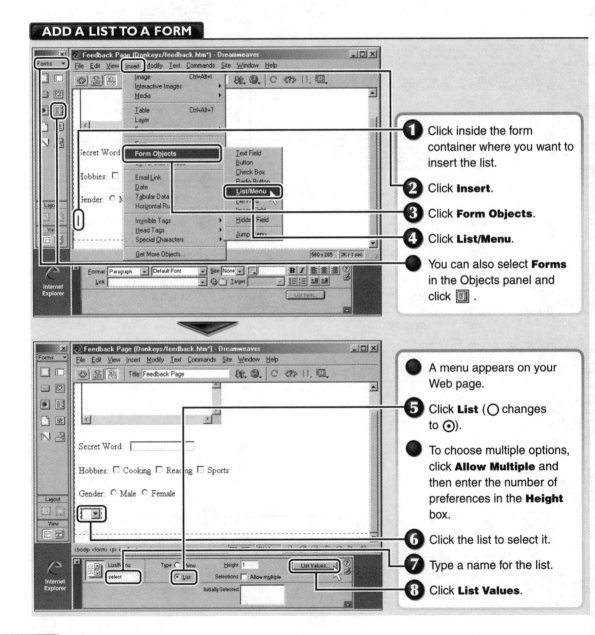

1 Click inside the form container where you want to insert the list.

2 Click **Insert**.

3 Click **Form Objects**.

4 Click **List/Menu**.

● You can also select **Forms** in the Objects panel and click 📧 .

● A menu appears on your Web page.

5 Click **List** (○ changes to ⊙).

● To choose multiple options, click **Allow Multiple** and then enter the number of preferences in the **Height** box.

6 Click the list to select it.

7 Type a name for the list.

8 Click **List Values**.

in an *instant*

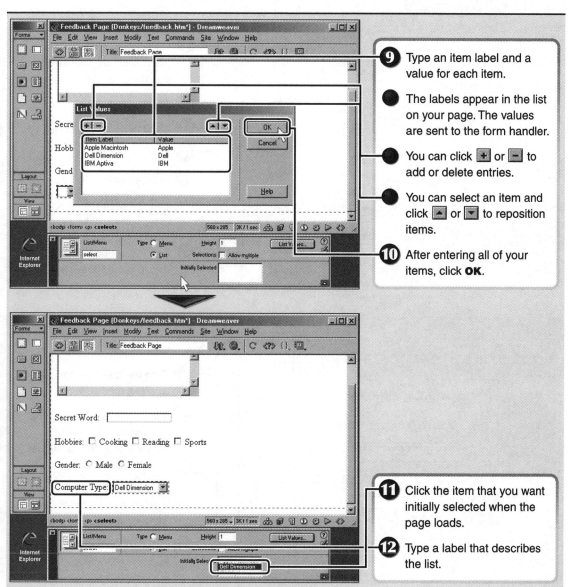

9 Type an item label and a value for each item.

● The labels appear in the list on your page. The values are sent to the form handler.

● You can click ➕ or ➖ to add or delete entries.

● You can select an item and click ▲ or ▼ to reposition items.

10 After entering all of your items, click **OK**.

11 Click the item that you want initially selected when the page loads.

12 Type a label that describes the list.

CREATE A JUMP MENU

A *jump menu* lets users easily navigate to other Web pages using the menu form object. Dreamweaver uses JavaScript to make the jump menu work.

CREATE A JUMP MENU

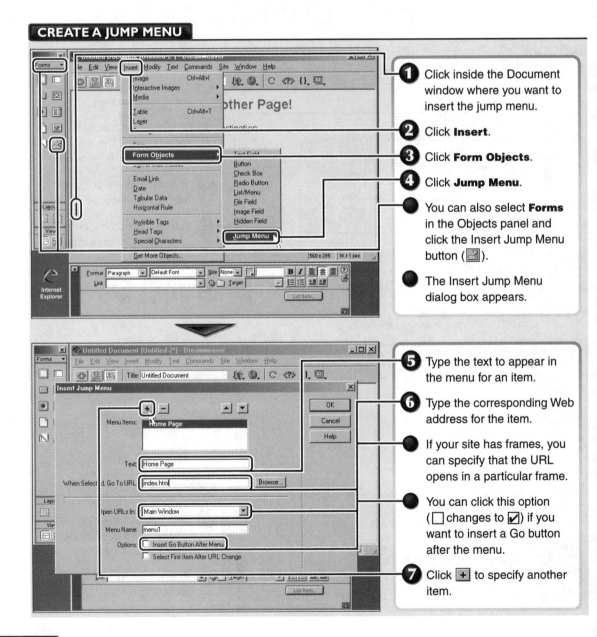

1 Click inside the Document window where you want to insert the jump menu.

2 Click **Insert**.

3 Click **Form Objects**.

4 Click **Jump Menu**.

You can also select **Forms** in the Objects panel and click the Insert Jump Menu button (⬚).

The Insert Jump Menu dialog box appears.

5 Type the text to appear in the menu for an item.

6 Type the corresponding Web address for the item.

If your site has frames, you can specify that the URL opens in a particular frame.

You can click this option (☐ changes to ☑) if you want to insert a Go button after the menu.

7 Click ⊞ to specify another item.

in an *instant*

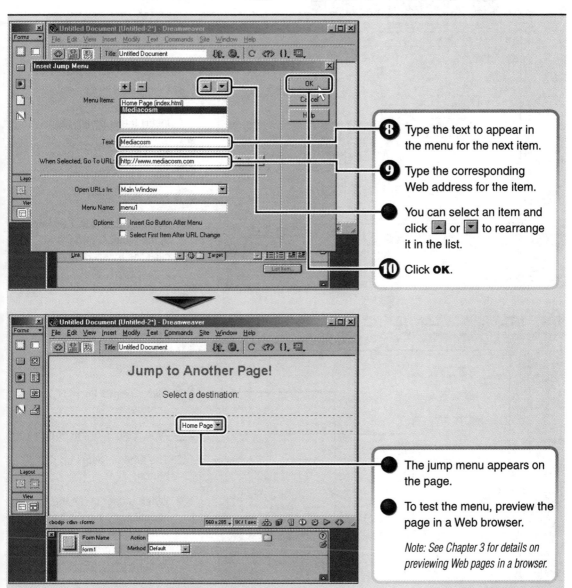

8 Type the text to appear in the menu for the next item.

9 Type the corresponding Web address for the item.

● You can select an item and click ▲ or ▼ to rearrange it in the list.

10 Click **OK**.

● The jump menu appears on the page.

● To test the menu, preview the page in a Web browser.

Note: See Chapter 3 for details on previewing Web pages in a browser.

ADD A SUBMIT BUTTON TO A FORM

You can add a button that enables users to submit information in a form, sending it to the specified form handler. To specify a form handler, see "Set Up a Form."

ADD A SUBMIT BUTTON TO A FORM

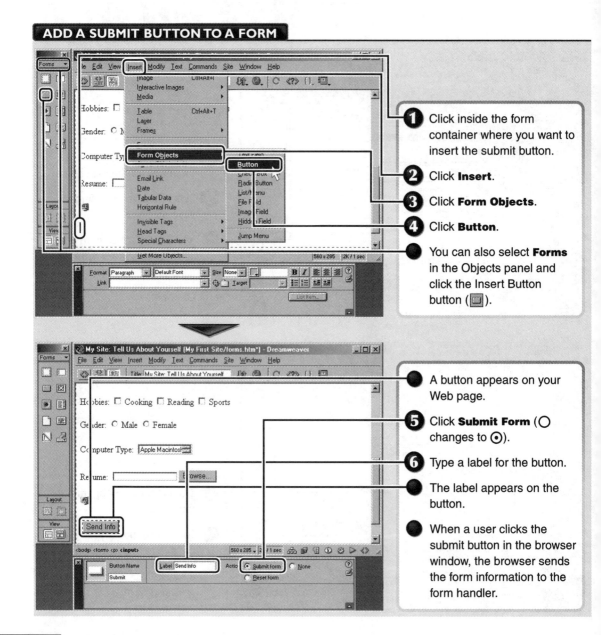

① Click inside the form container where you want to insert the submit button.

② Click **Insert**.

③ Click **Form Objects**.

④ Click **Button**.

⬤ You can also select **Forms** in the Objects panel and click the Insert Button button (▣).

⬤ A button appears on your Web page.

⑤ Click **Submit Form** (○ changes to ⊙).

⑥ Type a label for the button.

⬤ The label appears on the button.

⬤ When a user clicks the submit button in the browser window, the browser sends the form information to the form handler.

You can add a button that enables users to reset all elements
of a form to their initial values. This allows users to erase
their form entries so that they can start over again.

ADD A RESET BUTTON TO A FORM

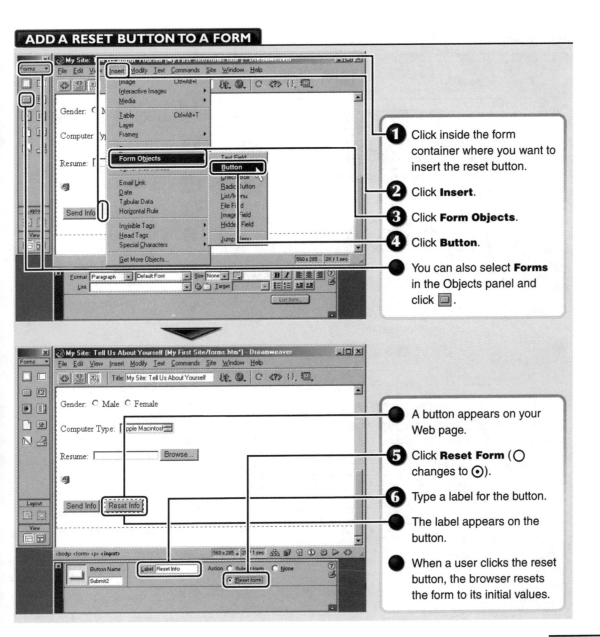

1 Click inside the form
container where you want to
insert the reset button.

2 Click **Insert**.

3 Click **Form Objects**.

4 Click **Button**.

■ You can also select **Forms**
in the Objects panel and
click ▣.

■ A button appears on your
Web page.

5 Click **Reset Form** (○
changes to ⊙).

6 Type a label for the button.

■ The label appears on the
button.

■ When a user clicks the reset
button, the browser resets
the form to its initial values.

VALIDATE A FORM

You can double-check the information a user enters in a form to make sure that it is valid. The validation process can include checking that postal codes have the correct number of characters and that e-mail addresses are in the correct format.

VALIDATE A FORM

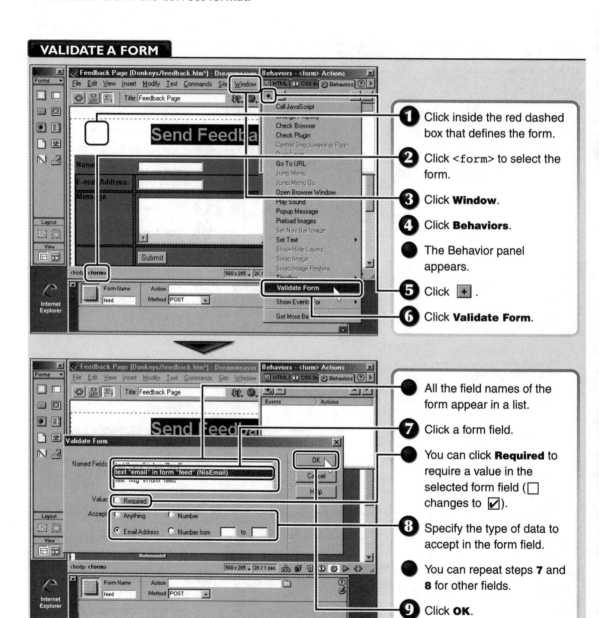

1 Click inside the red dashed box that defines the form.

2 Click <form> to select the form.

3 Click **Window**.

4 Click **Behaviors**.

● The Behavior panel appears.

5 Click ➕ .

6 Click **Validate Form**.

● All the field names of the form appear in a list.

7 Click a form field.

● You can click **Required** to require a value in the selected form field (☐ changes to ☑).

8 Specify the type of data to accept in the form field.

● You can repeat steps **7** and **8** for other fields.

9 Click **OK**.

in an *instant*

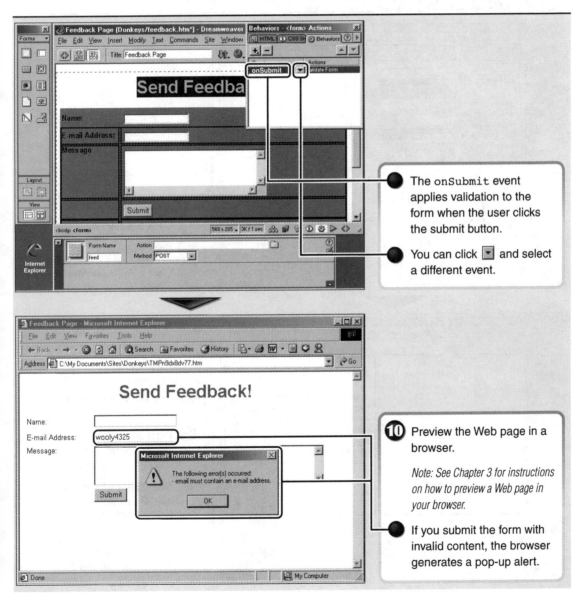

The onSubmit event applies validation to the form when the user clicks the submit button.

You can click ▼ and select a different event.

Send Feedback!

Name:

E-mail Address: wooly4325

Message:

Microsoft Internet Explorer

⚠ The following error(s) occurred:
- email must contain an e-mail address.

OK

🔟 Preview the Web page in a browser.

Note: See Chapter 3 for instructions on how to preview a Web page in your browser.

If you submit the form with invalid content, the browser generates a pop-up alert.

DIVIDE A PAGE INTO FRAMES

You can split a Document window vertically to create a frameset with left and right frames or split it horizontally to create a frameset with top and bottom frames.

DIVIDE A PAGE INTO FRAMES

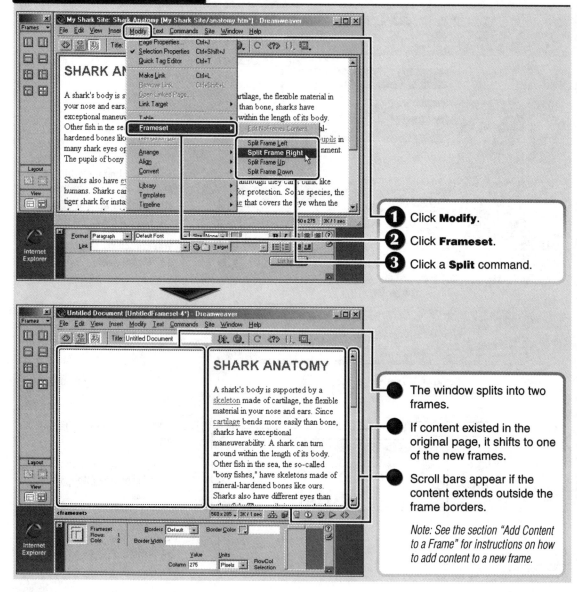

1 Click **Modify**.

2 Click **Frameset**.

3 Click a **Split** command.

● The window splits into two frames.

● If content existed in the original page, it shifts to one of the new frames.

● Scroll bars appear if the content extends outside the frame borders.

Note: See the section "Add Content to a Frame" for instructions on how to add content to a new frame.

You can easily create popular frame styles by using the predefined framesets located in the Objects panel.

INSERT A PREDEFINED FRAMESET

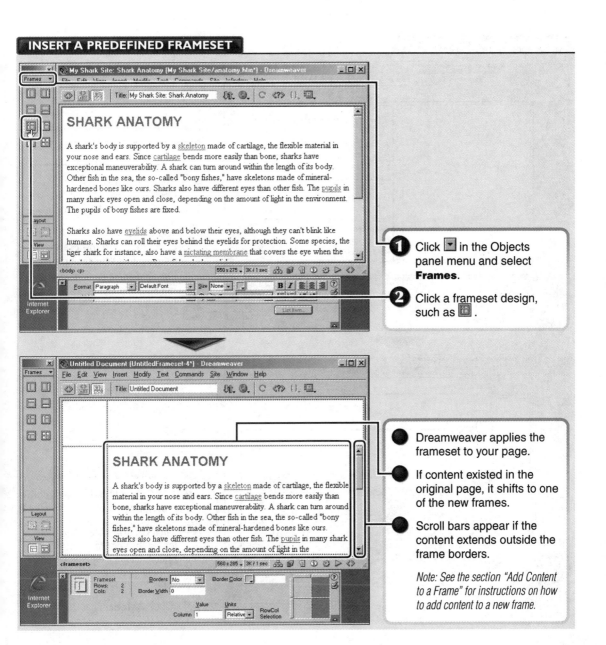

1 Click ⯆ in the Objects panel menu and select **Frames**.

2 Click a frameset design, such as ⬚.

● Dreamweaver applies the frameset to your page.

● If content existed in the original page, it shifts to one of the new frames.

● Scroll bars appear if the content extends outside the frame borders.

Note: See the section "Add Content to a Frame" for instructions on how to add content to a new frame.

ADD CONTENT TO A FRAME

You can add content to a frame by inserting an existing
HTML document into the frame. You can also add content
by typing text or inserting elements such as images and
tables, just as you would in an unframed page.

ADD CONTENT TO A FRAME

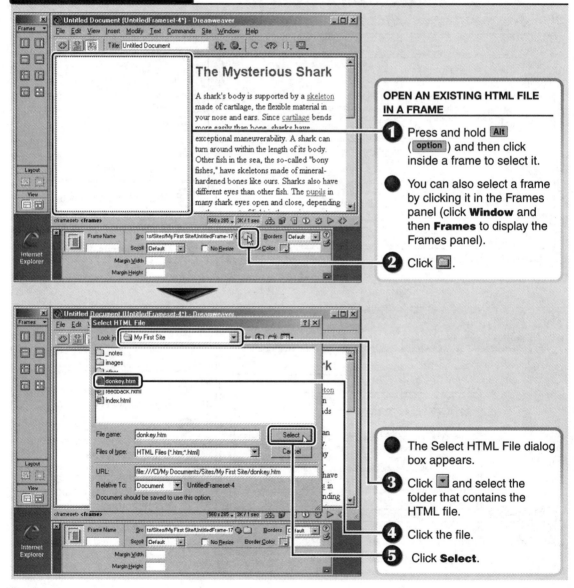

**OPEN AN EXISTING HTML FILE
IN A FRAME**

1 Press and hold **Alt**
(**option**) and then click
inside a frame to select it.

■ You can also select a frame
by clicking it in the Frames
panel (click **Window** and
then **Frames** to display the
Frames panel).

2 Click ▣.

■ The Select HTML File dialog
box appears.

3 Click ▾ and select the
folder that contains the
HTML file.

4 Click the file.

5 Click **Select**.

in an *instant*

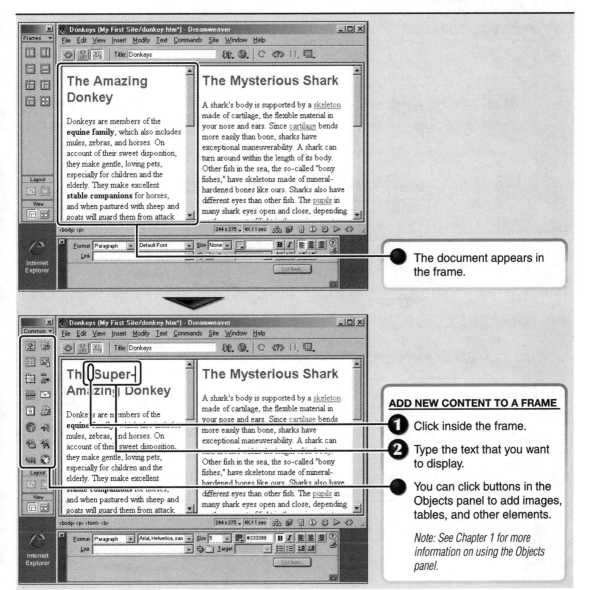

The document appears in the frame.

ADD NEW CONTENT TO A FRAME

1 Click inside the frame.

2 Type the text that you want to display.

You can click buttons in the Objects panel to add images, tables, and other elements.

Note: See Chapter 1 for more information on using the Objects panel.

SAVE A FRAMED SITE

Saving your framed site requires you to save the HTML documents that appear in the frames as well as the frameset that defines how the frames are organized. You need to save all the documents before you can upload your site.

SAVE A FRAMED SITE

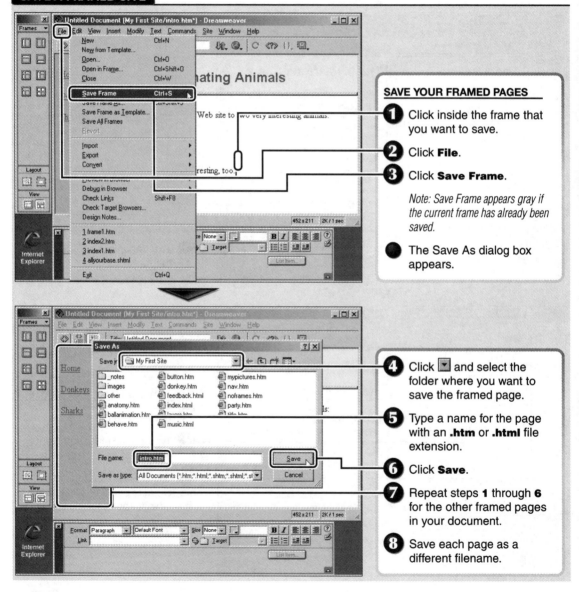

SAVE YOUR FRAMED PAGES

1 Click inside the frame that you want to save.

2 Click **File**.

3 Click **Save Frame**.

Note: Save Frame appears gray if the current frame has already been saved.

● The Save As dialog box appears.

4 Click ☑ and select the folder where you want to save the framed page.

5 Type a name for the page with an **.htm** or **.html** file extension.

6 Click **Save**.

7 Repeat steps **1** through **6** for the other framed pages in your document.

8 Save each page as a different filename.

in an instant

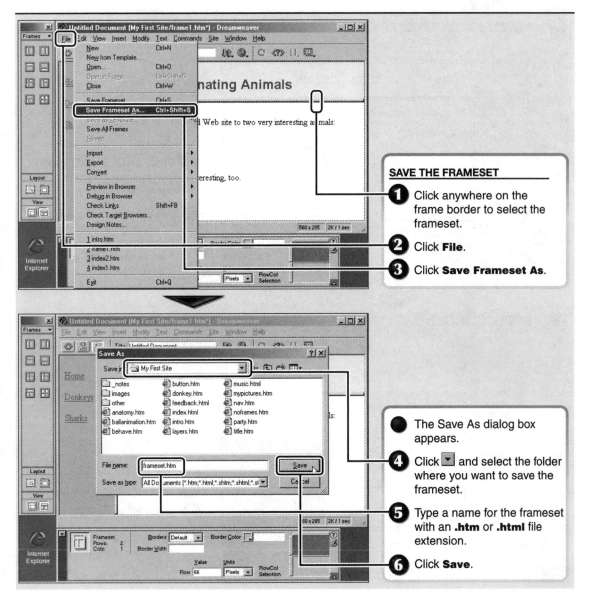

SAVE THE FRAMESET

1. Click anywhere on the frame border to select the frameset.

2. Click **File**.

3. Click **Save Frameset As**.

● The Save As dialog box appears.

4. Click ▣ and select the folder where you want to save the frameset.

5. Type a name for the frameset with an **.htm** or **.html** file extension.

6. Click **Save**.

NAME A FRAME

To create hyperlinks that work between your frames, you need to give your frames names. The name tells where the hyperlink destination should open in the frameset.

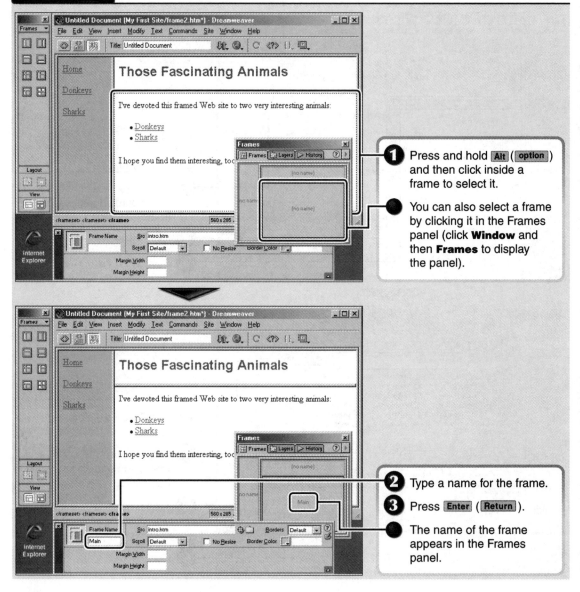

1 Press and hold **Alt** (**option**) and then click inside a frame to select it.

● You can also select a frame by clicking it in the Frames panel (click **Window** and then **Frames** to display the panel).

2 Type a name for the frame.

3 Press **Enter** (**Return**).

● The name of the frame appears in the Frames panel.

You can delete a frame if you want
to make your frameset less
complicated.

DELETE A FRAME

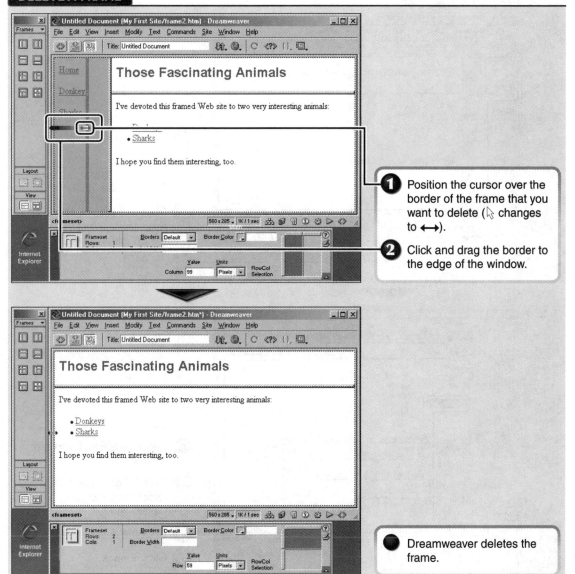

1 Position the cursor over the border of the frame that you want to delete (⇱ changes to ↔).

2 Click and drag the border to the edge of the window.

● Dreamweaver deletes the frame.

HYPERLINK TO A FRAME

You can create a hyperlink that opens a page in a different frame. You will want to do this for frames that contain navigation hyperlinks.

HYPERLINK TO A FRAME

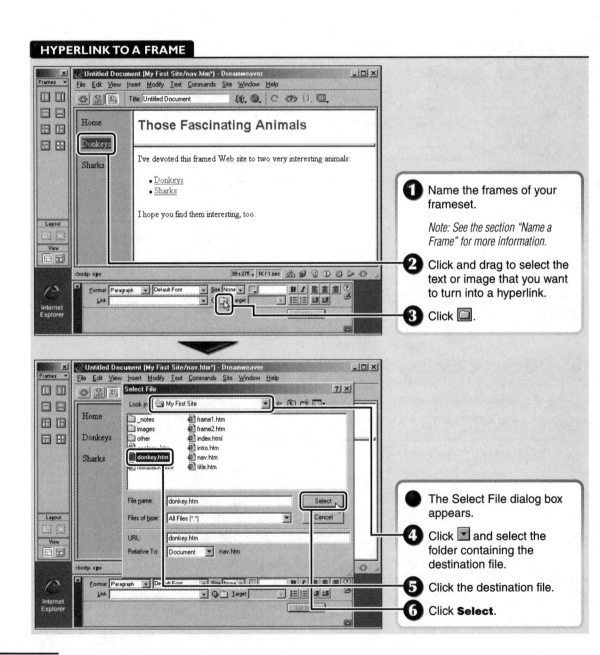

① Name the frames of your frameset.

Note: See the section "Name a Frame" for more information.

② Click and drag to select the text or image that you want to turn into a hyperlink.

③ Click ▣.

■ The Select File dialog box appears.

④ Click ▾ and select the folder containing the destination file.

⑤ Click the destination file.

⑥ Click **Select**.

in an instant

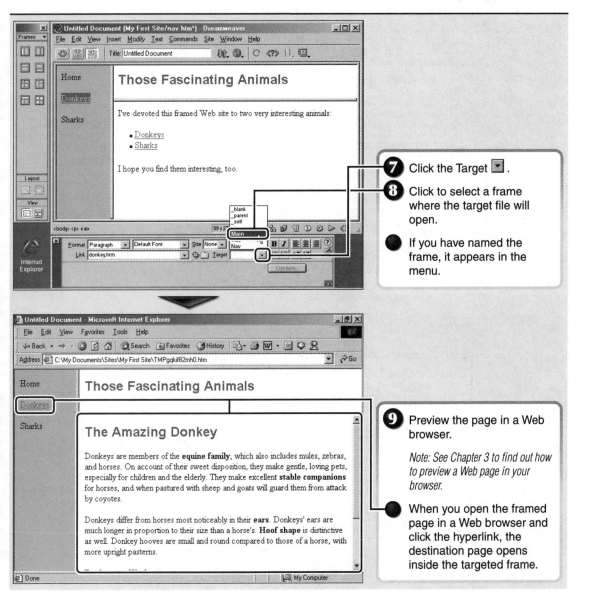

7 Click the Target ▼.

8 Click to select a frame where the target file will open.

● If you have named the frame, it appears in the menu.

9 Preview the page in a Web browser.

Note: See Chapter 3 to find out how to preview a Web page in your browser.

● When you open the framed page in a Web browser and click the hyperlink, the destination page opens inside the targeted frame.

CHANGE FRAME DIMENSIONS

You can change the dimensions of a frame to attractively and efficiently display the information inside it.

CHANGE FRAME DIMENSIONS

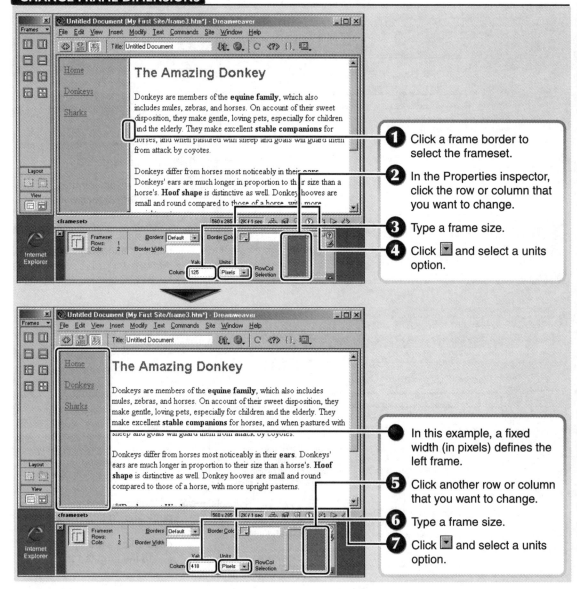

1 Click a frame border to select the frameset.

2 In the Properties inspector, click the row or column that you want to change.

3 Type a frame size.

4 Click ☑ and select a units option.

● In this example, a fixed width (in pixels) defines the left frame.

5 Click another row or column that you want to change.

6 Type a frame size.

7 Click ☑ and select a units option.

in an *instant*

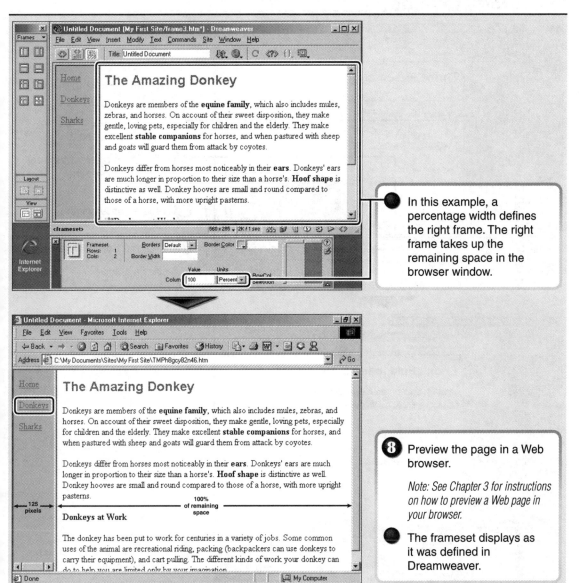

In this example, a percentage width defines the right frame. The right frame takes up the remaining space in the browser window.

8 Preview the page in a Web browser.

Note: See Chapter 3 for instructions on how to preview a Web page in your browser.

The frameset displays as it was defined in Dreamweaver.

FORMAT FRAME BORDERS

You can modify the appearance of your frame borders to make them complement the style of your Web site content. You can specify that borders be turned on or off, and you can set the color and width of your borders.

FORMAT FRAME BORDERS

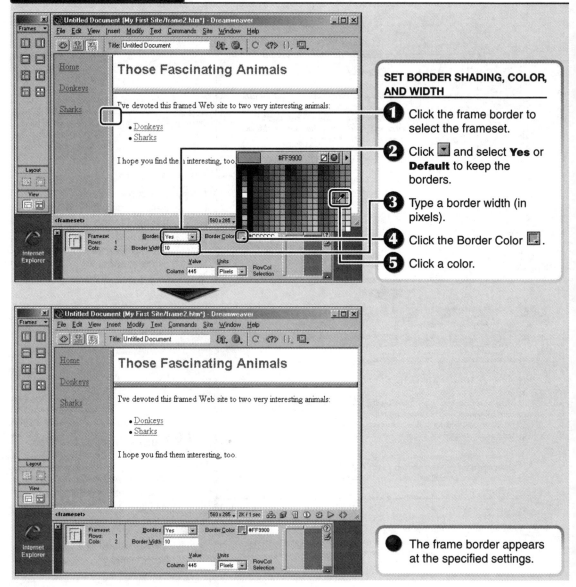

SET BORDER SHADING, COLOR, AND WIDTH

1 Click the frame border to select the frameset.

2 Click 🔽 and select **Yes** or **Default** to keep the borders.

3 Type a border width (in pixels).

4 Click the Border Color 🔲.

5 Click a color.

● The frame border appears at the specified settings.

in an *instant*

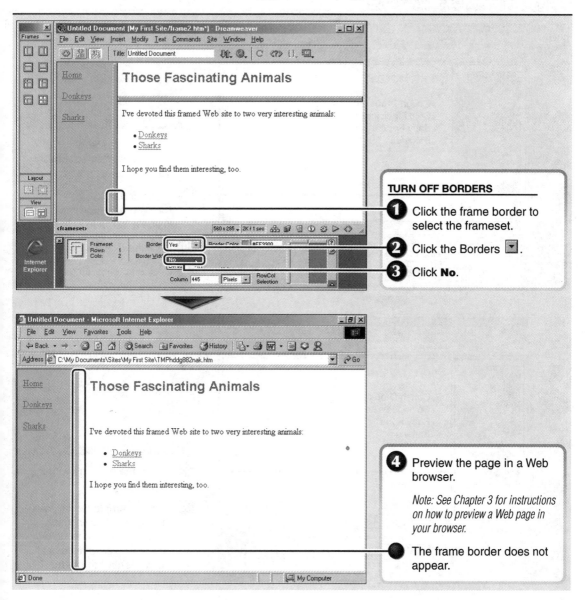

TURN OFF BORDERS

1 Click the frame border to select the frameset.

2 Click the Borders ▼.

3 Click **No**.

4 Preview the page in a Web browser.

Note: See Chapter 3 for instructions on how to preview a Web page in your browser.

● The frame border does not appear.

CONTROL FRAME SCROLL BARS

You can control whether scroll bars will appear in your frames. Hiding scroll bars enables you to have more control over the presentation of your site, but may also prevent some users from seeing all your site content.

CONTROL FRAME SCROLL BARS

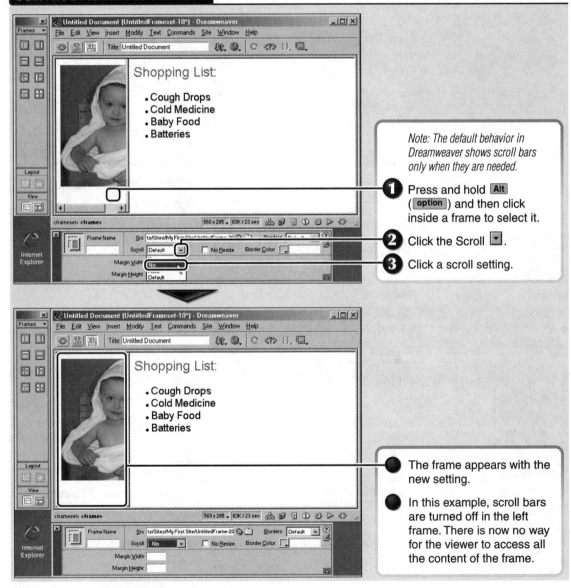

Note: The default behavior in Dreamweaver shows scroll bars only when they are needed.

1 Press and hold **Alt** (**option**) and then click inside a frame to select it.

2 Click the Scroll ▼.

3 Click a scroll setting.

● The frame appears with the new setting.

● In this example, scroll bars are turned off in the left frame. There is now no way for the viewer to access all the content of the frame.

The default behavior for most browsers allows users to resize frames by clicking and dragging frame borders. You can prevent users from resizing the frames of a site and protect the presentation of content.

CONTROL FRAME RESIZING

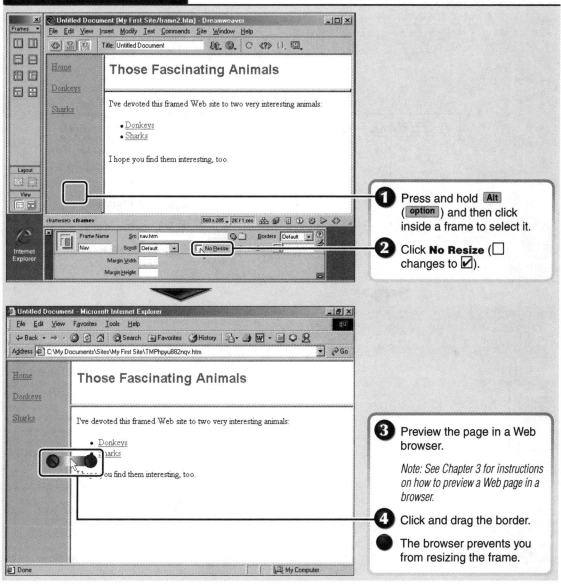

1 Press and hold **Alt** (**option**) and then click inside a frame to select it.

2 Click **No Resize** (□ changes to ☑).

3 Preview the page in a Web browser.

Note: See Chapter 3 for instructions on how to preview a Web page in a browser.

4 Click and drag the border.

● The browser prevents you from resizing the frame.

ADD NOFRAMES CONTENT

Not every user has a browser that can display frames. For these users, you can provide content that is displayed instead of frames.

ADD NOFRAMES CONTENT

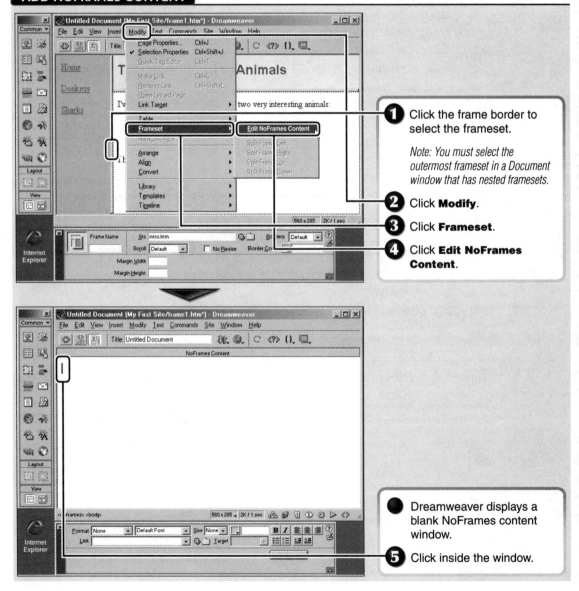

1 Click the frame border to select the frameset.

Note: You must select the outermost frameset in a Document window that has nested framesets.

2 Click **Modify**.

3 Click **Frameset**.

4 Click **Edit NoFrames Content**.

■ Dreamweaver displays a blank NoFrames content window.

5 Click inside the window.

in an *instant*

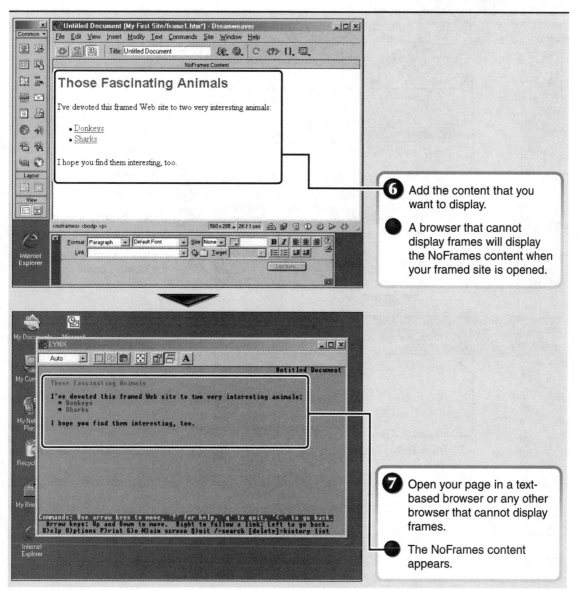

6 Add the content that you want to display.

● A browser that cannot display frames will display the NoFrames content when your framed site is opened.

7 Open your page in a text-based browser or any other browser that cannot display frames.

● The NoFrames content appears.

NEST PAGE FRAMES

You can subdivide a frame of an existing frameset to create nested frames. Nested frames enable you to organize the information in your site in a more complex way.

NEST PAGE FRAMES

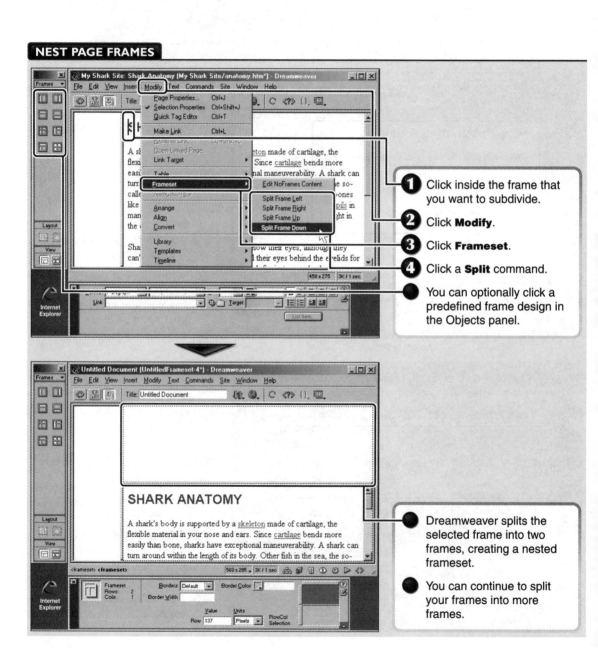

1 Click inside the frame that you want to subdivide.

2 Click **Modify**.

3 Click **Frameset**.

4 Click a **Split** command.

● You can optionally click a predefined frame design in the Objects panel.

● Dreamweaver splits the selected frame into two frames, creating a nested frameset.

● You can continue to split your frames into more frames.

VIEW LIBRARY ITEMS AND TEMPLATES

You can access the library and templates of a site by using commands in the Window menu. You can also access them via the Assets panel.

VIEW LIBRARY ITEMS AND TEMPLATES

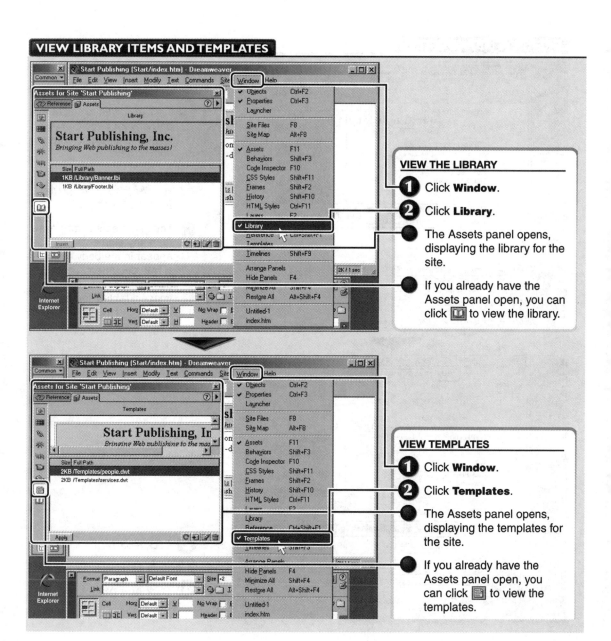

VIEW THE LIBRARY

1 Click **Window**.

2 Click **Library**.

■ The Assets panel opens, displaying the library for the site.

■ If you already have the Assets panel open, you can click 🕮 to view the library.

VIEW TEMPLATES

1 Click **Window**.

2 Click **Templates**.

■ The Assets panel opens, displaying the templates for the site.

■ If you already have the Assets panel open, you can click 🗐 to view the templates.

CREATE A LIBRARY ITEM

You can define text, images, and other Dreamweaver objects as library items. Library items enable you to insert page elements quickly without having to re-create them from scratch every time.

CREATE A LIBRARY ITEM

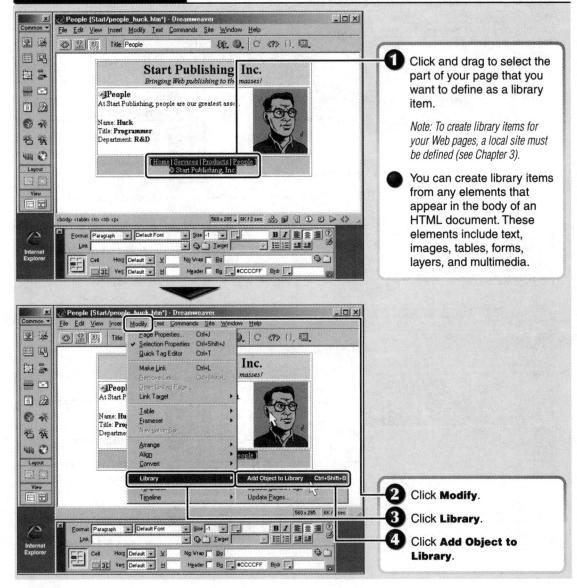

1 Click and drag to select the part of your page that you want to define as a library item.

Note: To create library items for your Web pages, a local site must be defined (see Chapter 3).

● You can create library items from any elements that appear in the body of an HTML document. These elements include text, images, tables, forms, layers, and multimedia.

2 Click **Modify**.

3 Click **Library**.

4 Click **Add Object to Library**.

in an *instant*

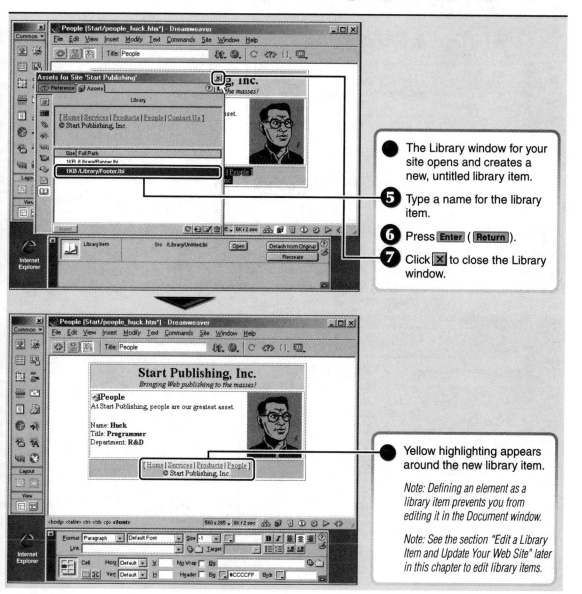

The Library window for your site opens and creates a new, untitled library item.

5 Type a name for the library item.

6 Press **Enter** (**Return**).

7 Click ☒ to close the Library window.

Yellow highlighting appears around the new library item.

Note: Defining an element as a library item prevents you from editing it in the Document window.

Note: See the section "Edit a Library Item and Update Your Web Site" later in this chapter to edit library items.

INSERT A LIBRARY ITEM

Inserting an element into your page from the library saves you from having to create it from scratch. It also ensures that the element is identical to other instances of that item in your site.

INSERT A LIBRARY ITEM

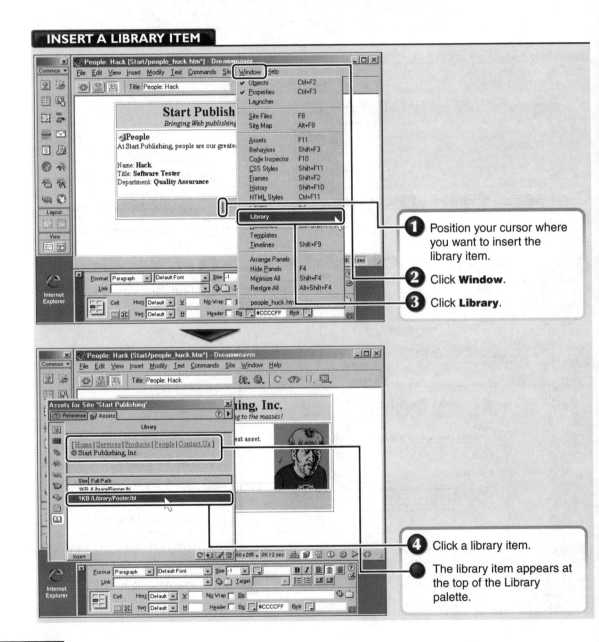

1 Position your cursor where you want to insert the library item.

2 Click **Window**.

3 Click **Library**.

4 Click a library item.

The library item appears at the top of the Library palette.

in an instant

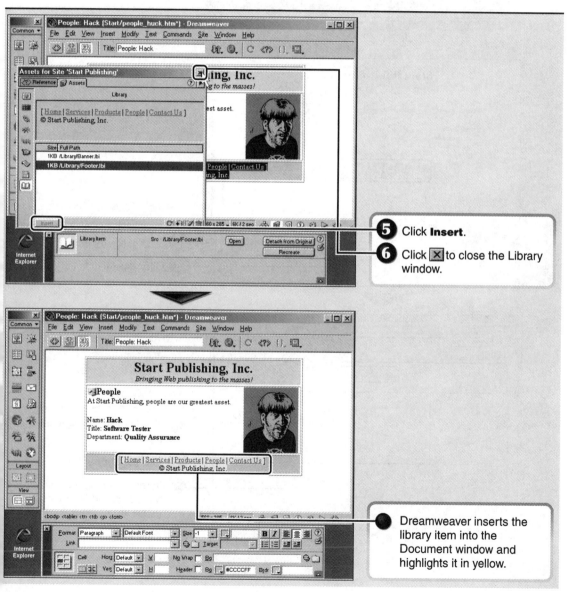

5 Click **Insert**.

6 Click ☒ to close the Library window.

● Dreamweaver inserts the library item into the Document window and highlights it in yellow.

EDIT A LIBRARY ITEM AND UPDATE YOUR WEB SITE

You can edit a library item and then automatically update all the pages in your site that feature that item. This feature can save you time when maintaining a Web site.

EDIT A LIBRARY ITEM AND UPDATE YOUR WEB SITE

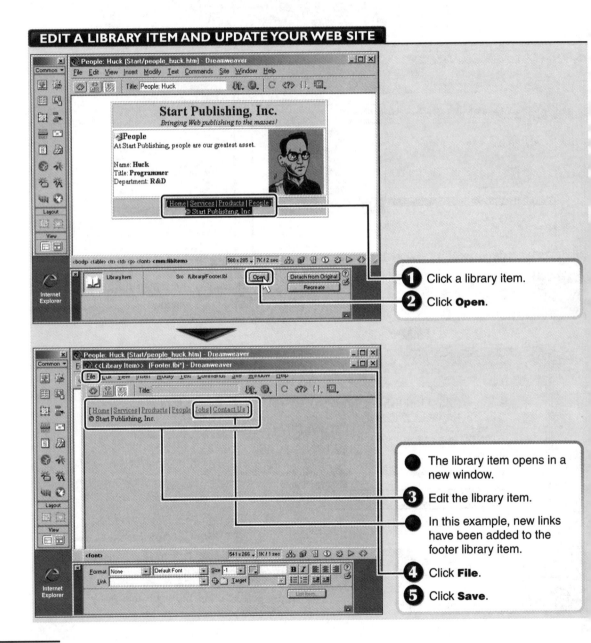

1 Click a library item.

2 Click **Open**.

● The library item opens in a new window.

3 Edit the library item.

● In this example, new links have been added to the footer library item.

4 Click **File**.

5 Click **Save**.

in an *instant*

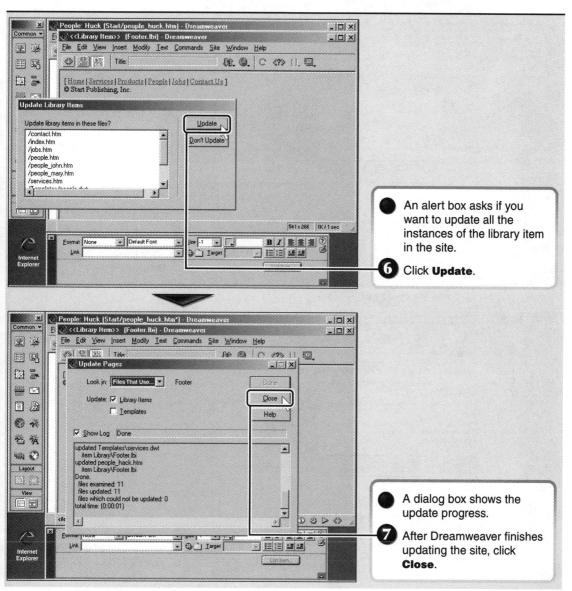

An alert box asks if you want to update all the instances of the library item in the site.

6 Click **Update**.

A dialog box shows the update progress.

7 After Dreamweaver finishes updating the site, click **Close**.

DETACH CONTENT FROM THE LIBRARY FOR EDITING

You can detach an instance of a library item from the library and then edit it just like regular content.

DETACH CONTENT FROM THE LIBRARY FOR EDITING

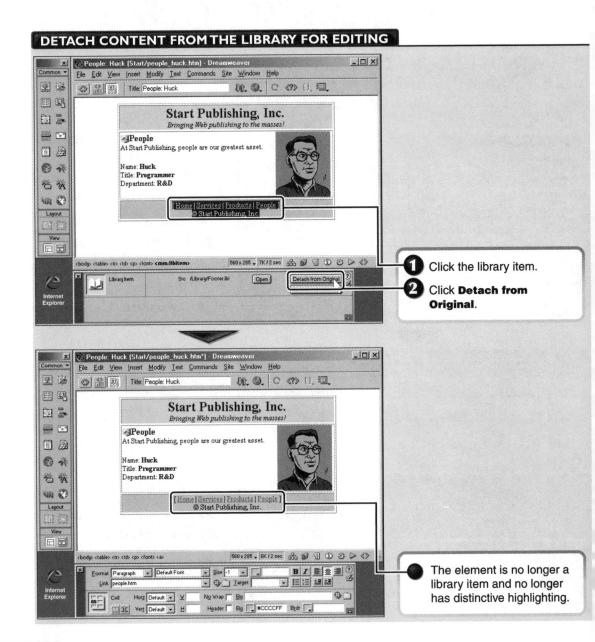

1 Click the library item.

2 Click **Detach from Original**.

● The element is no longer a library item and no longer has distinctive highlighting.

in an *instant*

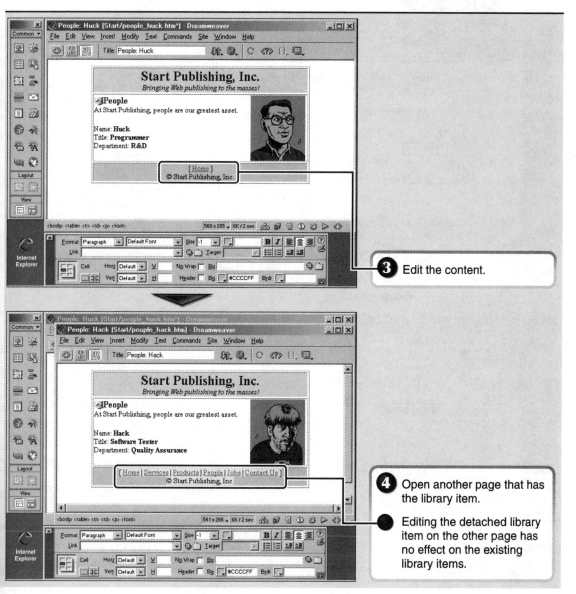

3 Edit the content.

4 Open another page that has the library item.

Editing the detached library item on the other page has no effect on the existing library items.

CREATE A TEMPLATE

To help you save time, you can create generic template pages to use as starting points for new pages.

CREATE A TEMPLATE

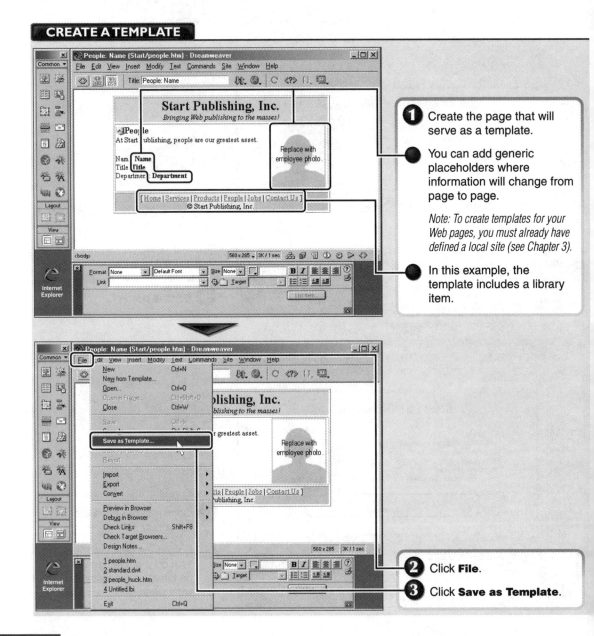

① Create the page that will serve as a template.

● You can add generic placeholders where information will change from page to page.

Note: To create templates for your Web pages, you must already have defined a local site (see Chapter 3).

● In this example, the template includes a library item.

② Click **File**.

③ Click **Save as Template**.

in an *instant*

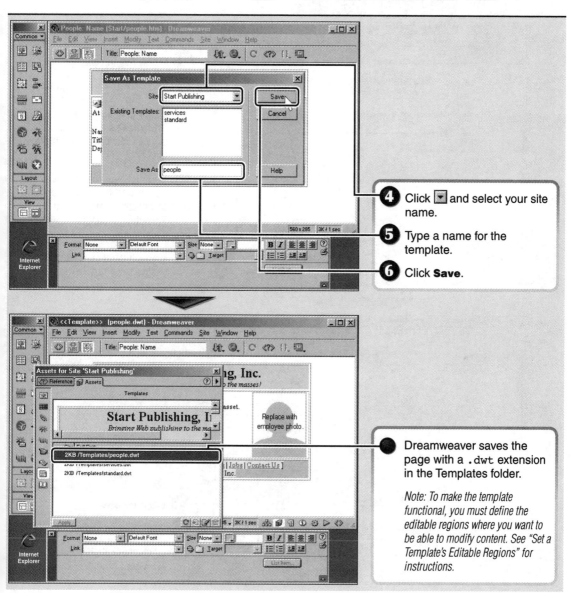

4 Click ▼ and select your site name.

5 Type a name for the template.

6 Click **Save**.

● Dreamweaver saves the page with a `.dwt` extension in the Templates folder.

Note: To make the template functional, you must define the editable regions where you want to be able to modify content. See "Set a Template's Editable Regions" for instructions.

SET A TEMPLATE'S EDITABLE REGIONS

After you create a Web page template, you must define which regions of the template are editable. These regions are changeable in a page according to its template design.

SET A TEMPLATE'S EDITABLE REGIONS

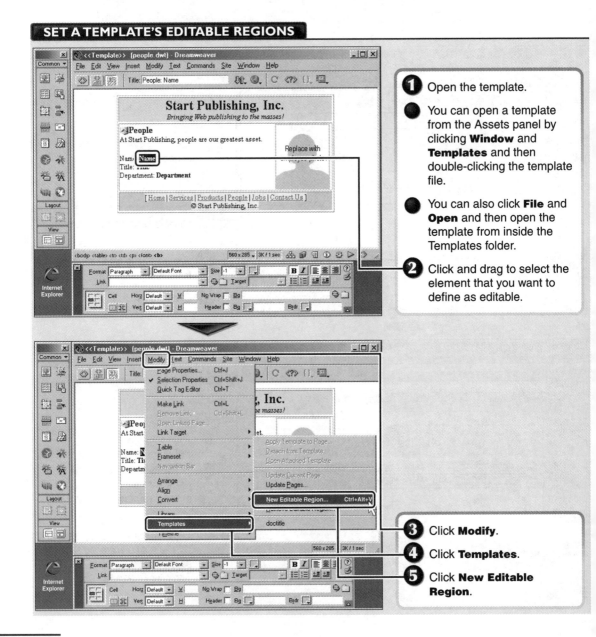

1 Open the template.

● You can open a template from the Assets panel by clicking **Window** and **Templates** and then double-clicking the template file.

● You can also click **File** and **Open** and then open the template from inside the Templates folder.

2 Click and drag to select the element that you want to define as editable.

3 Click **Modify**.

4 Click **Templates**.

5 Click **New Editable Region**.

in an *instant*

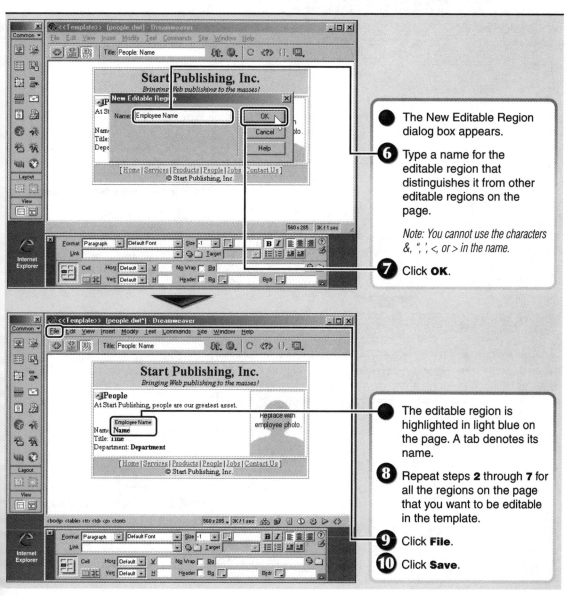

The New Editable Region dialog box appears.

6 Type a name for the editable region that distinguishes it from other editable regions on the page.

Note: You cannot use the characters &, " ' ; < , or > in the name.

7 Click **OK**.

The editable region is highlighted in light blue on the page. A tab denotes its name.

8 Repeat steps **2** through **7** for all the regions on the page that you want to be editable in the template.

9 Click **File**.

10 Click **Save**.

171

CREATE A PAGE BY USING A TEMPLATE

You can create a new Web page based on a template that you have already defined. This saves you from having to build all the generic elements that appear on many of your pages from scratch.

CREATE A PAGE BY USING A TEMPLATE

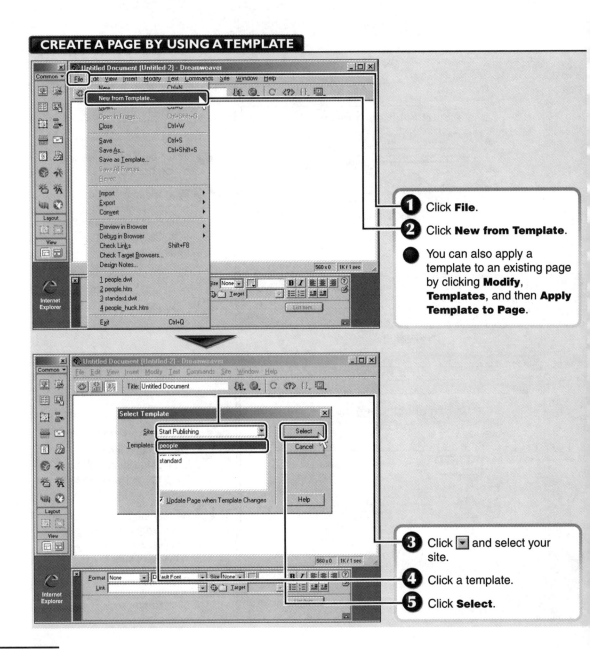

1 Click **File**.

2 Click **New from Template**.

● You can also apply a template to an existing page by clicking **Modify**, **Templates**, and then **Apply Template to Page**.

3 Click ▼ and select your site.

4 Click a template.

5 Click **Select**.

in an *instant*

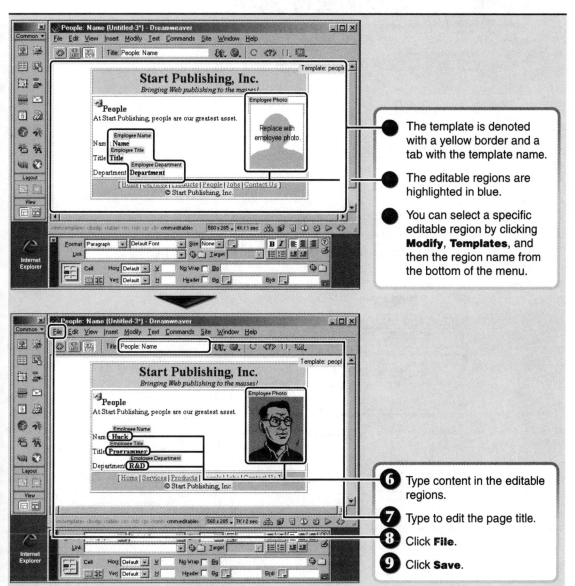

The template is denoted with a yellow border and a tab with the template name.

The editable regions are highlighted in blue.

You can select a specific editable region by clicking **Modify**, **Templates**, and then the region name from the bottom of the menu.

6 Type content in the editable regions.

7 Type to edit the page title.

8 Click **File**.

9 Click **Save**.

EDIT A TEMPLATE AND UPDATE YOUR WEB SITE

You can make changes to an original template file and then have Dreamweaver update other pages that were based on that template. This enables you to make changes to the page design of your site in seconds.

EDIT A TEMPLATE AND UPDATE YOUR WEB SITE

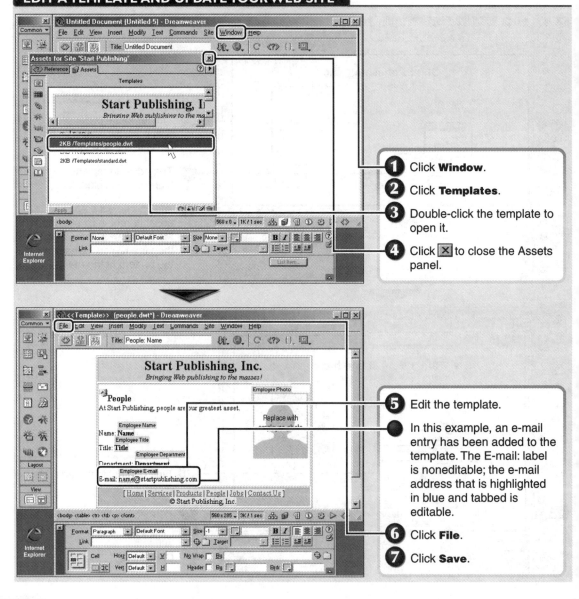

1. Click **Window**.

2. Click **Templates**.

3. Double-click the template to open it.

4. Click ☒ to close the Assets panel.

5. Edit the template.

● In this example, an e-mail entry has been added to the template. The E-mail: label is noneditable; the e-mail address that is highlighted in blue and tabbed is editable.

6. Click **File**.

7. Click **Save**.

in an instant

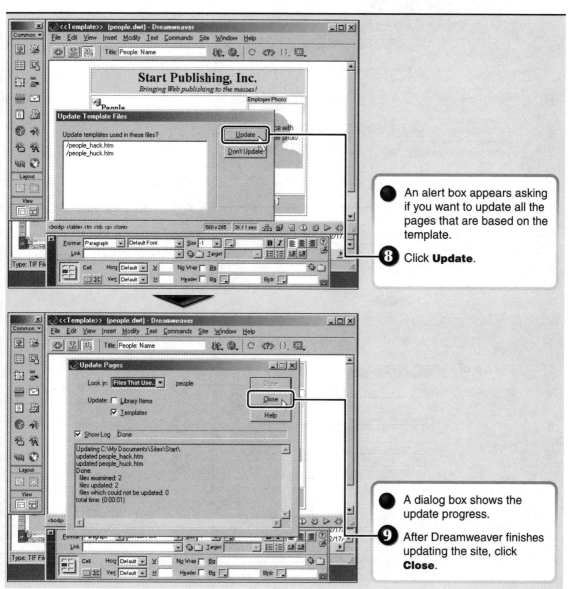

An alert box appears asking if you want to update all the pages that are based on the template.

8 Click **Update**.

A dialog box shows the update progress.

9 After Dreamweaver finishes updating the site, click **Close**.

CUSTOMIZE AN HTML TAG

You can use style sheets to customize the style that is applied by an HTML tag. This capability gives you control over how HTML makes the text and other content on your page appear.

CUSTOMIZE AN HTML TAG

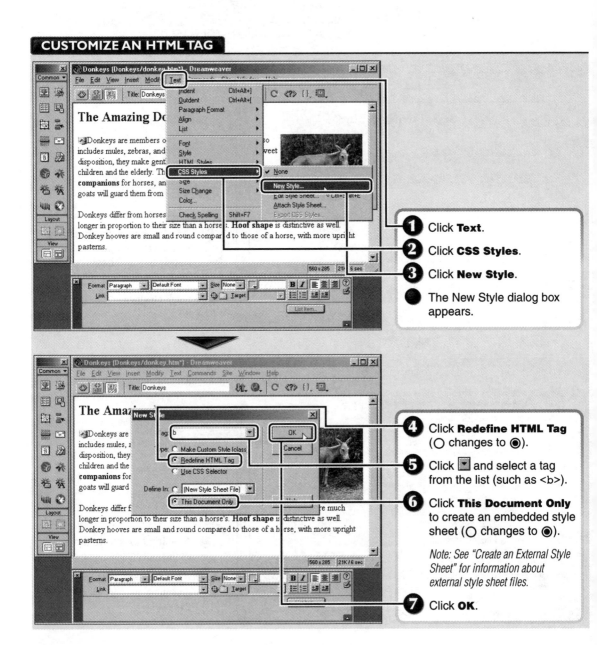

1. Click **Text**.

2. Click **CSS Styles**.

3. Click **New Style**.

● The New Style dialog box appears.

4. Click **Redefine HTML Tag** (○ changes to ◉).

5. Click ▼ and select a tag from the list (such as <b>).

6. Click **This Document Only** to create an embedded style sheet (○ changes to ◉).

   Note: See "Create an External Style Sheet" for information about external style sheet files.

7. Click **OK**.

in an *instant*

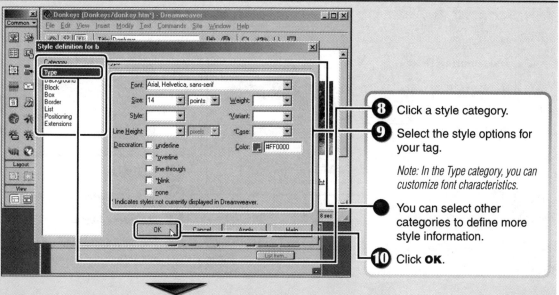

8 Click a style category.

9 Select the style options for your tag.

Note: In the Type category, you can customize font characteristics.

● You can select other categories to define more style information.

10 Click **OK**.

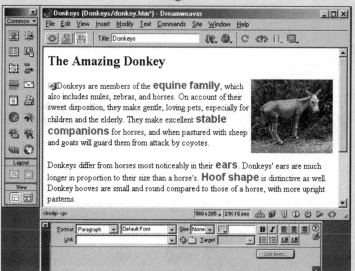

The Amazing Donkey

Donkeys are members of the **equine family**, which also includes mules, zebras, and horses. On account of their sweet disposition, they make gentle, loving pets, especially for children and the elderly. They make excellent **stable companions** for horses, and when pastured with sheep and goats will guard them from attack by coyotes.

Donkeys differ from horses most noticeably in their **ears**. Donkeys' ears are much longer in proportion to their size than a horse's. **Hoof shape** is distinctive as well. Donkey hooves are small and round compared to those of a horse, with more upright pasterns.

● Dreamweaver adds the new style to any content formatted with the redefined tag.

● You can also apply the style by formatting new content with the tag.

You can define specific style attributes as a style sheet *class*. You can then apply that class to elements on your Web page.

CREATE A CLASS

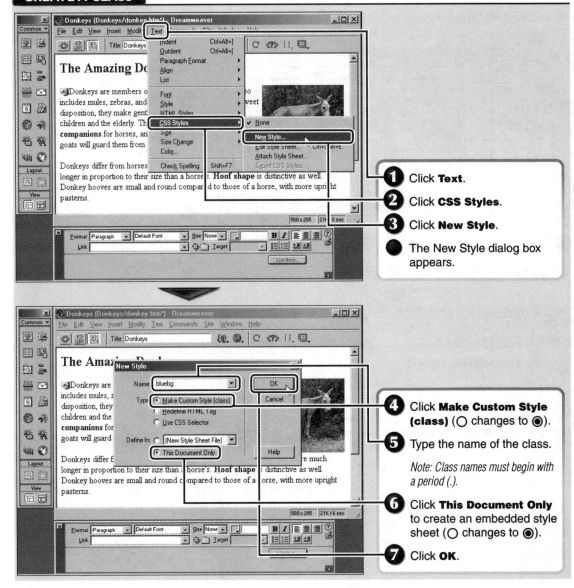

1 Click **Text**.

2 Click **CSS Styles**.

3 Click **New Style**.

● The New Style dialog box appears.

4 Click **Make Custom Style (class)** (○ changes to ⦿).

5 Type the name of the class.

Note: Class names must begin with a period (.).

6 Click **This Document Only** to create an embedded style sheet (○ changes to ⦿).

7 Click **OK**.

in an *instant*

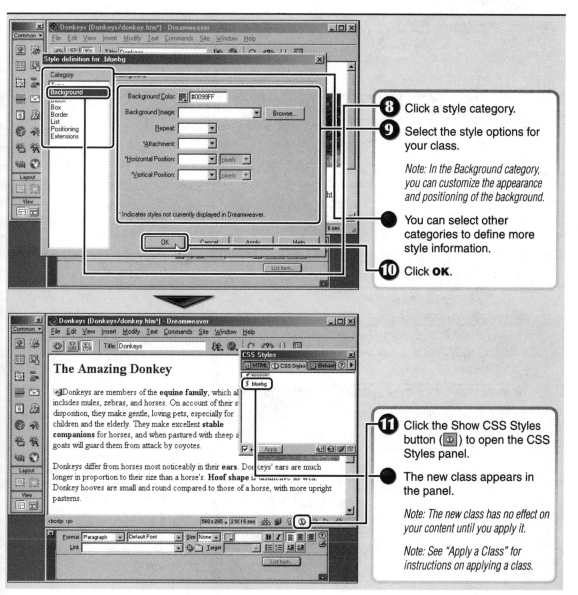

8 Click a style category.

9 Select the style options for your class.

Note: In the Background category, you can customize the appearance and positioning of the background.

● You can select other categories to define more style information.

10 Click **OK**.

11 Click the Show CSS Styles button (◉) to open the CSS Styles panel.

● The new class appears in the panel.

Note: The new class has no effect on your content until you apply it.

Note: See "Apply a Class" for instructions on applying a class.

APPLY A CLASS

You can apply a style sheet class to objects, paragraphs, or entire Web pages. This enables you to change the color, font, size, background, and other characteristics of content on your page.

APPLY A CLASS

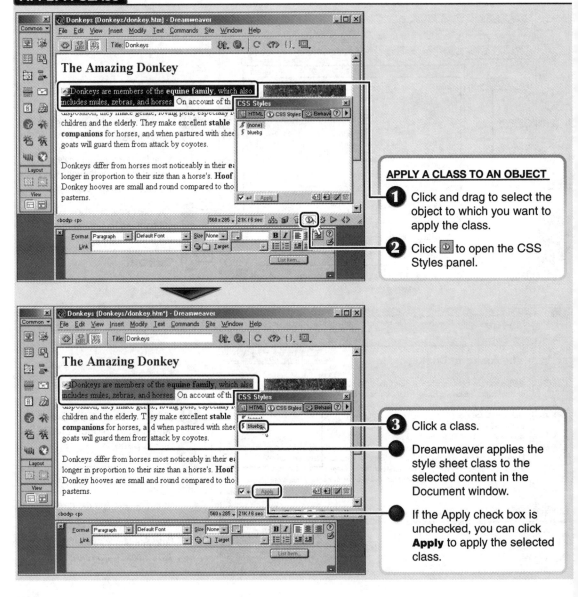

APPLY A CLASS TO AN OBJECT

1 Click and drag to select the object to which you want to apply the class.

2 Click ⊙ to open the CSS Styles panel.

3 Click a class.

Dreamweaver applies the style sheet class to the selected content in the Document window.

If the Apply check box is unchecked, you can click **Apply** to apply the selected class.

in an *instant*

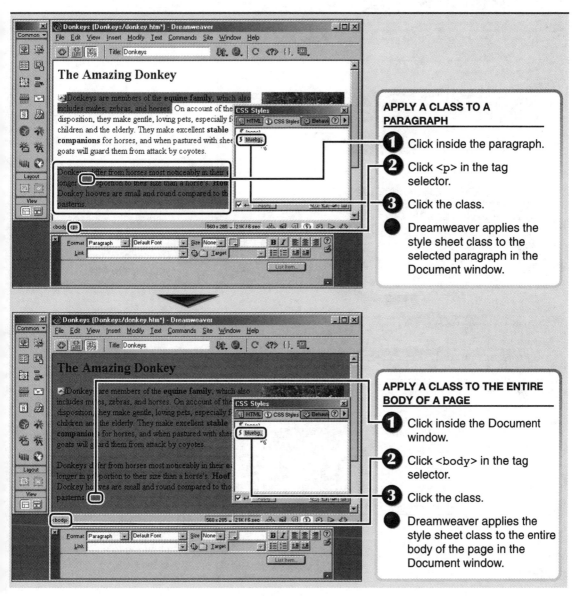

APPLY A CLASS TO A PARAGRAPH

1. Click inside the paragraph.

2. Click <p> in the tag selector.

3. Click the class.

● Dreamweaver applies the style sheet class to the selected paragraph in the Document window.

APPLY A CLASS TO THE ENTIRE BODY OF A PAGE

1. Click inside the Document window.

2. Click <body> in the tag selector.

3. Click the class.

● Dreamweaver applies the style sheet class to the entire body of the page in the Document window.

You can edit the style rules of a class. This will change all instances where you have applied the class on your pages.

EDIT A STYLE SHEET CLASS

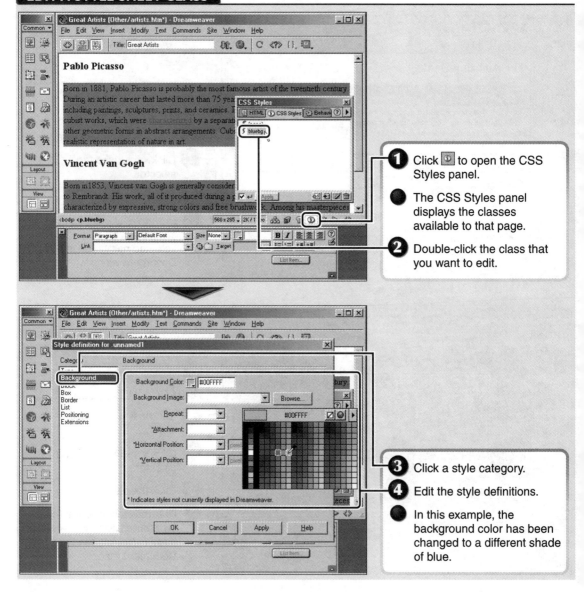

1 Click 🔘 to open the CSS Styles panel.

● The CSS Styles panel displays the classes available to that page.

2 Double-click the class that you want to edit.

3 Click a style category.

4 Edit the style definitions.

● In this example, the background color has been changed to a different shade of blue.

182

in an *instant*

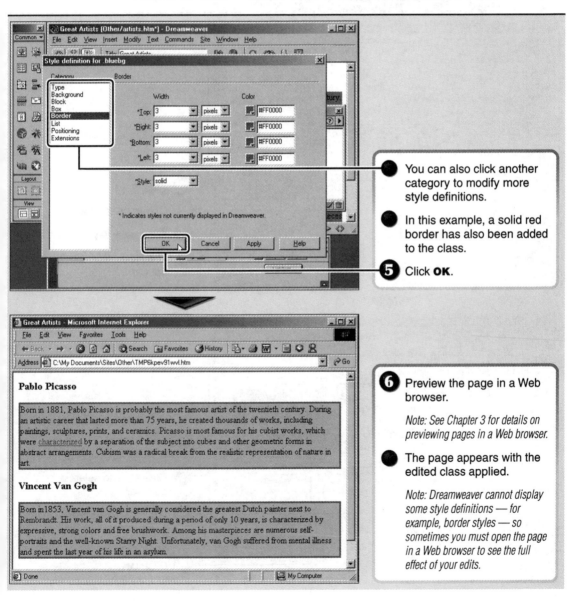

You can also click another category to modify more style definitions.

In this example, a solid red border has also been added to the class.

5 Click **OK**.

6 Preview the page in a Web browser.

Note: See Chapter 3 for details on previewing pages in a Web browser.

The page appears with the edited class applied.

Note: Dreamweaver cannot display some style definitions — for example, border styles — so sometimes you must open the page in a Web browser to see the full effect of your edits.

USING CSS SELECTORS TO MODIFY LINKS

You can use style sheet *selectors* to customize the links on your page. Selectors let you customize your links in ways that you cannot with HTML.

USING CSS SELECTORS TO MODIFY LINKS

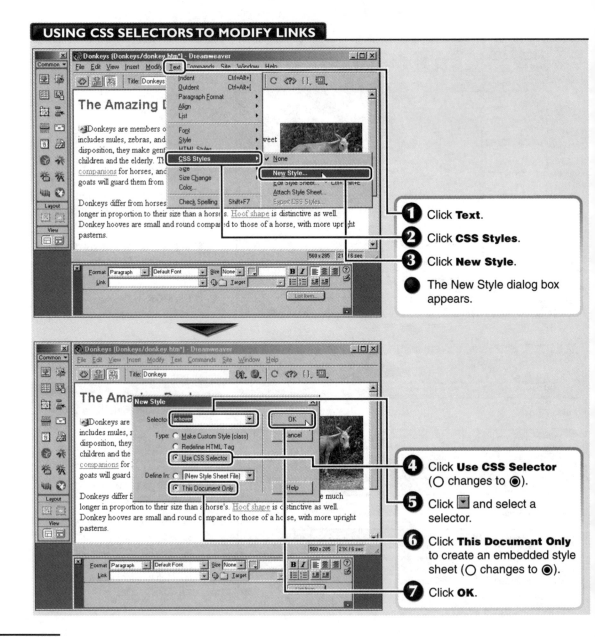

1 Click **Text**.

2 Click **CSS Styles**.

3 Click **New Style**.

■ The New Style dialog box appears.

4 Click **Use CSS Selector** (○ changes to ◉).

5 Click ▼ and select a selector.

6 Click **This Document Only** to create an embedded style sheet (○ changes to ◉).

7 Click **OK**.

in an *instant*

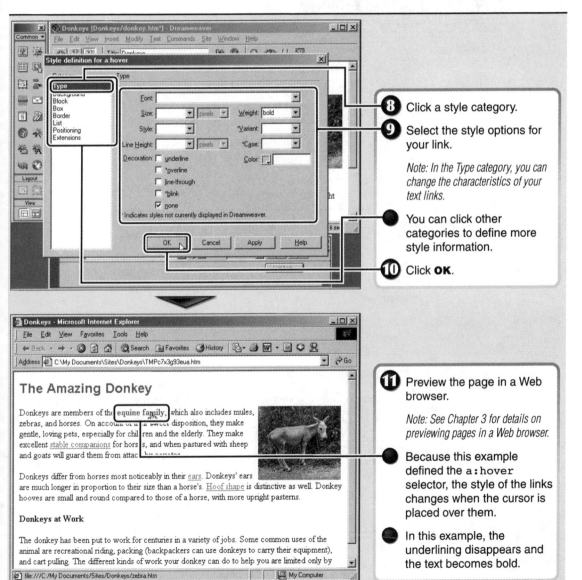

8 Click a style category.

9 Select the style options for your link.

Note: In the Type category, you can change the characteristics of your text links.

● You can click other categories to define more style information.

10 Click **OK**.

11 Preview the page in a Web browser.

Note: See Chapter 3 for details on previewing pages in a Web browser.

● Because this example defined the a:hover selector, the style of the links changes when the cursor is placed over them.

● In this example, the underlining disappears and the text becomes bold.

CREATE AN EXTERNAL STYLE SHEET

External style sheets enable you to define a set of style sheet rules and apply them to many different pages — even pages on different Web sites. This capability lets you keep a consistent look and feel across many pages and streamline style updates.

CREATE AN EXTERNAL STYLE SHEET

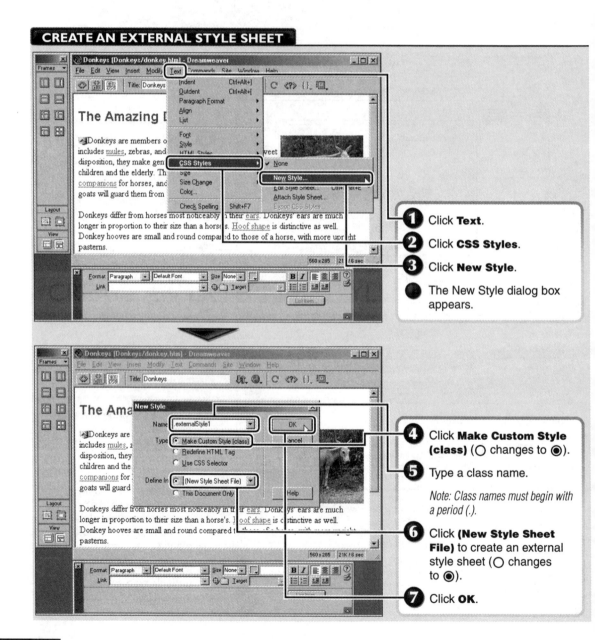

1 Click **Text**.

2 Click **CSS Styles**.

3 Click **New Style**.

■ The New Style dialog box appears.

4 Click **Make Custom Style (class)** (○ changes to ●).

5 Type a class name.

Note: Class names must begin with a period (.).

6 Click **(New Style Sheet File)** to create an external style sheet (○ changes to ●).

7 Click **OK**.

in an *instant*

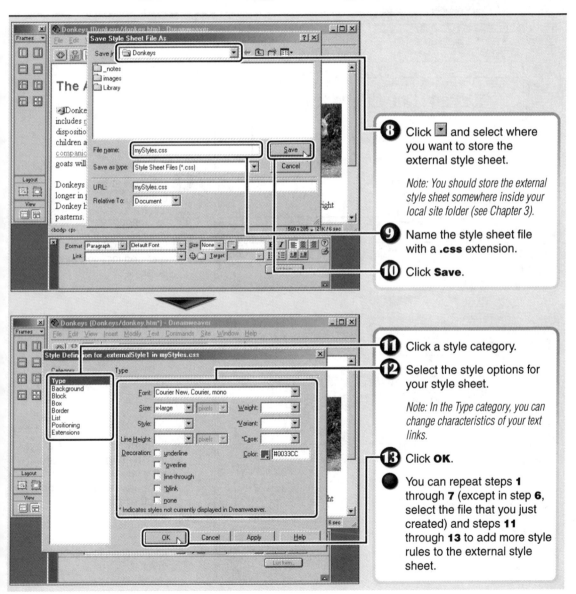

8 Click ☐ and select where you want to store the external style sheet.

Note: You should store the external style sheet somewhere inside your local site folder (see Chapter 3).

9 Name the style sheet file with a **.css** extension.

10 Click **Save**.

11 Click a style category.

12 Select the style options for your style sheet.

Note: In the Type category, you can change characteristics of your text links.

13 Click **OK**.

● You can repeat steps **1** through **7** (except in step **6**, select the file that you just created) and steps **11** through **13** to add more style rules to the external style sheet.

CREATE A LAYER

Layers let you create rectangular areas that float above the other content on your page. You can fill these blocks with different types of content and position them precisely in the browser window.

CREATE A LAYER

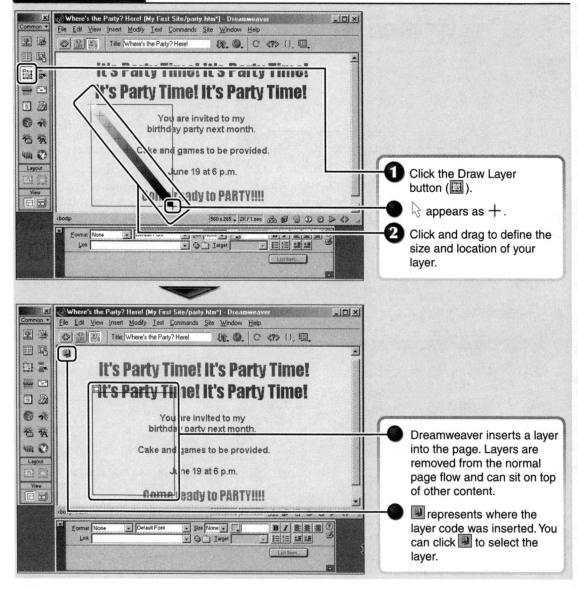

① Click the Draw Layer button (▥).

- ▷ appears as +.

② Click and drag to define the size and location of your layer.

● Dreamweaver inserts a layer into the page. Layers are removed from the normal page flow and can sit on top of other content.

● ▥ represents where the layer code was inserted. You can click ▥ to select the layer.

in an *instant*

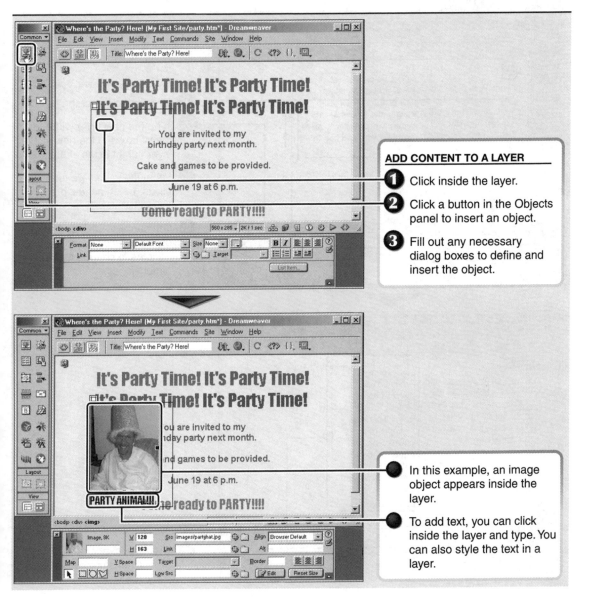

ADD CONTENT TO A LAYER

1 Click inside the layer.

2 Click a button in the Objects panel to insert an object.

3 Fill out any necessary dialog boxes to define and insert the object.

● In this example, an image object appears inside the layer.

● To add text, you can click inside the layer and type. You can also style the text in a layer.

RESIZE AND REPOSITION LAYERS

Every layer has specific position and dimension settings that define its place in the page. You can adjust the position and dimensions of a layer to make it fit attractively with the rest of the content on your page.

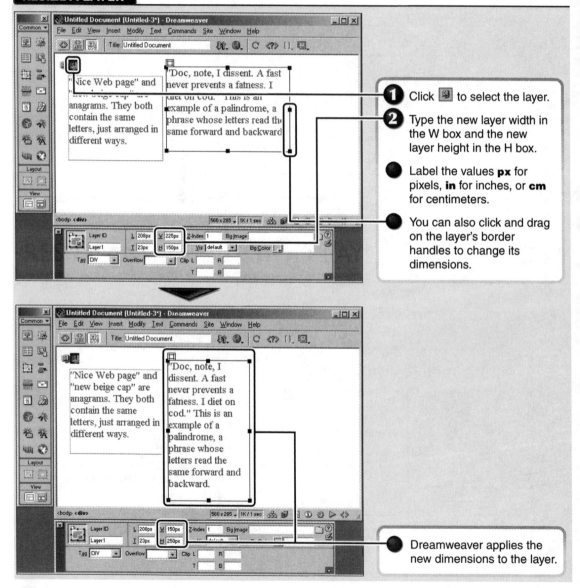

① Click  to select the layer.

② Type the new layer width in the W box and the new layer height in the H box.

● Label the values **px** for pixels, **in** for inches, or **cm** for centimeters.

● You can also click and drag on the layer's border handles to change its dimensions.

● Dreamweaver applies the new dimensions to the layer.

in an *Instant*

REPOSITION A LAYER

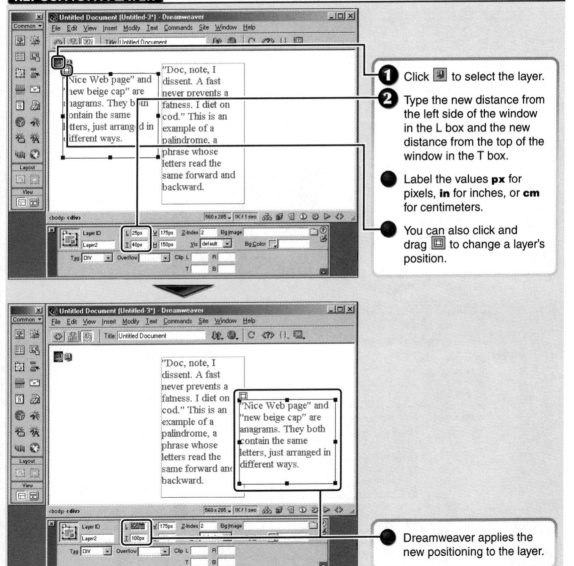

1 Click ⬛ to select the layer.

2 Type the new distance from the left side of the window in the L box and the new distance from the top of the window in the T box.

● Label the values **px** for pixels, **in** for inches, or **cm** for centimeters.

● You can also click and drag ⬛ to change a layer's position.

● Dreamweaver applies the new positioning to the layer.

ADD A BACKGROUND COLOR TO A LAYER

Setting the background color of a layer is similar to setting the background color of a page. By setting the background color, you can make a layer stand out or blend in on a page.

ADD A BACKGROUND COLOR TO A LAYER

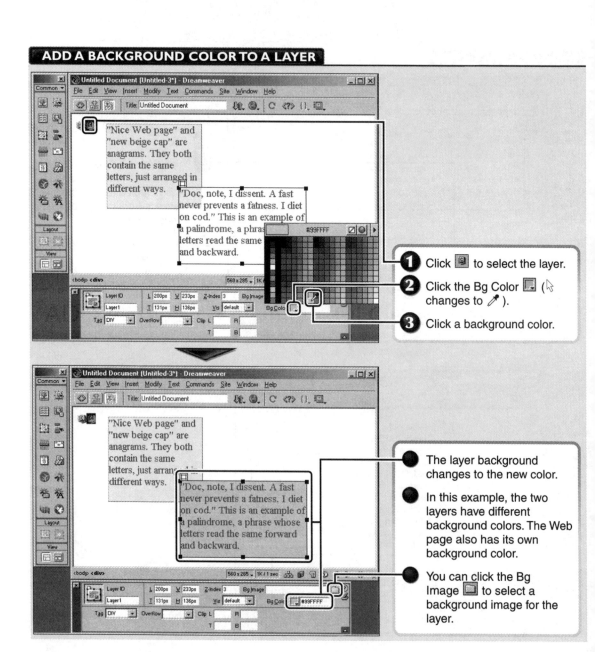

① Click 🖼 to select the layer.

② Click the Bg Color 🔲 (🖑 changes to ✐).

③ Click a background color.

● The layer background changes to the new color.

● In this example, the two layers have different background colors. The Web page also has its own background color.

● You can click the Bg Image 📁 to select a background image for the layer.

You can change the stacking order of layers on a page to change how they overlap one another. You can then hide parts of some layers under other layers.

CHANGE THE STACKING ORDER OF LAYERS

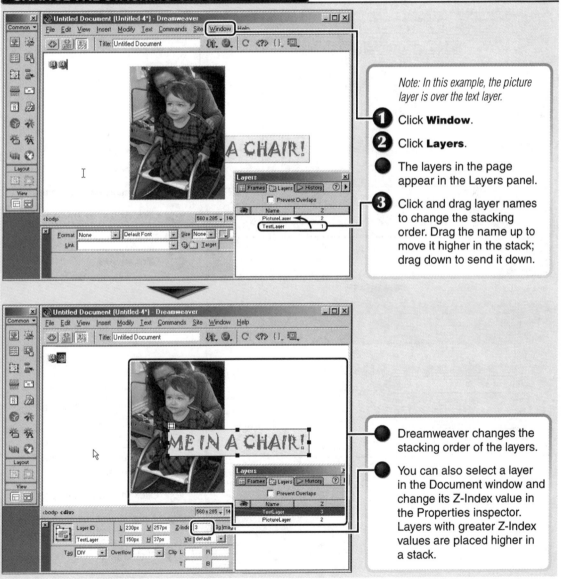

Note: In this example, the picture layer is over the text layer.

1 Click **Window**.

2 Click **Layers**.

■ The layers in the page appear in the Layers panel.

3 Click and drag layer names to change the stacking order. Drag the name up to move it higher in the stack; drag down to send it down.

■ Dreamweaver changes the stacking order of the layers.

■ You can also select a layer in the Document window and change its Z-Index value in the Properties inspector. Layers with greater Z-Index values are placed higher in a stack.

CREATE A ROLLOVER IMAGE

You can replace an image on your page with another in response to a cursor passing over it by using a *rollover* behavior. Rollover effects are often applied to navigation buttons, where passing your cursor over the button causes it to light up or appear depressed, like a real button.

CREATE A ROLLOVER IMAGE

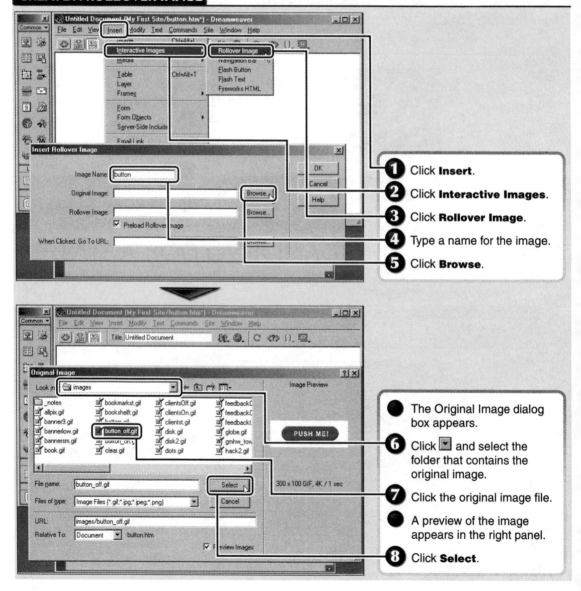

1 Click **Insert**.

2 Click **Interactive Images**.

3 Click **Rollover Image**.

4 Type a name for the image.

5 Click **Browse**.

● The Original Image dialog box appears.

6 Click ▾ and select the folder that contains the original image.

7 Click the original image file.

● A preview of the image appears in the right panel.

8 Click **Select**.

in an *instant*

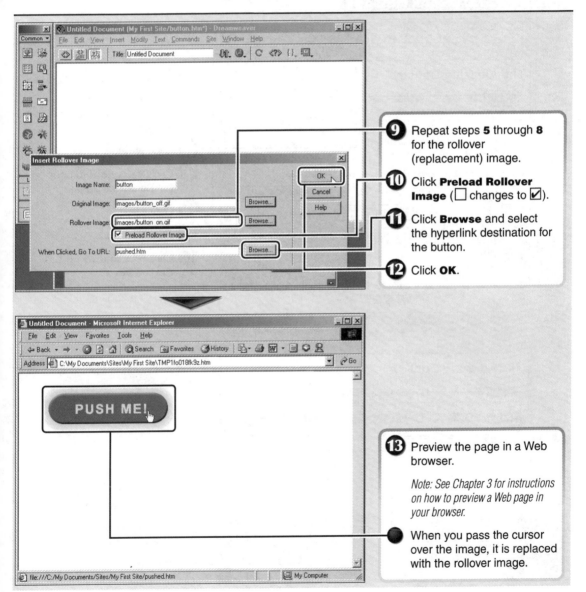

9 Repeat steps **5** through **8** for the rollover (replacement) image.

10 Click **Preload Rollover Image** (□ changes to ☑).

11 Click **Browse** and select the hyperlink destination for the button.

12 Click **OK**.

13 Preview the page in a Web browser.

Note: See Chapter 3 for instructions on how to preview a Web page in your browser.

● When you pass the cursor over the image, it is replaced with the rollover image.

CREATE A STATUS BAR MESSAGE

You can use a behavior to display a status bar message when a user rolls the cursor over a hyperlink. This message can describe where the hyperlink takes the user.

CREATE A STATUS BAR MESSAGE

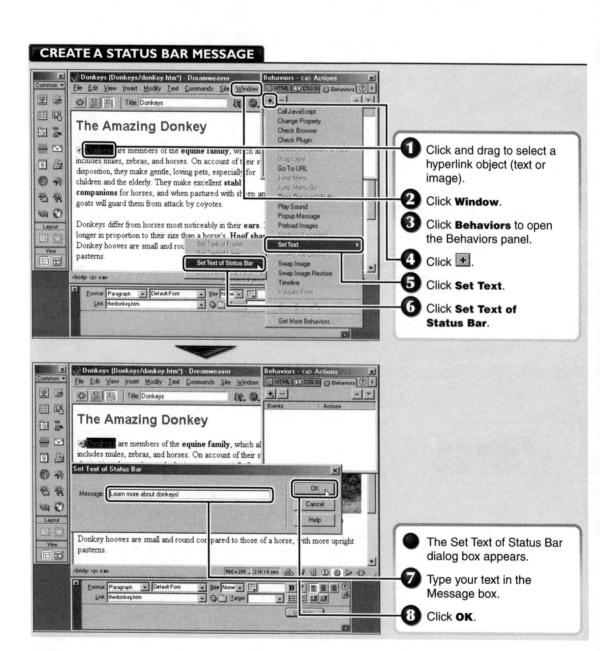

1 Click and drag to select a hyperlink object (text or image).

2 Click **Window**.

3 Click **Behaviors** to open the Behaviors panel.

4 Click 🞢.

5 Click **Set Text**.

6 Click **Set Text of Status Bar**.

● The Set Text of Status Bar dialog box appears.

7 Type your text in the Message box.

8 Click **OK**.

in an instant

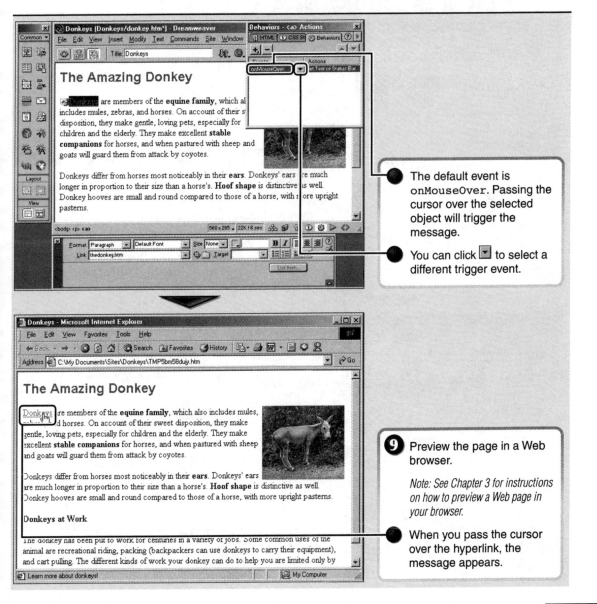

The default event is
onMouseOver. Passing the
cursor over the selected
object will trigger the
message.

You can click ▪ to select a
different trigger event.

⑨ Preview the page in a Web
browser.

*Note: See Chapter 3 for instructions
on how to preview a Web page in
your browser.*

When you pass the cursor
over the hyperlink, the
message appears.

You can use a behavior to open linked information in a new, customized browser window. This enables you to keep the page that contains the link open on the user's computer.

OPEN A CUSTOMIZED BROWSER WINDOW

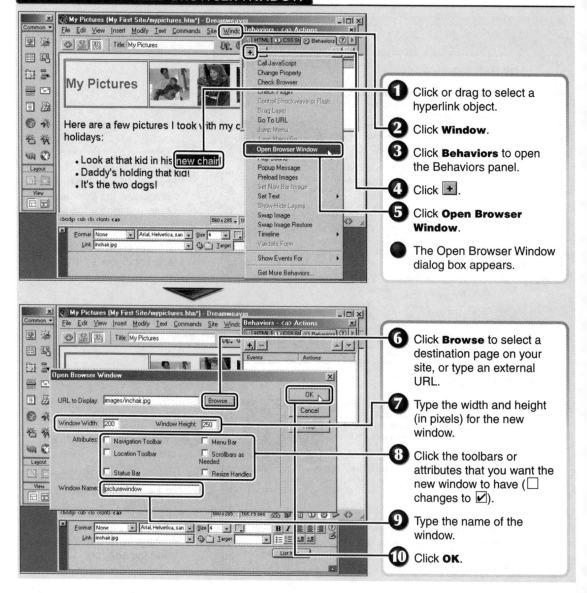

1 Click or drag to select a hyperlink object.

2 Click **Window**.

3 Click **Behaviors** to open the Behaviors panel.

4 Click ⊞.

5 Click **Open Browser Window**.

● The Open Browser Window dialog box appears.

6 Click **Browse** to select a destination page on your site, or type an external URL.

7 Type the width and height (in pixels) for the new window.

8 Click the toolbars or attributes that you want the new window to have (☐ changes to ☑).

9 Type the name of the window.

10 Click **OK**.

in an *instant*

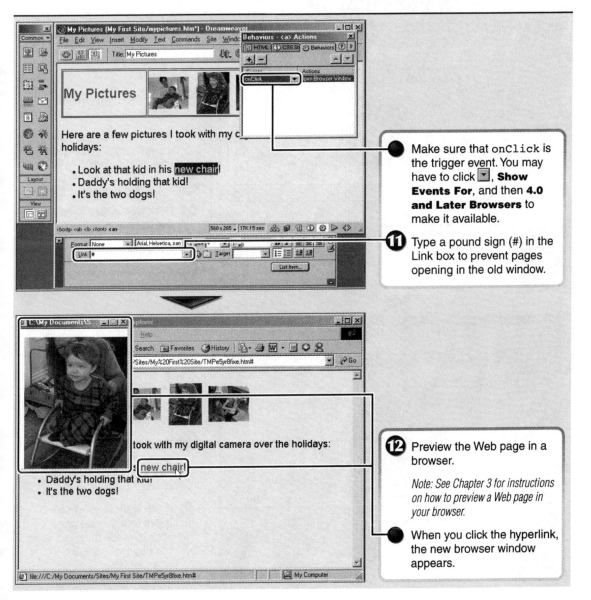

Make sure that `onClick` is
the trigger event. You may
have to click ▾, **Show
Events For**, and then **4.0
and Later Browsers** to
make it available.

11 Type a pound sign (#) in the
Link box to prevent pages
opening in the old window.

12 Preview the Web page in a
browser.

*Note: See Chapter 3 for instructions
on how to preview a Web page in
your browser.*

When you click the hyperlink,
the new browser window
appears.

CHECK A USER'S BROWSER VERSION

You can use a behavior to check the brand and version of a user's
browser and then forward the user to a page built specifically for
that browser. This lets you present advanced features only to the
users that can experience them.

CHECK A USER'S BROWSER VERSION

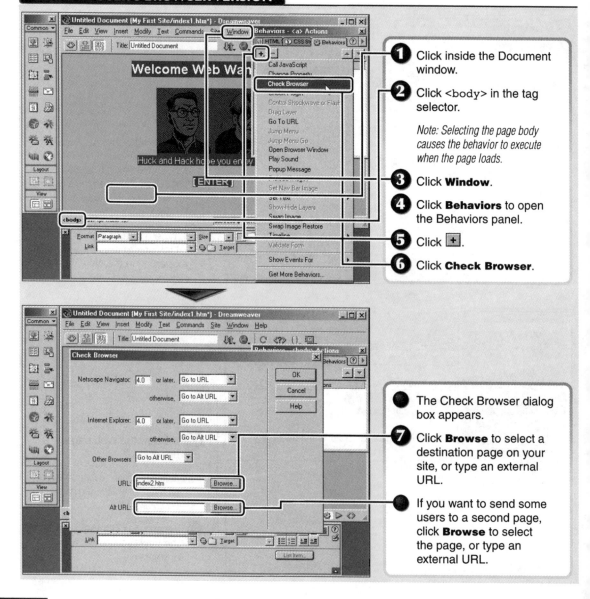

1 Click inside the Document window.

2 Click <body> in the tag selector.

Note: Selecting the page body causes the behavior to execute when the page loads.

3 Click **Window**.

4 Click **Behaviors** to open the Behaviors panel.

5 Click ➕.

6 Click **Check Browser**.

● The Check Browser dialog box appears.

7 Click **Browse** to select a destination page on your site, or type an external URL.

● If you want to send some users to a second page, click **Browse** to select the page, or type an external URL.

in an instant

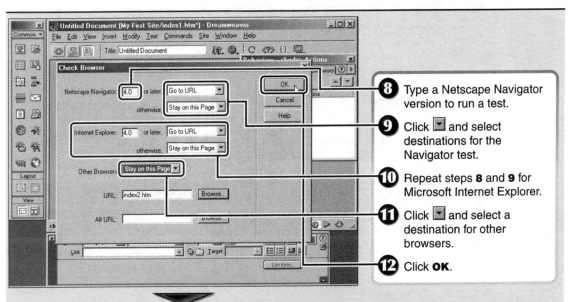

8 Type a Netscape Navigator version to run a test.

9 Click ▾ and select destinations for the Navigator test.

10 Repeat steps **8** and **9** for Microsoft Internet Explorer.

11 Click ▾ and select a destination for other browsers.

12 Click **OK**.

13 Preview the page in a Web browser.

Note: See Chapter 3 for instructions on how to preview a Web page in your browser.

● In this example, the Web page opens in Internet Explorer 5. The browser is forwarded to a custom page.

DEBUG JAVASCRIPT

JavaScript is a programming language that you can use to add interactivity to your Web page. Dreamweaver writes JavaScript code when you add behaviors to your page. You can use the debugger to analyze this code. You can also use the debugger to check any custom JavaScript that you have added to your page yourself to pinpoint errors.

DEBUG JAVASCRIPT

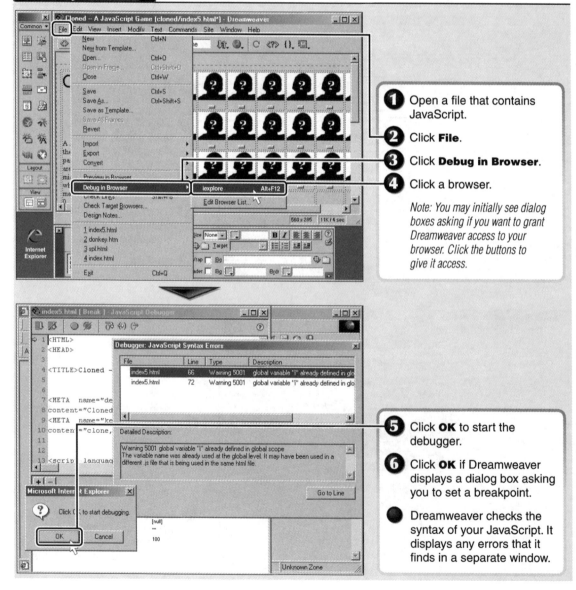

① Open a file that contains JavaScript.

② Click **File**.

③ Click **Debug in Browser**.

④ Click a browser.

Note: You may initially see dialog boxes asking if you want to grant Dreamweaver access to your browser. Click the buttons to give it access.

⑤ Click **OK** to start the debugger.

⑥ Click **OK** if Dreamweaver displays a dialog box asking you to set a breakpoint.

● Dreamweaver checks the syntax of your JavaScript. It displays any errors that it finds in a separate window.

in an *instant*

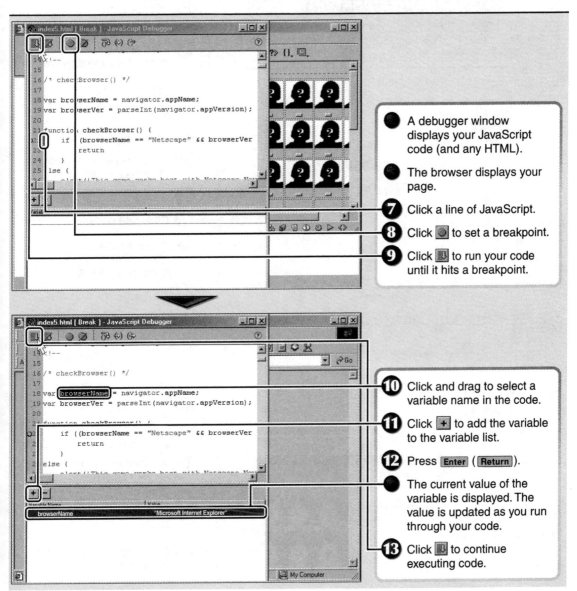

A debugger window displays your JavaScript code (and any HTML).

The browser displays your page.

7 Click a line of JavaScript.

8 Click ⊙ to set a breakpoint.

9 Click ▥ to run your code until it hits a breakpoint.

10 Click and drag to select a variable name in the code.

11 Click ⊞ to add the variable to the variable list.

12 Press **Enter** (**Return**).

The current value of the variable is displayed. The value is updated as you run through your code.

13 Click ▥ to continue executing code.

CREATE A STRAIGHT-LINE ANIMATION

You can create a timeline animation that moves a layer in a straight line on your page. A straight-line animation is a quick and easy way to enliven a page that otherwise consists of static text and images.

CREATE A STRAIGHT-LINE ANIMATION

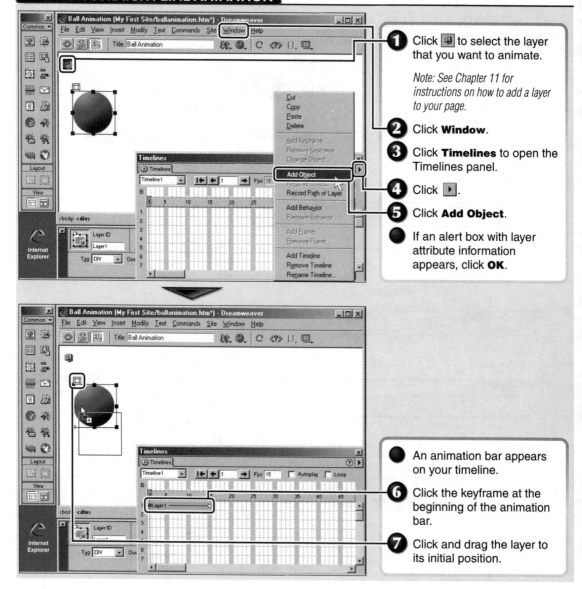

① Click 🖳 to select the layer that you want to animate.

Note: See Chapter 11 for instructions on how to add a layer to your page.

② Click **Window**.

③ Click **Timelines** to open the Timelines panel.

④ Click ▶.

⑤ Click **Add Object**.

● If an alert box with layer attribute information appears, click **OK**.

● An animation bar appears on your timeline.

⑥ Click the keyframe at the beginning of the animation bar.

⑦ Click and drag the layer to its initial position.

in an *instant*

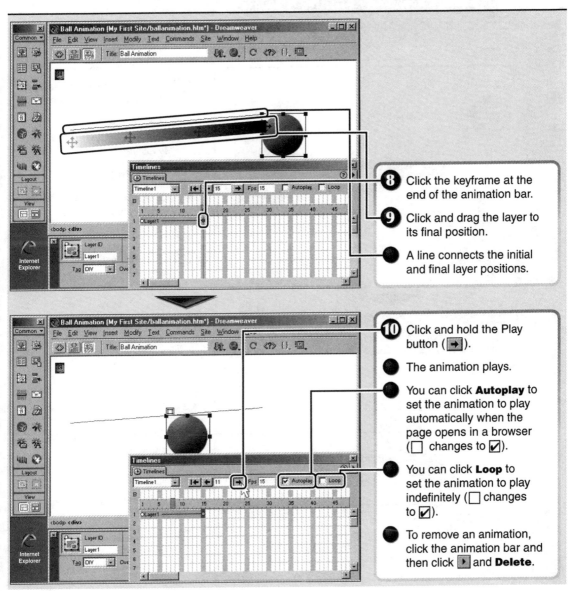

8 Click the keyframe at the end of the animation bar.

9 Click and drag the layer to its final position.

● A line connects the initial and final layer positions.

10 Click and hold the Play button (→).

● The animation plays.

● You can click **Autoplay** to set the animation to play automatically when the page opens in a browser (□ changes to ☑).

● You can click **Loop** to set the animation to play indefinitely (□ changes to ☑).

● To remove an animation, click the animation bar and then click ► and **Delete**.

CREATE AN ANIMATION BY DRAGGING A PATH

You can create animations that loop or curve by dragging a layer along the intended path and having Dreamweaver record the path as the layer moves. Recording a path can save time because it lets you avoid assigning keyframes.

CREATE AN ANIMATION BY DRAGGING A PATH

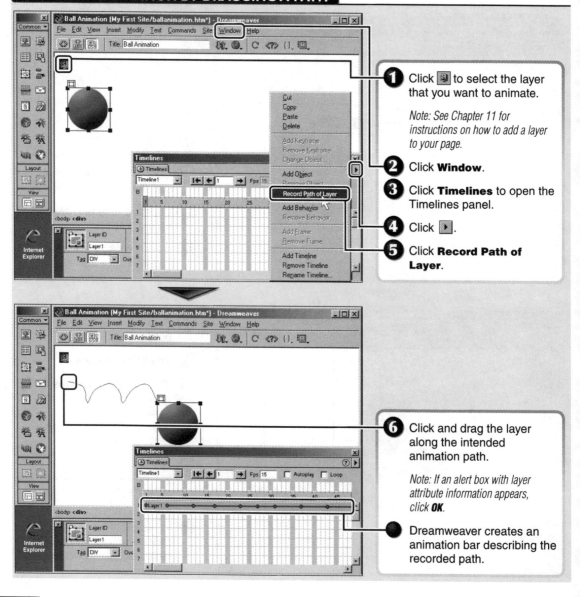

① Click 🖼 to select the layer that you want to animate.

Note: See Chapter 11 for instructions on how to add a layer to your page.

② Click **Window**.

③ Click **Timelines** to open the Timelines panel.

④ Click ▶.

⑤ Click **Record Path of Layer**.

⑥ Click and drag the layer along the intended animation path.

Note: If an alert box with layer attribute information appears, click OK.

● Dreamweaver creates an animation bar describing the recorded path.

in an *instant*

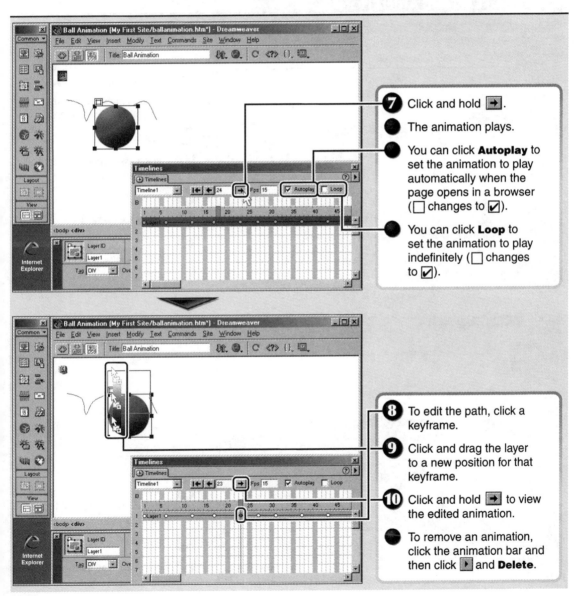

7 Click and hold ➡.

● The animation plays.

● You can click **Autoplay** to set the animation to play automatically when the page opens in a browser (☐ changes to ☑).

● You can click **Loop** to set the animation to play indefinitely (☐ changes to ☑).

8 To edit the path, click a keyframe.

9 Click and drag the layer to a new position for that keyframe.

10 Click and hold ➡ to view the edited animation.

● To remove an animation, click the animation bar and then click ▶ and **Delete**.

CREATE A FLASHING ANIMATION

To draw attention to part of a page, you can make content blink inside a layer by changing the visibility of the layer in a timeline.

CREATE A FLASHING ANIMATION

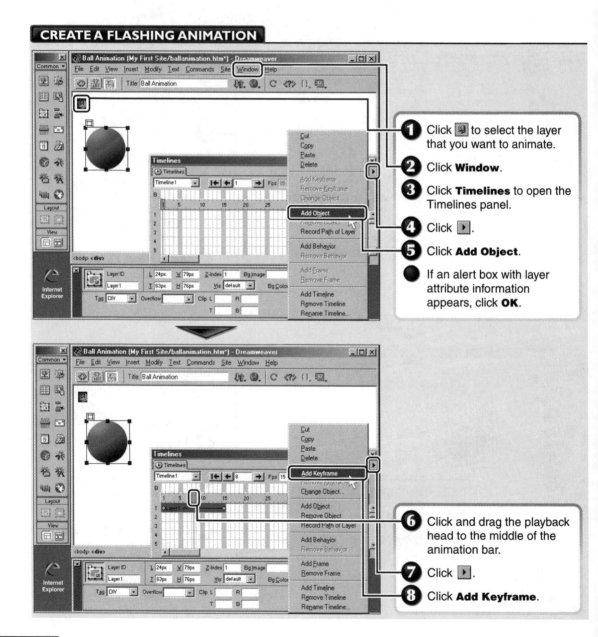

① Click 🔲 to select the layer that you want to animate.

② Click **Window**.

③ Click **Timelines** to open the Timelines panel.

④ Click ▶.

⑤ Click **Add Object**.

● If an alert box with layer attribute information appears, click **OK**.

⑥ Click and drag the playback head to the middle of the animation bar.

⑦ Click ▶.

⑧ Click **Add Keyframe**.

in an *instant*

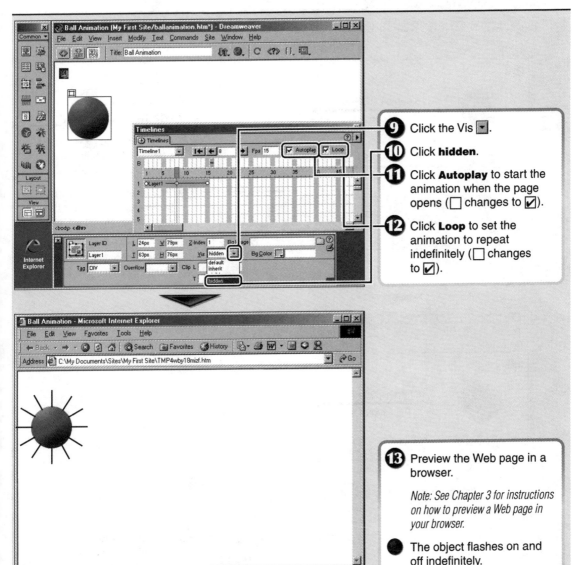

9 Click the Vis ▾.

10 Click **hidden**.

11 Click **Autoplay** to start the animation when the page opens (☐ changes to ☑).

12 Click **Loop** to set the animation to repeat indefinitely (☐ changes to ☑).

13 Preview the Web page in a browser.

Note: See Chapter 3 for instructions on how to preview a Web page in your browser.

● The object flashes on and off indefinitely.

CHANGE ANIMATION SPEED

You can speed up or slow down a timeline animation by changing its frame rate or by adjusting the number of frames that make up the animation.

CHANGE ANIMATION SPEED

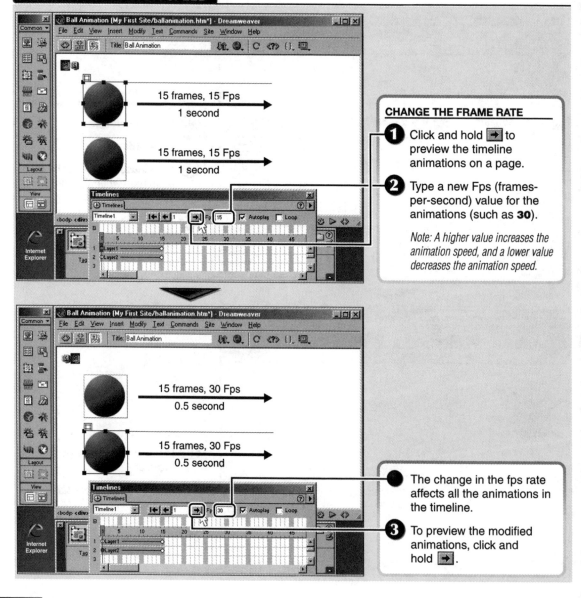

CHANGE THE FRAME RATE

① Click and hold ➡ to preview the timeline animations on a page.

② Type a new Fps (frames-per-second) value for the animations (such as **30**).

Note: A higher value increases the animation speed, and a lower value decreases the animation speed.

■ The change in the fps rate affects all the animations in the timeline.

③ To preview the modified animations, click and hold ➡.

in an *instant*

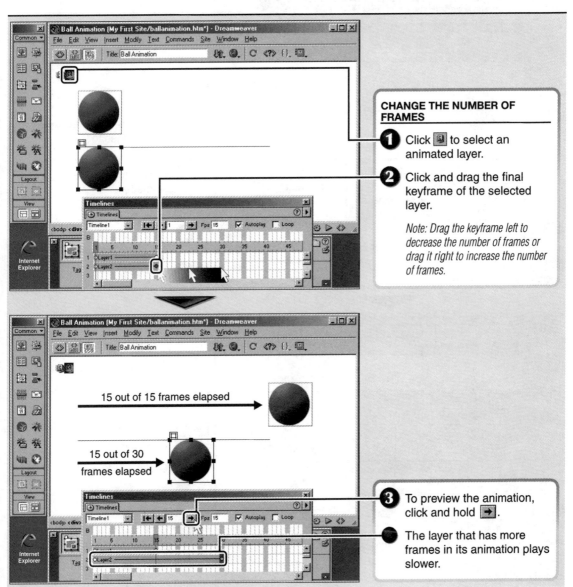

CHANGE THE NUMBER OF FRAMES

① Click 🔳 to select an animated layer.

② Click and drag the final keyframe of the selected layer.

Note: Drag the keyframe left to decrease the number of frames or drag it right to increase the number of frames.

15 out of 15 frames elapsed

15 out of 30 frames elapsed

③ To preview the animation, click and hold ➡️.

● The layer that has more frames in its animation plays slower.

TRIGGER AN ANIMATION WITH A BEHAVIOR

You can combine Dreamweaver behaviors and timelines so that clicking an image or hyperlink in your page plays an animation. This is an alternative to selecting Autoplay in the Timelines inspector, which causes an animation to automatically start when a page loads.

TRIGGER AN ANIMATION WITH A BEHAVIOR

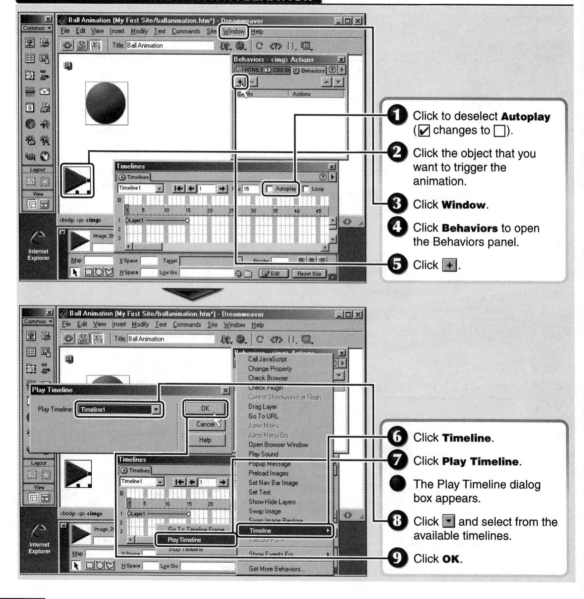

1 Click to deselect **Autoplay** (☑ changes to ☐).

2 Click the object that you want to trigger the animation.

3 Click **Window**.

4 Click **Behaviors** to open the Behaviors panel.

5 Click ➕.

6 Click **Timeline**.

7 Click **Play Timeline**.

● The Play Timeline dialog box appears.

8 Click ▼ and select from the available timelines.

9 Click **OK**.

in an *instant*

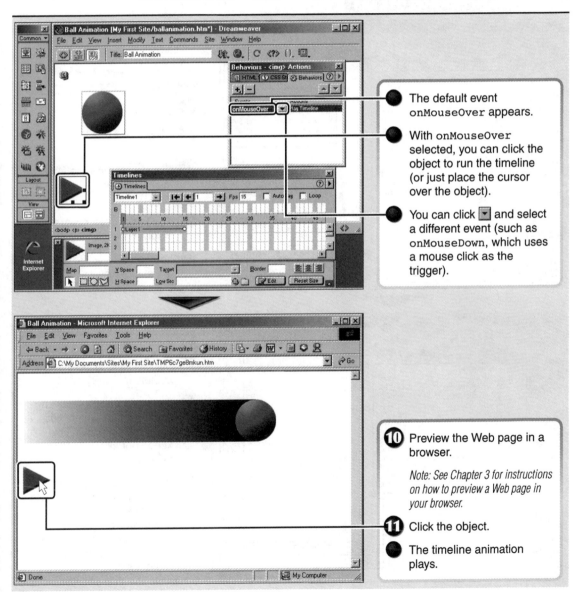

The default event
`onMouseOver` appears.

With `onMouseOver`
selected, you can click the
object to run the timeline
(or just place the cursor
over the object).

You can click ▼ and select
a different event (such as
`onMouseDown`, which uses
a mouse click as the
trigger).

⑩ Preview the Web page in a
browser.

*Note: See Chapter 3 for instructions
on how to preview a Web page in
your browser.*

⑪ Click the object.

The timeline animation
plays.

ORGANIZE FILES AND FOLDERS

You can use the Site window to organize the elements that make up your local and remote sites. The Site window lets you create and delete files and folders, as well as move files between folders.

ORGANIZE FILES AND FOLDERS

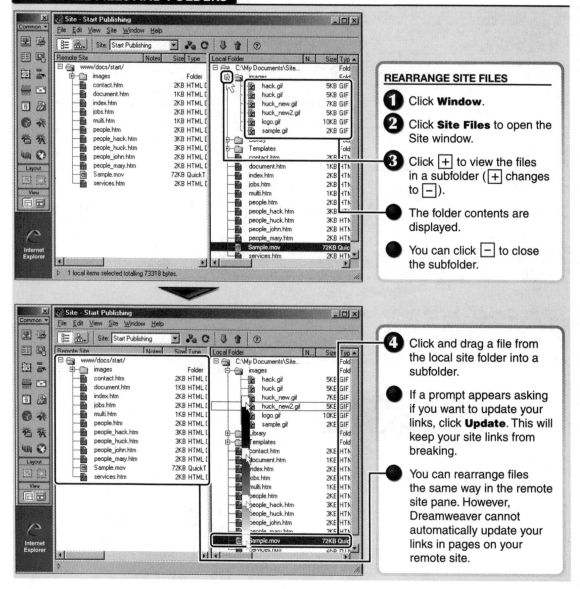

REARRANGE SITE FILES

1 Click **Window**.

2 Click **Site Files** to open the Site window.

3 Click ⊞ to view the files in a subfolder (⊞ changes to ⊟).

● The folder contents are displayed.

● You can click ⊟ to close the subfolder.

4 Click and drag a file from the local site folder into a subfolder.

● If a prompt appears asking if you want to update your links, click **Update**. This will keep your site links from breaking.

● You can rearrange files the same way in the remote site pane. However, Dreamweaver cannot automatically update your links in pages on your remote site.

in an instant

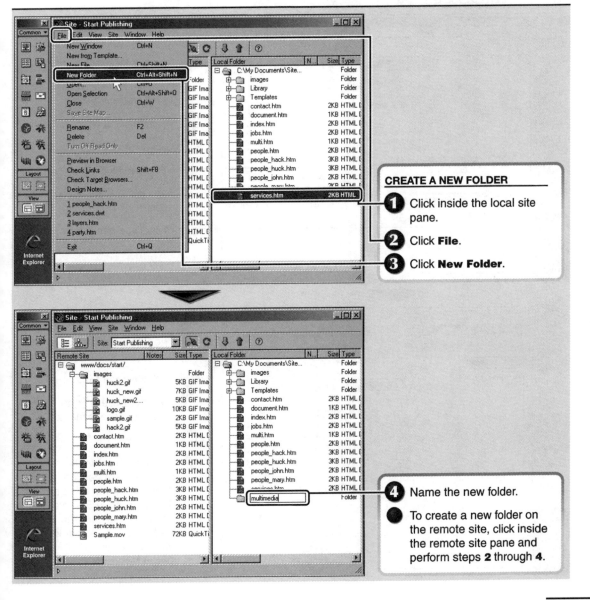

CREATE A NEW FOLDER

1 Click inside the local site pane.

2 Click **File**.

3 Click **New Folder**.

4 Name the new folder.

● To create a new folder on the remote site, click inside the remote site pane and perform steps **2** through **4**.

215

SET UP A REMOTE SITE

The remote site is the place where your site's files are made available to the rest of the world. You set up a remote site by specifying a directory on a Web server where your site will be hosted.

SET UP A REMOTE SITE

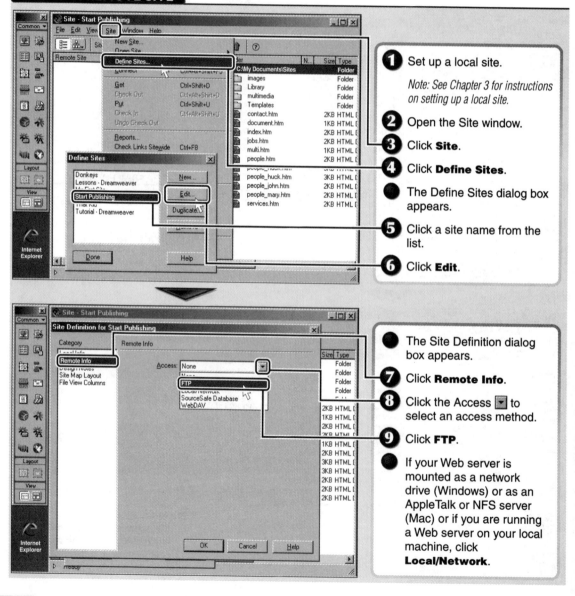

① Set up a local site.

Note: See Chapter 3 for instructions on setting up a local site.

② Open the Site window.

③ Click **Site**.

④ Click **Define Sites**.

■ The Define Sites dialog box appears.

⑤ Click a site name from the list.

⑥ Click **Edit**.

■ The Site Definition dialog box appears.

⑦ Click **Remote Info**.

⑧ Click the Access ■ to select an access method.

⑨ Click **FTP**.

■ If your Web server is mounted as a network drive (Windows) or as an AppleTalk or NFS server (Mac) or if you are running a Web server on your local machine, click **Local/Network**.

in an *instant*

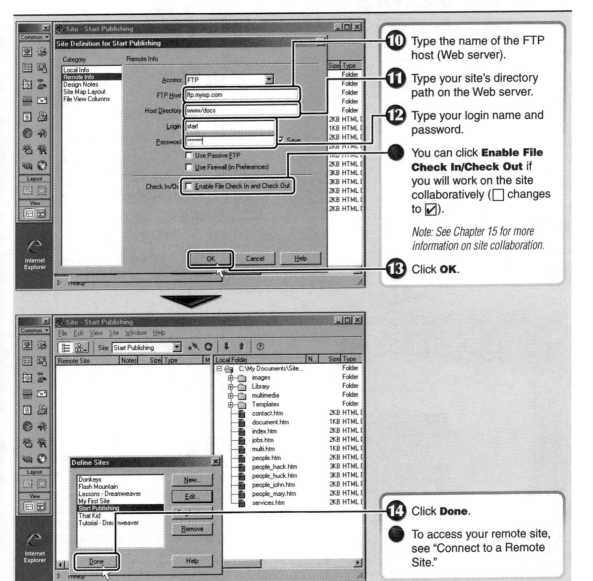

10 Type the name of the FTP host (Web server).

11 Type your site's directory path on the Web server.

12 Type your login name and password.

● You can click **Enable File Check In/Check Out** if you will work on the site collaboratively (☐ changes to ☑).

Note: See Chapter 15 for more information on site collaboration.

13 Click **OK**.

14 Click **Done**.

● To access your remote site, see "Connect to a Remote Site."

CONNECT TO A REMOTE SITE

You can connect to the Web server that hosts your remote site and transfer files between it and your computer. Dreamweaver connects to the Web server by a process known as *File Transfer Protocol,* or FTP.

CONNECT TO A REMOTE SITE

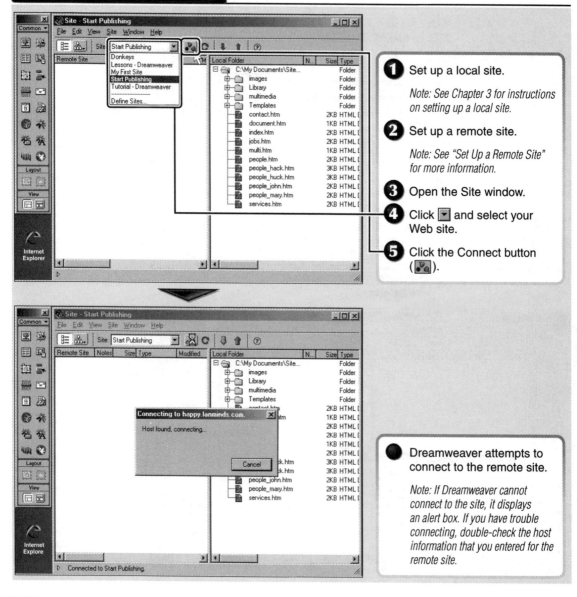

1 Set up a local site.

Note: See Chapter 3 for instructions on setting up a local site.

2 Set up a remote site.

Note: See "Set Up a Remote Site" for more information.

3 Open the Site window.

4 Click ▼ and select your Web site.

5 Click the Connect button (■).

● Dreamweaver attempts to connect to the remote site.

Note: If Dreamweaver cannot connect to the site, it displays an alert box. If you have trouble connecting, double-check the host information that you entered for the remote site.

in an *instant*

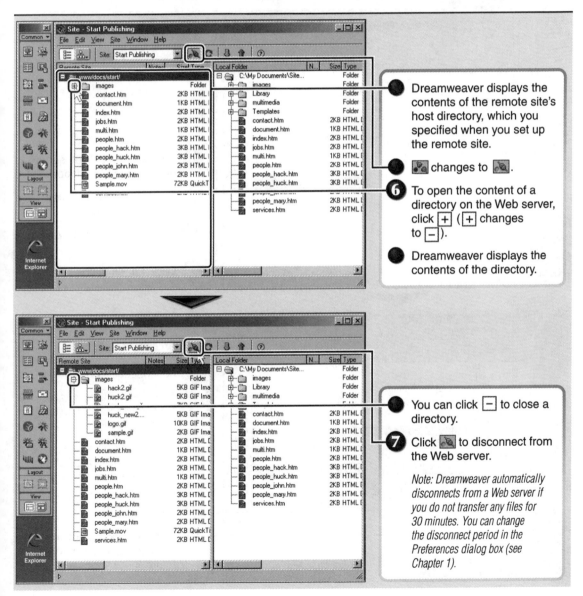

Dreamweaver displays the contents of the remote site's host directory, which you specified when you set up the remote site.

🔲 changes to 🔲.

6 To open the content of a directory on the Web server, click `+` (`+` changes to `-`).

Dreamweaver displays the contents of the directory.

You can click `-` to close a directory.

7 Click 🔲 to disconnect from the Web server.

Note: Dreamweaver automatically disconnects from a Web server if you do not transfer any files for 30 minutes. You can change the disconnect period in the Preferences dialog box (see Chapter 1).

UPLOAD FILES

You can upload site files from Dreamweaver to your remote site to make the files available to others on the Web.

UPLOAD FILES

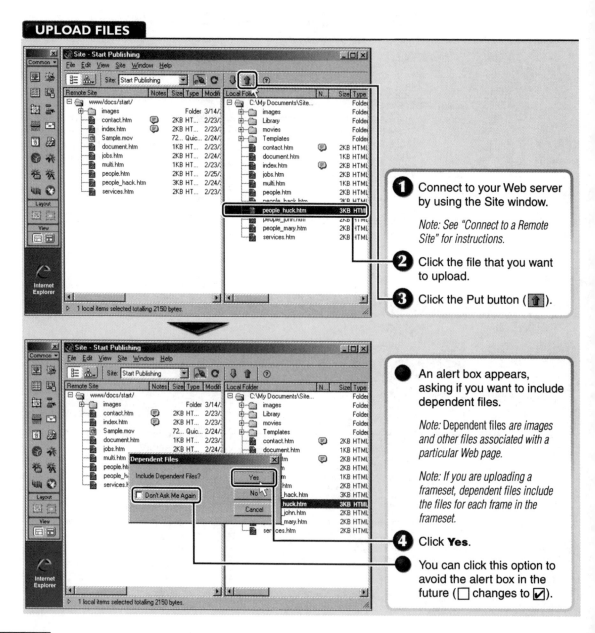

1 Connect to your Web server by using the Site window.

Note: See "Connect to a Remote Site" for instructions.

2 Click the file that you want to upload.

3 Click the Put button (⬆).

● An alert box appears, asking if you want to include dependent files.

Note: Dependent files are images and other files associated with a particular Web page.

Note: If you are uploading a frameset, dependent files include the files for each frame in the frameset.

4 Click **Yes**.

● You can click this option to avoid the alert box in the future (☐ changes to ☑).

in an instant

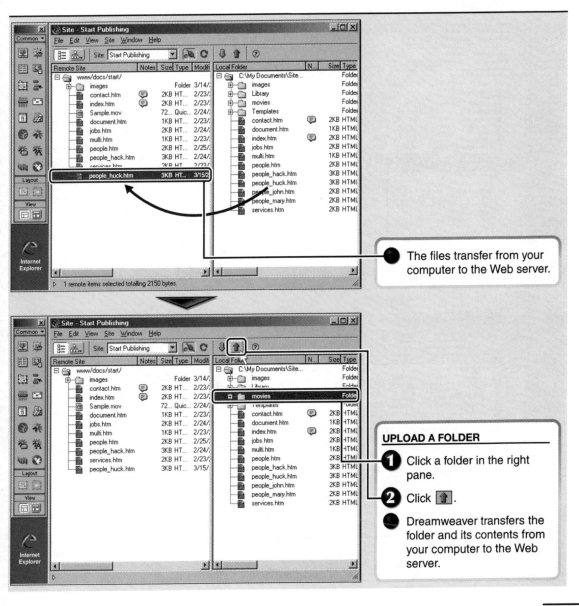

The files transfer from your computer to the Web server.

UPLOAD A FOLDER

1️⃣ Click a folder in the right pane.

2️⃣ Click .

Dreamweaver transfers the folder and its contents from your computer to the Web server.

DOWNLOAD FILES

You can download files from your remote site to Dreamweaver if you need to retrieve duplicate copies from the Web server.

DOWNLOAD FILES

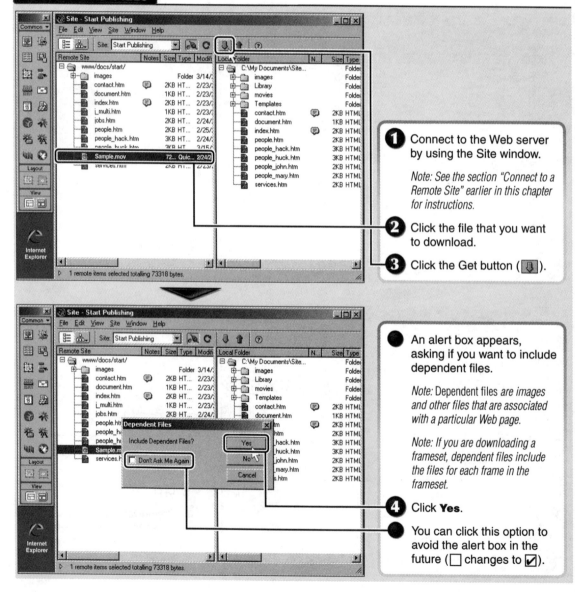

1 Connect to the Web server by using the Site window.

Note: See the section "Connect to a Remote Site" earlier in this chapter for instructions.

2 Click the file that you want to download.

3 Click the Get button (■).

An alert box appears, asking if you want to include dependent files.

Note: Dependent files are images and other files that are associated with a particular Web page.

Note: If you are downloading a frameset, dependent files include the files for each frame in the frameset.

4 Click **Yes**.

You can click this option to avoid the alert box in the future (□ changes to ☑).

in an instant

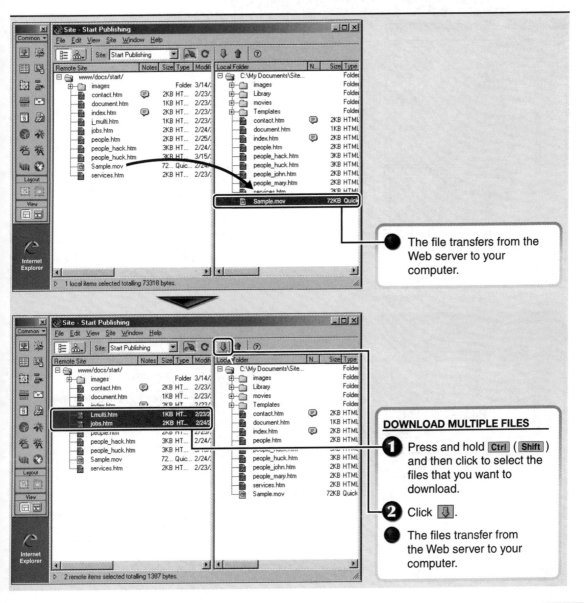

The file transfers from the Web server to your computer.

DOWNLOAD MULTIPLE FILES

1 Press and hold Ctrl (Shift) and then click to select the files that you want to download.

2 Click ⬇.

The files transfer from the Web server to your computer.

SYNCHRONIZE YOUR LOCAL AND REMOTE SITES

Dreamweaver can transfer files between your local and remote sites so that both sites have an identical set of the most recent files. This can be useful if other people are editing files on the remote site and the files on your local site may not be the most recent.

SYNCHRONIZE YOUR LOCAL AND REMOTE SITES

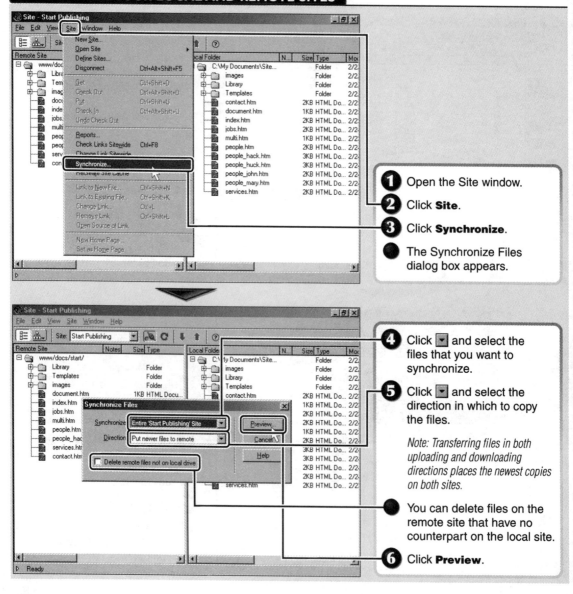

① Open the Site window.

② Click **Site**.

③ Click **Synchronize**.

● The Synchronize Files dialog box appears.

④ Click ▼ and select the files that you want to synchronize.

⑤ Click ▼ and select the direction in which to copy the files.

Note: Transferring files in both uploading and downloading directions places the newest copies on both sites.

● You can delete files on the remote site that have no counterpart on the local site.

⑥ Click **Preview**.

in an *instant*

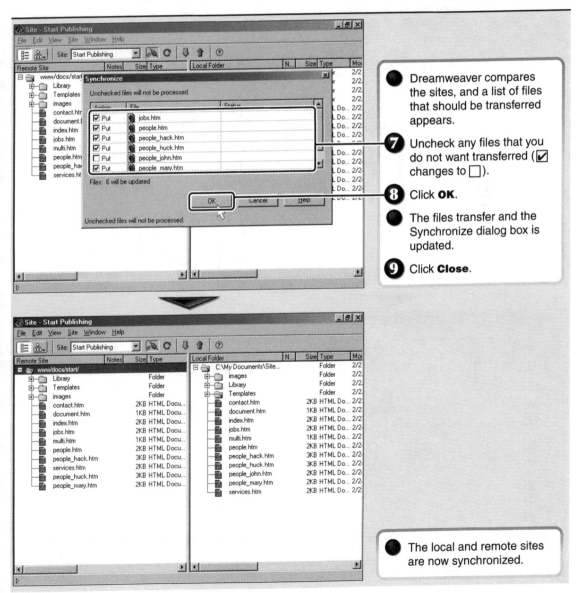

Dreamweaver compares the sites, and a list of files that should be transferred appears.

⑦ Uncheck any files that you do not want transferred (☑ changes to ☐).

⑧ Click **OK**.

The files transfer and the Synchronize dialog box is updated.

⑨ Click **Close**.

The local and remote sites are now synchronized.

USING THE SITE MAP

The Site Map view enables you to see your site in a flowchart form with link lines connecting document icons. This view highlights pages that have broken internal links, which can help you maintain your site.

USING THE SITE MAP

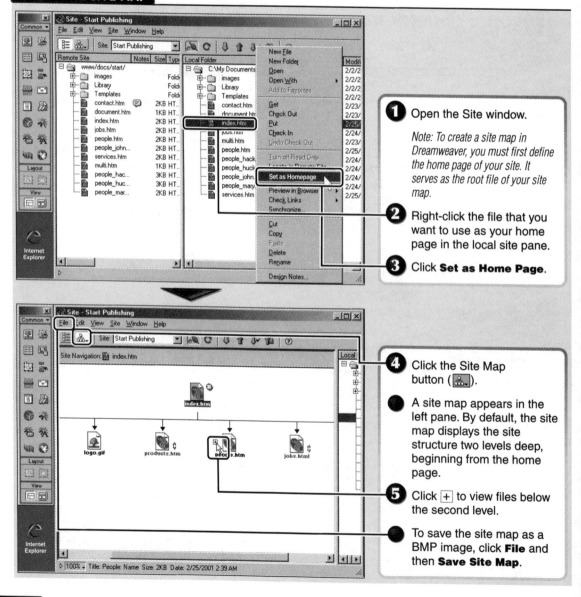

1 Open the Site window.

Note: To create a site map in Dreamweaver, you must first define the home page of your site. It serves as the root file of your site map.

2 Right-click the file that you want to use as your home page in the local site pane.

3 Click **Set as Home Page**.

4 Click the Site Map button ().

A site map appears in the left pane. By default, the site map displays the site structure two levels deep, beginning from the home page.

5 Click + to view files below the second level.

To save the site map as a BMP image, click **File** and then **Save Site Map**.

in an *instant*

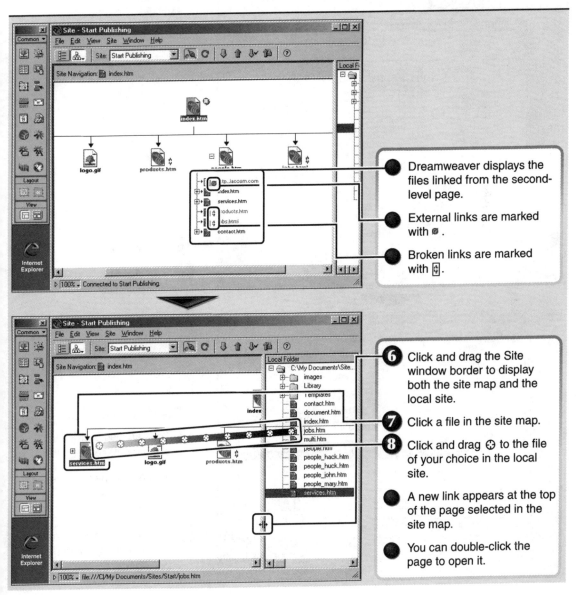

Dreamweaver displays the files linked from the second-level page.

External links are marked with ⌀ .

Broken links are marked with ⬍.

6 Click and drag the Site window border to display both the site map and the local site.

7 Click a file in the site map.

8 Click and drag ⊕ to the file of your choice in the local site.

A new link appears at the top of the page selected in the site map.

You can double-click the page to open it.

MANAGE SITE ASSETS

You can view and manage important elements that appear in the pages of your site with the Assets panel.

MANAGE SITE ASSETS

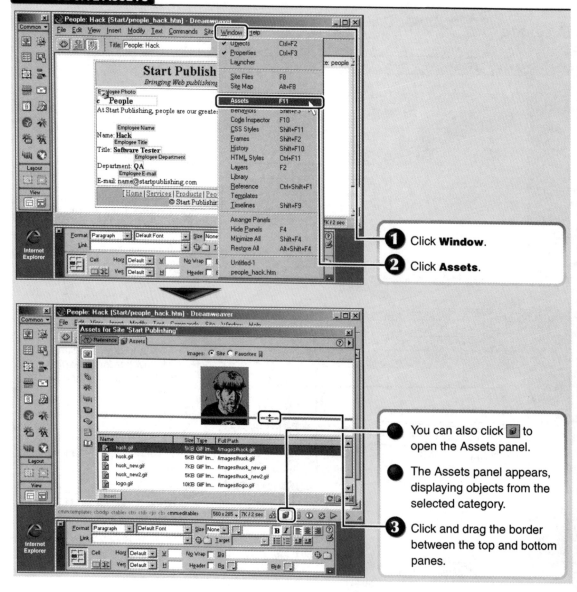

1 Click **Window**.

2 Click **Assets**.

● You can also click 🖼 to open the Assets panel.

● The Assets panel appears, displaying objects from the selected category.

3 Click and drag the border between the top and bottom panes.

228

in an instant

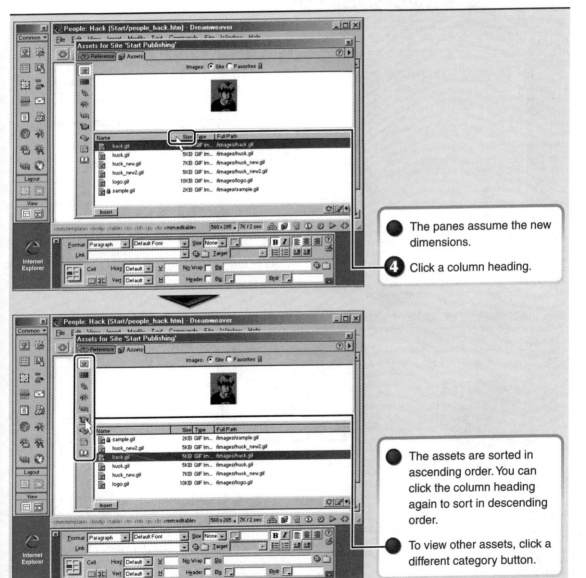

The panes assume the new dimensions.

4 Click a column heading.

The assets are sorted in ascending order. You can click the column heading again to sort in descending order.

To view other assets, click a different category button.

You can add frequently used content to your site directly from the Assets panel. This technique can be more efficient than using a menu command or the Objects panel.

ADD CONTENT BY USING THE ASSET PANEL

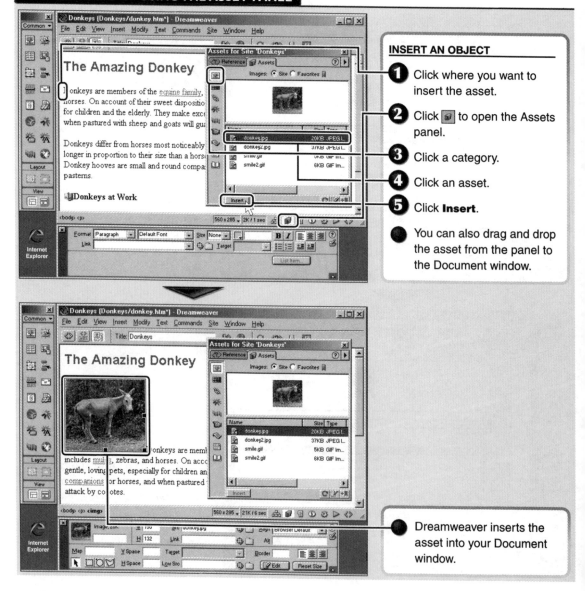

INSERT AN OBJECT

1 Click where you want to insert the asset.

2 Click 🗐 to open the Assets panel.

3 Click a category.

4 Click an asset.

5 Click **Insert**.

■ You can also drag and drop the asset from the panel to the Document window.

■ Dreamweaver inserts the asset into your Document window.

in an **instant**

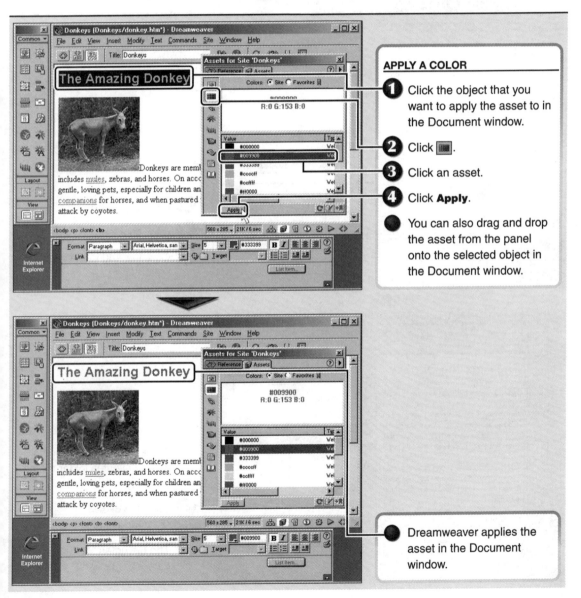

APPLY A COLOR

1 Click the object that you want to apply the asset to in the Document window.

2 Click 🖩.

3 Click an asset.

4 Click **Apply**.

● You can also drag and drop the asset from the panel onto the selected object in the Document window.

● Dreamweaver applies the asset in the Document window.

SPECIFY FAVORITE ASSETS

To make your asset lists more manageable, you can
organize assets that you use often into a Favorites list
inside each asset category.

SPECIFY FAVORITE ASSETS

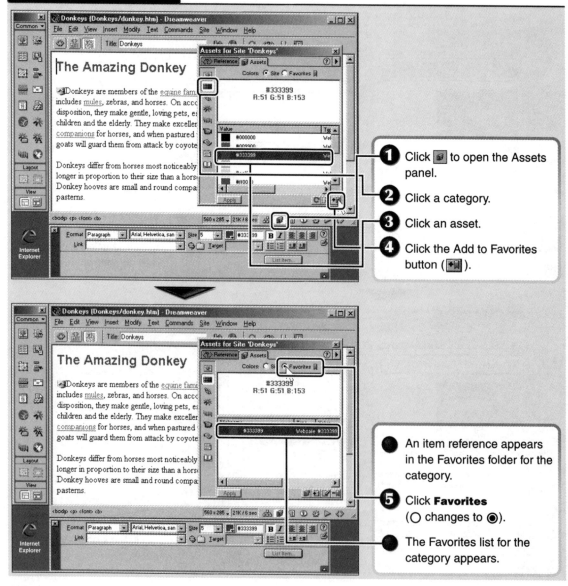

① Click 🖼 to open the Assets panel.

② Click a category.

③ Click an asset.

④ Click the Add to Favorites button (🔳).

● An item reference appears in the Favorites folder for the category.

⑤ Click **Favorites** (○ changes to ◉).

● The Favorites list for the category appears.

in an *instant*

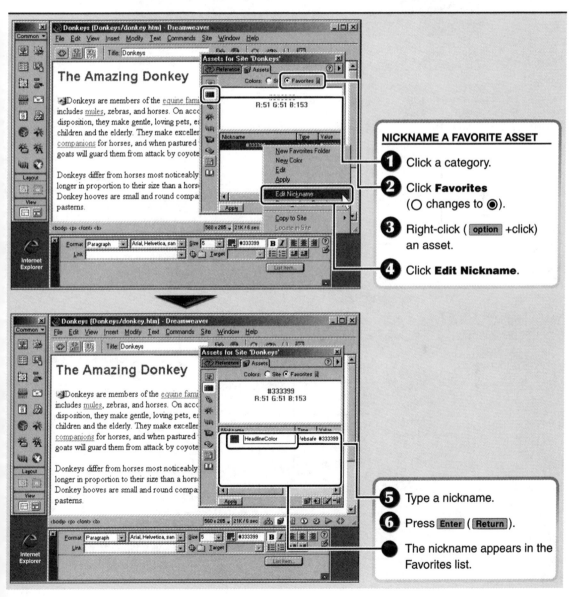

NICKNAME A FAVORITE ASSET

1 Click a category.

2 Click **Favorites**
(○ changes to ◉).

3 Right-click (option +click)
an asset.

4 Click **Edit Nickname**.

5 Type a nickname.

6 Press Enter (Return).

● The nickname appears in the
Favorites list.

CHECK A PAGE IN OR OUT

Dreamweaver provides a Check In/Check Out system that enables several people to work collaboratively on Web site files. When this system is in use, others cannot work on site files that are checked out.

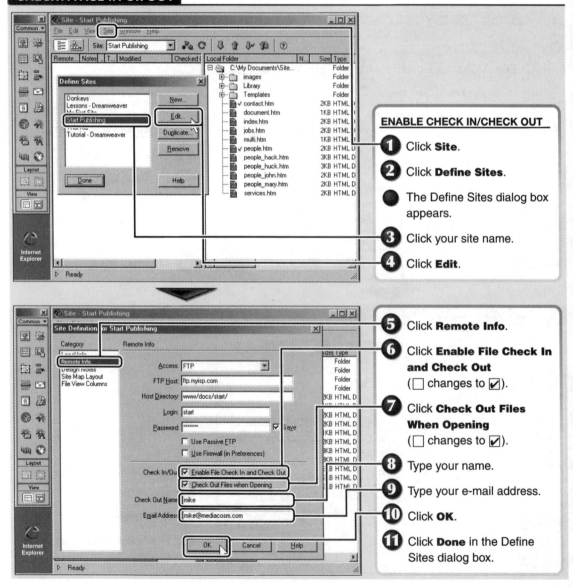

ENABLE CHECK IN/CHECK OUT

1 Click **Site**.

2 Click **Define Sites**.

● The Define Sites dialog box appears.

3 Click your site name.

4 Click **Edit**.

5 Click **Remote Info**.

6 Click **Enable File Check In and Check Out** (☐ changes to ☑).

7 Click **Check Out Files When Opening** (☐ changes to ☑).

8 Type your name.

9 Type your e-mail address.

10 Click **OK**.

11 Click **Done** in the Define Sites dialog box.

in an instant

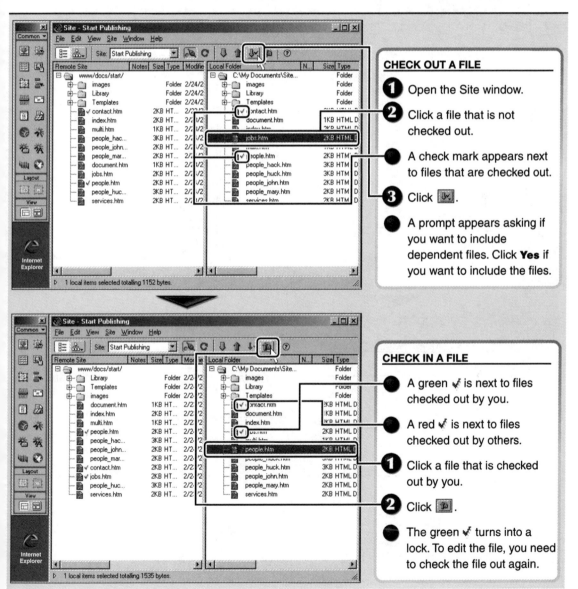

CHECK OUT A FILE

1 Open the Site window.

2 Click a file that is not checked out.

● A check mark appears next to files that are checked out.

3 Click ⟨⟩.

● A prompt appears asking if you want to include dependent files. Click **Yes** if you want to include the files.

CHECK IN A FILE

● A green ✓ is next to files checked out by you.

● A red ✓ is next to files checked out by others.

1 Click a file that is checked out by you.

2 Click ⟨⟩.

● The green ✓ turns into a lock. To edit the file, you need to check the file out again.

MAKE DESIGN NOTES

You can attach accessory information, such as editing history and an author name, to your Web pages with design notes. Such notes can be useful if you are working on a site collaboratively because they let you add information about the development status of a file.

MAKE DESIGN NOTES

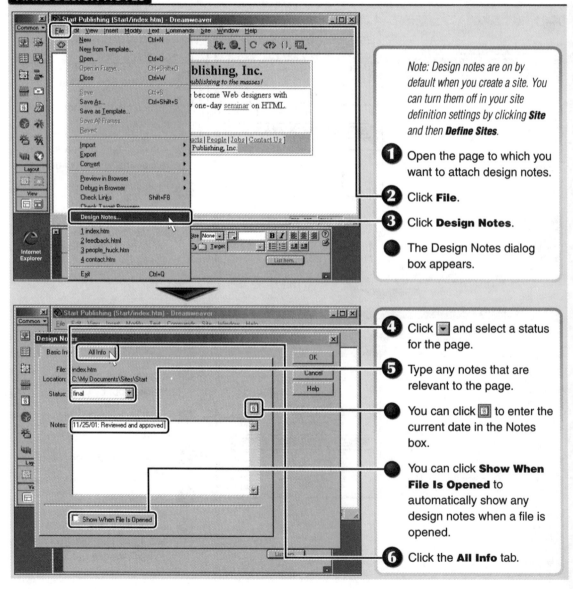

*Note: Design notes are on by default when you create a site. You can turn them off in your site definition settings by clicking **Site** and then **Define Sites**.*

① Open the page to which you want to attach design notes.

② Click **File**.

③ Click **Design Notes**.

● The Design Notes dialog box appears.

④ Click ▼ and select a status for the page.

⑤ Type any notes that are relevant to the page.

● You can click 📅 to enter the current date in the Notes box.

● You can click **Show When File Is Opened** to automatically show any design notes when a file is opened.

⑥ Click the **All Info** tab.

in an *instant*

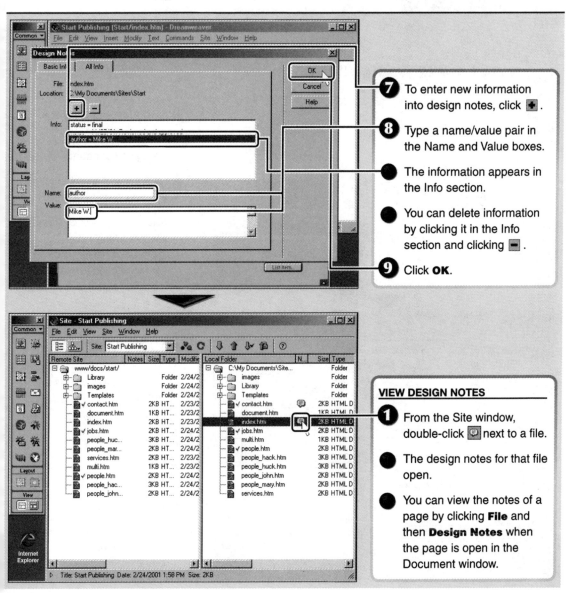

7 To enter new information into design notes, click ✚.

8 Type a name/value pair in the Name and Value boxes.

● The information appears in the Info section.

● You can delete information by clicking it in the Info section and clicking ➖.

9 Click **OK**.

VIEW DESIGN NOTES

1 From the Site window, double-click 💬 next to a file.

● The design notes for that file open.

● You can view the notes of a page by clicking **File** and then **Design Notes** when the page is open in the Document window.

FIND AND REPLACE TEXT

The Find and Replace feature is a powerful tool for making changes to text elements that repeat across many pages. You can find and replace text on your Web page, text in your source code, or specific HTML tags in your pages.

FIND AND REPLACE TEXT

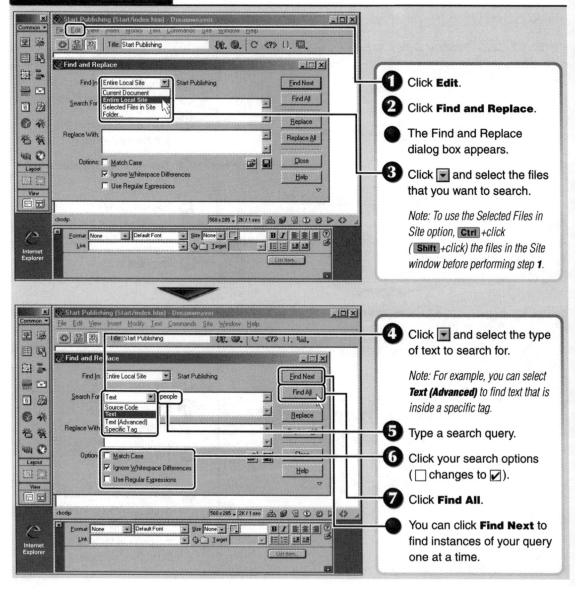

1 Click **Edit**.

2 Click **Find and Replace**.

● The Find and Replace dialog box appears.

3 Click ▾ and select the files that you want to search.

Note: To use the Selected Files in Site option, **Ctrl** *+click* (**Shift** *+click) the files in the Site window before performing step* **1**.

4 Click ▾ and select the type of text to search for.

Note: For example, you can select **Text (Advanced)** *to find text that is inside a specific tag.*

5 Type a search query.

6 Click your search options (☐ changes to ☑).

7 Click **Find All**.

● You can click **Find Next** to find instances of your query one at a time.

in an *instant*

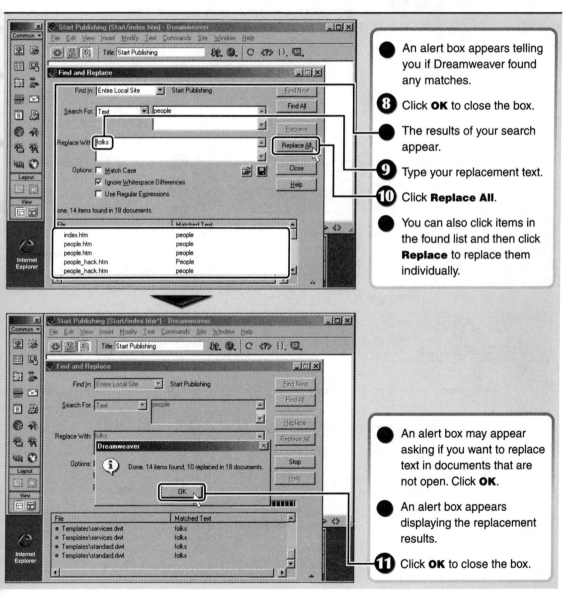

An alert box appears telling you if Dreamweaver found any matches.

8 Click **OK** to close the box.

The results of your search appear.

9 Type your replacement text.

10 Click **Replace All**.

You can also click items in the found list and then click **Replace** to replace them individually.

An alert box may appear asking if you want to replace text in documents that are not open. Click **OK**.

An alert box appears displaying the replacement results.

11 Click **OK** to close the box.

239

CHANGE A LINK SITEWIDE

You can search for and replace all the hyperlinks on your
site that point to a specific address. This is helpful when
a page is renamed or deleted and hyperlinks to it need
updating.

CHANGE A LINK SITEWIDE

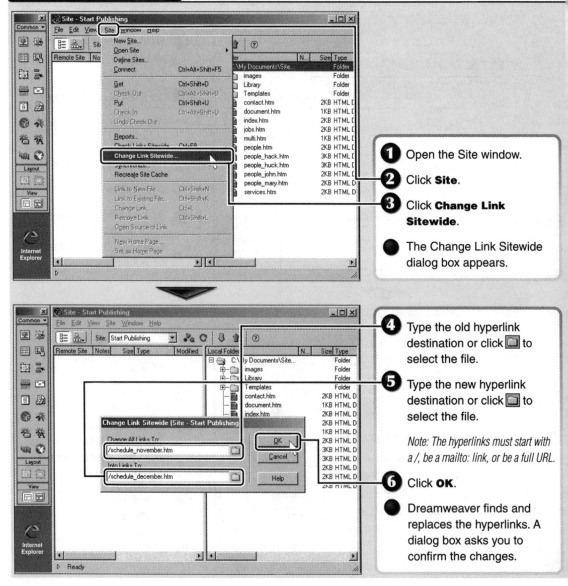

① Open the Site window.

② Click **Site**.

③ Click **Change Link Sitewide**.

● The Change Link Sitewide dialog box appears.

④ Type the old hyperlink destination or click 📁 to select the file.

⑤ Type the new hyperlink destination or click 📁 to select the file.

Note: The hyperlinks must start with a /, be a mailto: link, or be a full URL.

⑥ Click **OK**.

● Dreamweaver finds and replaces the hyperlinks. A dialog box asks you to confirm the changes.

240

A site report pinpoints any redundant
HTML and missing descriptive information
in your pages. It is a good idea to run a
site report before you upload your site to
a Web server.

RUN A SITE REPORT

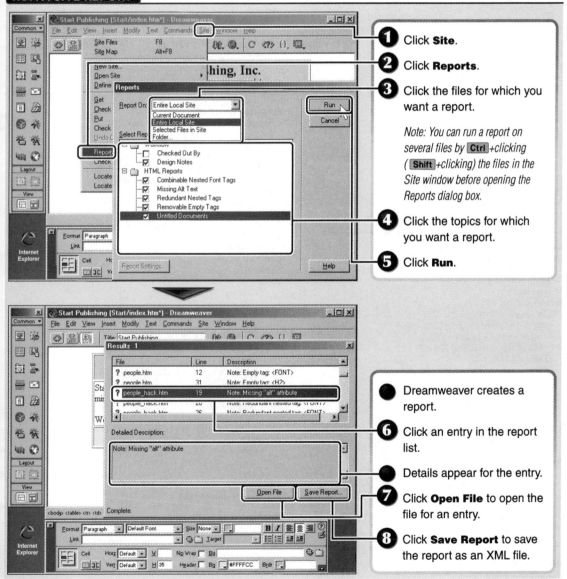

1 Click **Site**.

2 Click **Reports**.

3 Click the files for which you
want a report.

*Note: You can run a report on
several files by* **Ctrl** *+clicking
(* **Shift** *+clicking) the files in the
Site window before opening the
Reports dialog box.*

4 Click the topics for which
you want a report.

5 Click **Run**.

■ Dreamweaver creates a
report.

6 Click an entry in the report
list.

■ Details appear for the entry.

7 Click **Open File** to open the
file for an entry.

8 Click **Save Report** to save
the report as an XML file.

241

INDEX

INDEX

INDEX

Other Visual Series That Help You Read Less - Learn More™

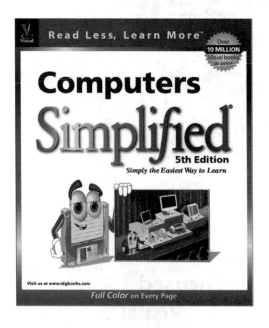

Simplified®

Teach Yourself VISUALLY™

Master VISUALLY™

Visual Blueprint

Available wherever books are sold